Public Policy and Local Governance

NEW HORIZONS IN PUBLIC POLICY

General Editor: Wayne Parsons
Professor of Public Policy, Queen Mary and Westfield College,
University of London, UK

This series aims to explore the major issues facing academics and
practitioners working in the field of public policy at the dawn of a new
millennium. It seeks to reflect on where public policy has been, in both
theoretical and practical terms, and to prompt debate on where it is going.
The series emphasises the need to understand public policy in the context of
international developments and global change. New Horizons in Public
Policy publishes the latest research on the study of the policy making process
and public management, and presents original and critical thinking on the
policy issues and problems facing modern and post-modern societies.
  Titles in the series include:

Public Policy and Local Governance

Institutions in Postmodern Society

Peter Bogason

Roskilde University
Denmark

NEW HORIZONS IN PUBLIC POLICY

Edward Elgar

Cheltenham, UK • Northampton, MA, USA

Published by
Edward Elgar Publishing Limited
Glensanda House
Montpellier Parade
Cheltenham
Glos GL50 1UA
UK

Edward Elgar Publishing, Inc.
136 West Street
Suite 202
Northampton
Massachusetts 01060
USA

A catalogue record for this book
is available from the British Library

Library of Congress Cataloguing in Publication Data
Bogason, Peter.
    Public policy and local governance : institutions in postmodern society / Peter Bogason.
        (New Horizons in public policy)
    1. Local government. 2. Political planning. 3. Postmodernism—Political aspects. I. Title. II. Series.

    JS141 .B64 2000
    306.2—dc21   99–045191

ISBN 1 84064 349 8

Printed in the United Kingdom at the University Press, Cambridge

Contents

Preface

Most academic work is written in contact with colleagues. I want to thank the members of the research group I am associated with in Roskilde, the Center for Local Institutional Research, for support and challenges over the years. A very first draft of this book was written during a stay as a Netherlands Interuniversity Institute of Government visiting professor in the Department of Public Administration, Leiden University, the Netherlands. The second draft was completed later at the Center for Public Administration and Policy at Virginia Tech, Falls Church, Virginia, USA. I thank both these institutions for their hospitality.

Thus, the various drafts have been discussed in different settings across two continents and five countries. I thank the following individuals for comments and various forms of help: Helle Sundgaard Andersen, Eric Austin, Tom R Burns, Lars Carlsson, Gunnar Gjelstrup, Charles T Goodsell, Herman van Gunsteren, Allan Dreyer Hansen, Anton Hemerijck, Lars Hulgård, Philip A Idenburg, Peter John, Birgit Jæger, Sandra Kensen, Pekka Ketunen, Christine Mica, Marie-Louise van Muijen, Hanne Warming Nielsen, Asbjørn Sonne Nørgaard, Elinor Ostrom, Vincent Ostrom, Anne Reff Pedersen, Ove K Pedersen, Jos Raadschelders, Johan Smed, Eva Sørensen, Kåre Thomsen, Theo A J Toonen, Jochen de Vries, Henk Waagenaar, Gary L Wamsley, Orion F White, Jim F Wolf, and an anonymous referee from Edward Elgar. Furthermore, I owe a class of students at Roskilde University a thank you for a critical discussion of a draft version of the book in October 1999.

I also want to thank the series editor, Wayne Parsons, for introducing me to the Edward Elgar Publishing House. The staff of Edward Elgar has been very helpful in finishing the manuscript.

The usual disclaimers regarding the responsibilities of all these people for the final result apply. But let me retort to one specific comment, namely applicability: Why not let the contents of the book address areas of trouble as in Eastern Europe and the Third World? Those areas ought to be of my concern. The answer is simple: they concern me as an individual and private observer, but not as a scholar, because I do not have the insight necessary to get involved very far in scholarly debates. So I had better accept the constraints and make reservations accordingly - the book mainly concerns Western Europe, North America and other areas of a similar politico-socio-economic type.

Roskilde and Rungsted Kyst
Peter Bogason

1. Introduction

This book is about institutional analysis of networks. It discusses how to analyse collective action in the locality, linked to the public sector because the actors need resources in terms of money, expertise or legitimacy; in effect they create public policies for a number of purposes at the local level. So the book is a search for links between the analysis of such collective action which becomes *public action*, and the analysis of the creation of *public policy*. Since the trend is, as we shall see, for public policies to be no longer created by one formal organization-in-charge, the approach of such analyses should be to combine actions by several formal organizations, but at the same time one must understand the role of individual actors. We want to analyse the strategic actor using institutional arrangements as both constraints and assets for present and future action.

The book's approach is based on an understanding of what we may call institutional settings for networks, and the research perspective is "bottom-up". This means that it is based on the perceptions of those vested with daily responsibilities for making things work (and often acting across organizational boundaries), rather than on perceptions from the top of a particular organization.

The introduction below sketches out the basic understanding of the rest of the book. The approach is based on several social science disciplines: political science, public administration, policy analysis and organizational sociology. In terms of some of the debates that come up in those disciplines, the approach is placed somewhere inside a triangle between New Public Management, New Normativists and Discourse Theorists, seeking compromises between important elements of all three; we shall return to these below.

COLLECTIVE PUBLIC ACTION UNDER POSTMODERN CONDITIONS

A basic perception of this book is that those who are living in the Western democracies are becoming challenged by new forms of societal features, which we for want of a better expression may call postmodern conditions.

We can only be sure of one thing: these conditions differ from the modern society in some important aspects. If and when we know more about those conditions, we may be able to find better concepts to characterize them. Chapter 2 will deal with those questions in more detail, below we just outline the most crucial factors.

But first a few words about why the changes around us deserve scholarly reaction. At the end of the 19th century, Emile Durkheim and Max Weber were defining the field of a new discipline, sociology, dealing with the changes of society from the traditional (rural) society to the modern (urban) society. Durkheim and Weber analysed the activities of the élites of their time, in the processes of constructing new systems of production and organizing private and public activities on a large scale. They were struggling to conceptualize and analyse change, working on the basis of (or in opposition to) their predecessors in social analysis - Comte, Marx, Tönnies and others - and they did not know the answers to their questions beforehand. But their concepts and ideas were not coming from an abstract world of theories, they were heavily dependent on what was going on in their contemporary societies - industrialization, bureaucratization, and urbanization.

Those social science theories, then, which many see as very general theories, may also be seen as theories that were to a large extent dependent on observations of the contemporary society, in those cases *fin de siècle* of 19th century France and Germany. Therefore, one hundred years later, and on the threshold of a new century, we should discuss whether the conceptualizations and research methods of those founders of the modern social sciences are still relevant in all aspects. A negative answer does not necessarily mean that they are irrelevant with regard to a great deal of questions such as problematics linked to the facets of the modern society. But for other questions, we may need conceptualizations and research methods adapted to societal features that differ from those of the modern society.

Below, some main features of social change apart from the generally acknowledged features of the modern society are sketched out as a basis for discussing conceptual problems.

The *modern* society is characterized by *rationalization*, the systematic use of reason based on an overarching vision. Its main organizational forms are industrialization and bureaucratization where rational organizational measures are used to perfection. Units of a plant, or the offices of a large organization, are highly specialized as elements of an elaborate division of labor in the production process. Each plant or organization may itself even be an element in a nationwide or even world-wide division of labor of a large-scale production. The resulting high degree of differentiation raises demands for some degree of coordination which is mainly found as attempts to centralize powers at the top of the organizations or the peak associations and political systems that are attempting to control the activities of the modern society. There finally is a high degree of formalization of decision-making processes, demanding standardized and formal communication which can be stored for future use and reference. The general aim, then, of these processes is to create coherence and integration of a highly sophisticated system of decision-making which has in it some potential for differentiation.

Under *postmodern* conditions - which coexist with the modern society - many have given up coordinating in the fashion of the modern society, so differentiation plays a major role. Instead of rationalization, we see different actors involved in processes of *reasoning* from very different and practical vantage points. Overall visions are replaced by localized and often creative insights. Consequently, there is a high degree of fragmentation. There is a high degree of individualism, based on an unprecedented system of social security rooted in the modern society. The nation state becomes of less and less importance in politics, in the economy and in cultural affairs; international regimes take over where national boundaries limited exchange in the modern society. We see an organizational segregation with many types of interests involved in decision-making across formal organizational boundaries, and a decentralization of powers to production units and local systems of governance. Large national corporate structures become less important, localism blossoms in an internationalized world.

The trends towards postmodern conditions have serious consequences for policy analysis. In the modern society, the centralized systems of control and goal-setting processes bound to the top executives legitimized analyses of outputs and outcomes of political interventions in society from that perspective, top-down. But the decentralized and fragmented postmodern conditions defy such clear and top-heavy understanding of policy aims and outcomes. There is larger differentiation and thus fewer generally applicable standards. There is room for local maneuver and adaptation. There are legitimate differences at the local level which must be taken into account.

In particular, this affects the applicability of the top-down approach to policy analysis. It may never have been the best way of analysing policy implementation, but changes in society create problems for analysis of that sort within more and more policy fields. The model of evaluation based on generalized goals and command-control implementation does not fit in general any more. We need models that take diversity into account, going across formal organizational boundaries, and developing an understanding for problematics of people such as field workers and "clients", the latter less as one-way dependents and more as active individuals. Constructing such models requires better understanding of processes rather than stability, of structuration rather than structure.

One might think that collective action becomes archaic under the post-modern conditions where individuality reigns. But it is not necessarily so. The trends towards fragmentation may create problems for those who do not have the material resources to solve problems of (public) services individually. There is still a perceived need for coordinated services, but the solutions offered by public organizations are increasingly challenged. So people may have a need to develop new ways of collective action, away from the centralized system of new corporatism, and within a framework that is within the communicative reach for people in the locality.

Consequently, we are interested in discussing and analysing collective action that in some measure is linked to the resources - in their broadest sense - of the public sector and thus constitutes a type of public policy process. The rationale for this interest is that in spite of trends towards individualism and fragmentation, which we shall deal with in more detail in the next chapter, most people need the support of other people to overcome many of the challenges in their daily lives. In particular, there is a need for a number of services which may become more affordable and better quality when provided by a collectivity. This is precisely what the advanced welfare state has done, but it is being challenged by forces from both left and right, and there is an increasing consensus, even among European Socialists, that a number of alternatives should be tried out. Alternatives may not be so radical as the word sounds. Basically, what we see is moderate change where in particular the production of services is carried out under new auspices, making the traditional professional, public organization less relevant. But the road towards more radical alternatives is open for those who want to pursue it.

One area arising from this change is the need for new ways of organiz-ing. Another is how we are to analyse these new ways of organizing, and the consequences for public policy. This is the main subject of the rest of the book. We take for granted that some changes are occurring, and since there is less unification in the organizational patterns, researchers must have tools that can work for them in identifying and analysing the new ways of acting.

In Chapter 3, we shall elucidate the possible meanings of the concept of collective action. Here it may suffice to say that, in principle, we include actions involving more than one individual interested in achieving the same goal without having to compete with one another or to dominate by force. A special interest deals with the provision of common good(s) of common interest to a group of people in the locality. There is a considerable need for people to pool resources to solve matters of common interest. At the same time, however, one must consider the postmodern thesis of a considerable fragmentation of the organizational and political pattern, usually vested with the task of organizing collective action. The corollary is that research cannot adequately grasp what is going on if one starts the research process with those organizations and particularly their managerial top. Therefore, it is better to start with the activities in the locality rather than the perceptions of such managers who think that they have an overview of what goes on.

This development is reflected in organizational theory. Weber found the bureaucratic organization to be the perfect match for the demands of modern society. The bureaucratic organization is based on excessive specialization among bureaux and employees, the organization design is the hierarchy, its powers are exercised on the basis of general rules, and its employees expect a life-long career within the organization, based on their merits. This sort of organization supports the needs of the modern society in the direction of stability, predictability, centralized responsibility and responsiveness to planned demands. Organization under postmodern conditions is the negation of these elements (Clegg 1990). It employs generalists who are, however, trained so that they can quickly adapt to new demands for skills, and in this sense there is a specialization, but only in some functions, not as an inherent characteristic of the employees. The organization design has hierarchical elements, but in a "flat" system with few layers, and it is constantly changing at the personal level to reflect the changes in the production process needs; a version of the matrix organization. General rules are few, *ad hoc* decisions must be taken all the time to prompt reaction to the changes needed for the organization to respond to new demands. The employees do not stay for life in the organization; they go from one organization to another as job opportunities open and close, and take on different types of responsibilities. They may also work in a self-employed capacity in between. In order to grasp such trends, the challenge for organizational theory is to become more situation-oriented and to reconsider the usability of covering laws as vehicles to produce testable hypotheses about organizational developments.

The modern state and its rational organizations, then, are undergoing change through many forces which may be somewhat at odds with one another. The state is not disappearing, however, but some of its agents are becoming challenged. The core of the state is still extremely relevant for social action, this core being the *public power*, a phenomenon derived from a constitutional system giving it legitimacy to the citizens, and discussed in more detail in Chapter 2. The public power is one feature that agents in the society are searching for in order to use it for their purposes. The public power involves resources of immense strength and scope. It gives actors legitimacy to act on behalf of the state, it can supply them with, first of all, money, and second, legitimacy to act in ways no private citizen could do on his or her own. Therefore, individuals and groups are interested in getting aid from the public power, and thus the state still becomes important under the postmodern conditions, although its modern versions of organization are undermined. People just want to use the public power in accordance with postmodern conditions. They do so by attempting to include the public power in their collective action schemes. There is no given magnitude of the demand for the public power, this depends on the circumstances of the interplay between actors and the problems they face.

In a society where precisely that type of rationalized action is under heavy fire, one may not be surprised that the scientific concepts themselves, and among them the rational organization, become undermined. Within our sphere of interest, networks of interaction within or across organizational boundaries become particularly interesting. Such interaction does not take place *in vacuo*, it is embedded in what will be conceptualized as institutional arrangements, channeling interests and guiding behavior towards solutions of common interest, rather than conflict over scarce resources. The institutional arrangements, however, are not like relatively rigid organizations and their standard procedures for action; they only persevere as a result of the acceptance of the individuals acting within them, and they are continually subject to change in so far as they become at odds with the desires of important actors to reach a workable solution. They disappear once actors stop regarding them as part of their practical activities.

The new institutionalism(s) and the concepts of institution become pertinent for this understanding of the state, and will be discussed in Chapter 4. The contention is that we need not commence an analysis with the conceptualization of social problematics as seen by existing public organizations. Such a perspective only covers the ideas of the politicians and public managers and their principles developed for controlling the organization rather than solving the problems found under postmodern conditions.

Instead, one can start out with the problems that create some degree of need for collective action, and from there one must unroll possible patterns of organizing, emerging from the cooperative endeavors by participants to solve each problem according to their needs. The new institutionalism(s) of the last 10 to 15 years are applicable since they to some degree reflect the trends towards postmodern conditions. The science of the modern society stresses the goal-oriented rationality of human action and uses various forms of the modern society's instruments to direct social development, first of all organization theory and systems theory. Postmodern conditions are not susceptible to control in the above sense. There is no lack of means of control, and there are numerous attempts to get control over specific developments in the society, but the overarching master concept of modern control is becoming disputed. Solutions are *ad hoc* and actors are willing to modify in the process of acting, much in accordance with the ideas of flexible specialization within the production of consumer goods.

Thus the task of the analyst is not so much to understand the principles of the (public) organizations as to grasp the dynamics of interaction networks which may change from day to day. At the same time, organizations do exist, and they are likely to have some degree of stability, but their ways of operation have adapted to the networking institutional systems. Therefore, people are working as much with employees in other organizations as they are cooperating with peers in their own bureau. The important features, then, are the processual aspects rather than traditional organizational (managerial) concepts.

With Giddens (1984), one may speak of structuration rather than structure. There is a long-standing discussion of the actor-structure problem within the social sciences, and although the way Giddens has conceptualized this is not final, it helps underscore the point that the dynamic side of the interaction is what we are after. We shall return to this in Chapter 4.

So we want to carry out institutional analysis of policy networks. Why not restrict it to institutional analysis, or to network analysis alone? The aim is to bring together network analyses - which would analyse any kind of network - and institutional analysis - which would analyse any kind of institution. Bringing those two together in an analysis means that we reduce a large range of action patterns by looking for norms, purpose and rules for action, thus ruling out forms of networks that are not used for strategic action, and ignoring institutional arrangements such as large scale systems of general behavioral control (religion, democracy and so on). So we step beyond the loose notions of networks by using institutional concepts, and we loosen the narrow understandings of institution by using network analysis to catch more unstable factors of purposeful action.

RESEARCH PROCESSES AND SCHOOLS OF RESEARCH

Researchwise, this processual understanding is the passage to an adoption of an institutional bottom-up research design which will be discussed in detail in Chapter 5 and applied in Chapter 6. This research design challenges a number of "received views" within public administration, policy analysis, evaluation and organizational theory. The application I then suggest makes compromises between approaches like New Public Management, New

Normativists (including New Institutionalists) and Postmodern Discourse Analysis.

The bottom-up approach is the antidote to the top-down problem: The top-down approach takes the perspective of the organizational top - the politicians in the parliament, the bureaucratic leadership, the people in charge - and uses it for categorizing the problems to be researched. It has become most visible in the implementation research analysing why there might be problems in implementing the intents of a particular law or statute. Usually, top-downers find problems with the organizational setting or disinterest from social actors in the problematics addressed by the formal organization, and they advise the formal decision-makers on that basis without challenging the perspective of that particular organization. Bottom-uppers, in contrast, start out with the policy problem and then have the role of the (public) organizations as a hypothesis rather than a given. Thus they are able to put the instruments of the public into perspective; they can address any interaction linked to the problem instead of being tied up with a particular definition by one organization which may, after all, only be part of the solution seen from a societal perspective.

The more postmodern conditions prevail, the more the bottom-up approach becomes appropriate for an understanding of public collective action in the locality, because the more we will see new ways of citizen involvement in different affairs in ways that the actors of the modern public organization have not been able to comprehend. Therefore, they cannot give direction for researchers as to how to explore the problems of the society - their understanding is linked to the concepts of class, gender, interest organizations, party politics and so on, concepts of modernity that are challenged by postmodern conditions. But even under those conditions, public policy is created, and maybe increasingly by individuals who may superficially fall under those categories. But under present conditions people may behave differently than they did under modernity, and therefore they deserve closer scrutiny in new ways rather than a routinized repetition of a research design that was valid twenty years ago.

Social research is undergoing change. As we saw above, the social sciences were to a large degree established with a modern paradigm one hundred years ago. With postmodern conditions, the modern paradigm is challenged from many sides, and there is no clear alternative emerging. But alternatives are becoming clearer, and from the perspective of this book the trends within organizational sociology, policy analysis and evaluation are of particular interest. They abandon the modern approaches of the disinterested outside observer, and instead work on the basis of social constructivism where empirical evidence in a form that is disclosable to outsiders is created in a process of interaction between researcher and research subjects. Requirements for such research are that there is intersubjectivity: that the subjects can recognize what the researcher wants to express, and that the research can be reported to and discussed by the scientific community.

The approach may be applied to other problems of research. The focus of the book is on public collective action in the locality. One might argue that similar trends are found at the national and even international level in systems of functional differentiation, but these are not explored in this book.

How is this approach located in the universe of the research school? It is eclectic, but to illustrate the scope, one can relate to the schools of public administration of the 1990s (McSwite 1998). New Public Management theorists represented by authors like Osborne and Gaebler (1993) have called for more market and less bureaucracy. There is a certain agreement in the skepticism towards (big) bureaucracy inherent in the approach, but this in no way means that the only cure is to be found in the marketplace. Markets may enhance economic efficiency, but there are other values that must be adhered to in public action; an important one is democracy which is supposed to promote equality, in some cases in spite of the fact that costs become bigger. Furthermore, it is possible to replace large bureaucracies with a number of smaller organizations that are more responsive in serving their clients or constituencies than the big ones. Bureaucratic costs are then replaced by transaction costs, but at the same time greater flexibility becomes built into the resulting system.

Another school may be called the New Normativists. Approaches include the sociological versions of the New Institutionalism (March and Olsen 1989) and the Blacksburg Manifesto group (Wamsley, *et al.* 1990). Those groups call for an organizational or agency perspective; a perspective that carries on certain norms and cultures, maintaining a continuing concern about matters that are at the core of public activity. The approach in this book does not deny the importance of organizational norms and values, but it calls for more attention to the norms of the users of organizations, and the variety of democratic norms that may be played out, also in the locality. Organizations have tended to become professionalized, and professional norms may do good by calling for an equal treatment of equal cases, but they may hinder things being done differently, and hence block greater involvement of people in the locality to satisfy local needs.

A third school is the Postmodern Discourse Analysis, a quite disparate field, but one can mention representatives like Fox and Miller (1995) and Farmer (1998). They emphasize the need to understand communication between individuals as language and either try to reconstruct it as part of a sincere exchange of views, or deconstruct the resulting texts that come out of public agencies to show their internal inconsistency. The approach in this book would emphasize the need to understand communication, but it would also stress the need to understand the peculiarities of the situation in which the interaction takes place, and comprehend the problems at stake for those involved in order to (actively) reconstruct action situations that help to achieve a desired outcome. The approach therefore is not so much about how to analyse as how to analyse (for) strategic action.

In other words, this approach has elements of all of these schools of research, stressing the possibilities of flexibility of the New Public Management, the importance of norms of the Normativists, and the interest in discourse of the Postmodernists, but it does not share, or is at odds with, other aspects of those approaches. Why such eclecticism? The simplest explanation is that if one wants to carry out empirical research, none of the straight approaches seem to be readily applicable; their proponents struggle for theoretical recognition of principles and pay little attention to most of the problems linked to making them work as research tools. To this author, the necessity for actually carrying out empirical research comes first, and therefore, the compromises between principles of theory get first priority.

THE PLAN OF THE BOOK

The overarching theme of this book is institutional analysis of policy networks, and in pursuing this, the concept of institution is used throughout, but in somewhat varying ways in accordance with the different sources used. A more precise definition is not found until Chapter 5, and until then the concept of institution is broadly understood as a set of rules guiding and constraining the behavior of individuals and groups in relation to some problematic. The discussion above has touched upon the many themes of the book. Below we outline the contents of each chapter.

Chapter 2 develops the analytical understanding of the modern and postmodern societies as sketched out above, and introduces the concept of the public power. It addresses some of the uses of the theories of the largest entity of collective action, the state. The modern state has become a vast apparatus, but increasingly dependent on a continuing series of relationships with private actors as representatives of strong societal interests. Political parties have lost some of their powers on that account. A consequence of this development is that the state is losing its distinction as a conceptual variable in its original form. Many forms of social action are becoming to some degree political because of the resulting mix of actors. But if one plays down the importance of the organizational features of the state, first of all the bureaucracy, there remains a number of relationships or networks between actors which may be understood as rooted in the public power. The public power gives these actors resources for action with the special legitimacy which the state enjoys. The precondition is that it must have links back to a constitutional construct - which may be national or international (regimes like the declaration of human rights) - which then is the formal backbone securing recognition of those powers as legitimate. This public power is one of the main vehicles for many sorts of collective action, and hence the widespread interest in interacting with those who can be instrumental in obtaining the right to use it.

Chapter 3 discusses theories of collective action. The theories of collective action follow a methodological dividing line. This is mainly based on whether the analyst belongs in the scientific camp of methodological individualism or in the camp of the opponents, the collectivists. Methodological individualists explain why people, each acting on the basis of their preferences, do not cooperate unless very particular circumstances come about. Collectivists show that they do cooperate, because structural setups make them realize the potential of the collectivity. Therefore, a theme pervading the whole book is introduced: the actor-structure problematic. The apparent methodological divide may not be very fruitful to pursue, and a middle road is suggested which probably is what many empirical analysts - that is, researchers outside the laboratory or computer simulation settings - follow anyway. The real issue, however, is not so much individualism versus collectivism, but rather the character of the analytic assumptions permitting the actor to engage in cooperative behavior. These actors do not have to engage in consensual relations, but they must be able to exchange points of view and adapt their principles in the light of this information. So the development of the relationships and the points of view of the actors are interesting, instead of having preferences of the actors locked. Therefore collective action is possible and does take place when institutional arrangements facilitate exchange of views and thus endorse bargaining relations between individuals and groups.

Chapter 4 is reserved for basic elements of institutional theory. First, the historical roots of institutional theory within political science, economics and sociology are sketched out, and then the problems of how to define an institution are addressed on the basis of the well-known distinctions between macro and micro approaches. As the reader might expect, both schools are found wanting, and steps are taken to make a compromise between them in the general spirit of structuration, but with an aim to sort out more precisely what the components of a dynamic institutional analysis might look like. It is important to understand the consequences of human interaction and the processes that are developed as a consequence. In particular, the change of resources into action capabilities is important to understand, a move from "organization" to "organizing". Such a pattern is seen in the development of implementation theory. The first implementation researchers started their analysis with clarifying the goals for a policy, and then followed the chain of command to see how the goals were transformed into action. The second generation of implementation researchers concentrated more on a careful analysis of how the final parts of the chain from principle to action behaved. Some took the position of the street-level bureaucrats, some followed actors in the locality, no matter what their formal relationships to the implementation procedure were. These "bottom-up" approaches are used as points of departure for institutional analysis of collective action.

Chapter 5 is a further step towards approaching an institutional analysis of problems in the localities. A precise definition of the concept of institution is offered, and the components of the definition - policy problems, positions and networks, norms and rules, and order and meaning - are discussed in some detail. Based on past research, these elements of the institutional definition are discussed to create further conceptual clarification for analysis, and illustrations of how researchers have solved their problems in operational research are supplied.

Chapter 6 places research bottom-up in a meta-theoretical context and gives examples of research within several schools. The chapter groups research into three clusters - a (post)positivistic camp, a hermeneutic and critical theory segment, and a social constructivistic set - to illustrate a range of research from realists to relativists, and how they all contain representatives of bottom-up research. This is not to say, then, that any of those three types of research must be bottom-up. There is broad disagreement among the groups and within the groups, reflecting the fact that the social sciences have not reached any state of internal coherence; by some this is seen as a lack of maturity, by others it is a relief since they do not see any reason to "grow up" in that sense. The chapter is concluded by a discussion of a case from a locality; the top down version is linked to an adversarial cut-back policy process in a local government, the bottom-up version brings in a more sophisticated understanding of the rationales of many actors and broadens the perspective from interests in conflict to perseverance of a neighborhood; from a zero-sum to a positive-sum game.

Chapter 7 sums up the argument of the book and concludes the discussion of institutional bottom-up analysis of collective action under postmodern conditions. In so far as this means a change towards a social constructivist research paradigm, it indicates that the traditional value neutrality and external objectivity within research must be reconsidered.

2. Modernity, Postmodern Conditions and the Public Power

In this chapter we shall first discuss the development of society towards something which we for want of a better term may call postmodern conditions, and second, discuss some facets of state theory that are important in understanding prerequisites of local collective action relating to public resources. We want to analyse the quest for *the public power*, which is what we find to be the central element of the state under postmodern conditions.

Space precludes a comprehensive discussion of modernity and postmodern conditions like Arvidsson, Berntson and Dencik (1994), Crook, Pakulski and Waters (1992), Giddens (1990), Therborn (1995), Inglehart (1997) and many others. And it should be stressed that the line followed is not that there is now a full-fledged new societal form in place as Bauman (1992) argues. It is, however, necessary to spell out the basic elements of an understanding of changes in society. By doing that, we must necessarily generalize and neglect aspects that may be important from a specific American, German or other point of view.

The discussion of modernity and postmodern conditions is formed as an essay. Consequently, the reader may find the referencing wanting. But it is worth stressing that we do not expect to prove that a full-fledged postmodern society is in existence, but only patterns towards change, towards postmodern conditions. Consequently, there is not as much to report on in the traditional scholarly way. The chapter is mainly to be read as reflections upon reflections, combining the ideas of many observers, some of them mentioned above. These ideas are presented by types rather than by broad description, disregarding the variety, which under other circumstances we value.

THE MODERN SOCIETY

There is no general agreement about when the modern society became dominant over the traditional (feudal) society. But many observers concur that the modern society has its theoretical roots in the Enlightenment and its more practical roots in the time of the French Revolution. It gained pace with the industrialization during the 19th century and became fully developed in the 20th century.

We shall illustrate the core of the modern society by the concept of *rationalization* - the systematic use of a global and generalizing reason. This is to be understood on the basis of the historical development. The principles of modern society were developed in Europe and the USA during the 19th century, based on the era of the Enlightenment in the 18th century when philosophers like Voltaire, Montesquieu, Rousseau, Hume and Adam Smith did away with the remnants of religious fanaticism and superstition to define the understanding of man and his surroundings. Instead, facts based on scientific theories were to dominate our understanding of the environment, and the natural sciences proliferated.

During the 19th century processes of rationalization increasingly came to penetrate social practice, especially in the second half of the century, and advanced even more during the 20th century. The principles were particularly spelled out in the processes of industrialization and bureaucratization.

Industrialization first meant a systematic use of machines to make products practically identical and, due to constraints in generating and distributing power, machines were mostly pooled in large buildings, the industrial plant. At a later stage, the assembly line was introduced to reduce the amount of idle time for each worker and to refine their specific skills to perfection within a rather small part of the production process. This made standardized mass production possible. The workers lost control of both the quality of the product and the production process, and instruments of planning and tooling the production process into minute details had to be invented to make management feasible.

Bureaucratization is the parallel to industrialization within the production of paper based services and processes of control. The first step was to pool human beings in relation to an archive which formed the knowledge basis for the organization. Thus the office was created, based on communication in writing. This creation came before the Enlightenment, but over time there followed a specialization of functions between experts, who were subdivided into organizational entities, and the work flow was standardized, often based on categories within forms filled out by applicants. Thus the clerks gradually lost control of the contents of the service as functions became more and more isolated from the total process. Instruments for planning the work flow and systems of control and review had to be invented to make management from the top more feasible.

There are strong parallels in the two forms of production of goods (industrialization) and services (bureaucratization). An important feature is the loss of control over both work content and work process for the individual worker, and a corresponding empowerment of a system of managers whose roles are to plan content and process, and supervise the implementation of that plan. These roles may also be set up in a sophisticated division of labor between planning and supervision, and particularly between types of supervision. Thus an elaborate hierarchical system is constructed, based on the explicitly stated and hence known contents of a large number of functions and corresponding human roles, serving the purpose of standardizing the production of goods and services.

Such systems are examples of processes of rationalization where actions are predictable, maybe even calculable, and where action is dependent on skills acquired within roles rather than on the whimsies of the individual employee. Examples around us abound: take the automobile or the computer factory, where components come from different places and are assembled as identical cars and computers. Within services witness the operations of a McDonald's restaurant or a retail chain store, each identical to the other outlets in colors and basic layout and, in the restaurants, subject to strict norms for the product contents and cooking processes. Within office operations take examples of tax returns, applications for public benefits and so on, all subject to computer handling all the way to the response in (laser)writing which is composed from a computerized data base.

Rationalization by industrialization and bureaucratization has three implications for social action which are to be discussed below: specialization, centralization, and formalization.

Specialization is inherent in the process of creating some degree of division of labor. The more that processes of producing goods and services are subdivided into separate tasks, the more each role performing that task gets specialized. There are, however, several sides to such processes. One is a reduction in autonomy because the task is so simple that anyone can perform it after a short period of on-the-job training. The simplicity may be relative, however, in that it may be required for the role incumbent to have a fairly high level of education before being trained for the task - for instance, testing laboratory samples or welding. Still, the task is simple for such a person; examples are any kind of assembly line production. Another side of the process is a professional specialization where an increase of organizational autonomy may take place. This happens with a growth of demand for highly trained professionals to cover a field of operations within the organization. Here we see a subdivision based not on specific tasks, but on a wider array of problematics which are to be addressed and refined by such professionals. Modern hospitals form one example, with specialization in medical subdisciplines and a high degree of autonomy for the doctors in each department.

At the level of the society, the role of the family is reduced as more and more people get employed in a sophisticated production system of goods and services in a national and international setting. The reduction of family roles creates its own demand for machines for former household chores, professional care for children and for the elderly, food catering and so on.

There are other sides to specialization than just division of labor. One may see the development as one of differentiation, where no question is asked regarding the division of a function into sub-functions; rather we just see an increasing separation of units in the society. The more this development goes on, the more we may see special cultures emerging, linked to the special understanding of the world that integrates the separated unit.

Centralization is a consequence of the desire to keep control over the processes of specialization. This is relatively clear in cases of assembly line specialization where the whole process simply cannot proceed without managers directing the allocation of workers, directing the input of raw material and/or prefabricated components and directing the whole flow in time. This requires a hierarchical line of command and a flow of relevant information along those lines. When we speak of professional specialization, the logic is less clear-cut. Highly skilled people are able to work without much supervision, and they tend to do so; if their autonomy is challenged, they tend to respond by subtle means trying to regain their autonomy. Within the group of professionals, there will often exist some sort of hierarchy, maybe informal, but in relation to the environment, hierarchical relations are strongly restrained and mostly reduced to matters outside the professional knowledge like working hours, pay, budget and so on. Professional matters are only subject to control formulated in general terms as missions or such like.

Modern information processing techniques have added to the degree of centralization in those cases where the management has control over access to data. Computers facilitate tedious tasks of combining data to highly sophisticated information, given that the key to combining data is available. In so far as insight into types of individual data may be spread in the organization, but an overview of types of data is reserved for the leadership, managers of hierarchical systems are put into more powerful positions in the organization.

At the societal level, there is a tendency towards centralization within standardized industrial production and raw material delivery into multinational corporations. The same goes for channels of financing investments where banks and brokers merge into large entities, mostly also multinational.

States grow into sophisticated systems of societal control with large data bases of citizen information, and they develop strong systems of taxation to finance their activities. Over time, particularly in Western Europe, a system of institutionalized links has built up between trade unions, employers' unions and in many cases also state agents, forming a sort of neo-corporate system of interaction. These leave little room for maneuver at the local level which is reduced to having a say only in a few matters of local adaptation.

The third feature of the rationalization process is *formalization*. The stronger the degree of centralization within an organization, the more all aspects of making the processes work must be spelled out and subject to rigorous control, which cannot be tacit and/or informal. Actions and transactions are recorded in archives.

At the societal level, strong specialization means that all transactions must take place within the sphere of a measuring system, mostly money (including budgetary systems), and transactions are recorded by formal systems. Barter and friendly exchanges of services wither away. Roles in the shadows like housewives caring for children and the elderly disappear as all able members of society become members of the work force or become occupied in schools, broadly understood. The former family roles become formal wage earner tasks in centers for day care. Thus the number of formal transactions between individuals is increased as modernity is developed into differentiated activities which earlier - such as child care - were an integrated part of family life. Some may call it a commodification process (Crook, Pakulski and Waters 1992:6-8) indicating that activities like care are being changed into a product that is sold, but one should take note that it is often not a product that is part of transactions at a market value, hence use of the term "commodification" may disturb the analytic meaning of the essence of the differentiation process.

What are the consequences of the processes of rationalization of the modern society? We may stress *integration* or *coherence* as an important aspect. In the process of specialization, only certain aspects of the product (in the assembly line) or the problem solving process (as seen by professionals) are taken into consideration, but those facets are refined to perfection within the limits defined, and therefore may be considered as integrated in a small scale perspective. But what about the larger picture? There is a need to coordinate the parts to a whole and, indeed, there is no doubt that the forces of specialization are working to produce a society of differentiation. A large degree of differentiation, however, is seen as unwarranted by many actors, and they therefore counteract such a process. The *deliberate* process of integration in a larger context in modernity is taken care of by the processes of centralization. Each segment of a production plant may pursue its goal because the chain of management sees to it that the overall goals for production are reached. Likewise, the central state may be seen as an instrument of coordinating public activities - and restraining private activities - to fulfill the general political goals of the society. Thus there are several activities aiming at - though hardly guaranteeing - system integration. The processes of formalization may ensure that activities take place within a system of information enhancing the potential for coherence and integration; nobody of a certain level of education is left uninformed if he or she wants to pursue a topic that is recorded.

Thus, centralization and formalization may be understood as means to offset adverse consequences of the processes of specialization - from disintegration at the system level to integration. Durkheim (1965) pointed to trade unions as important for coordinating many activities in the modern specialized society. Weber (1978) discussed the role of the bureaucracy for controlling processes of both private and public production of goods and services. And Parsons developed his famous AGIL acronym - adaptation, goal-attainment, integration and latency - for the analysis of functions that a system must perform in order to survive the challenges of differentiation (Parsons, Bales and Shils 1953).

POSTMODERN CONDITIONS

Features of the postmodern conditions began to show around the 1960s. Observers do not agree on a date, and there is hardly any reason to fix one, since we are discussing trends, not absolute and irreversible features of development, and the idea is not to claim that we have reached a specific end-state of affairs.

It should, however, be stressed at the outset that the modern society certainly has not vanished. It is there, dominating large parts of our lives, particularly for those who have few working skills. But there are movements towards something new, movements that seem particularly to concern the educated élite, the Academy, and performers of the arts. In addition, alternatives are found among the young, particularly those who are smart, relatively unbound to maintaining constant (high) levels of income and eager to explore the limitations of normal life. Those are the potential postmodernists, people who are in the process of defining the parameters for the society to come. That society is not going to be an end-state either. In that sense the whole process of analysis below is the equivalent of shooting at a moving target.

If the hallmark of the modern society is processes of rationalization intended (but certainly not always successful) to lead to integration or coherence, the signposts of the postmodern conditions are processes of *reasoning* where there is no overarching rationale, but rather competing sources of understanding. Reasoning is a process of creating (temporary) connections between fragments. The grand and global vision of the modern society is replaced by practical discourses linked to one another in a series of deliberations among various actors (Fischer 1995:236). The actors have discrete goals and no intention of reaching an overall congruent state-of-the-world. Consequently, the postmodern conditions lead to disaggregation or *fragmentation* in a world where the processes of control based on rationalization fail and hence integration policies cannot be pursued, at least not by modern hierarchical means. It follows that individuals and organizations pursue their own separate goals and are not effectively subject to coordination measures that they do not accept.

Postmodern conditions are negating the measures of integration of modernity - but not in the sense of returning to what was before modern times. Therefore, there are no particular designs for organizing the production of goods and services like the industrial plant or the bureaucratic office to characterize the postmodern conditions. To illustrate the complexity and to some degree the non-coherence of thoughts about postmodern conditions, we can summarize - maybe unjustly, in a way too crude and a little mind-boggling - what Gibbins (1989:15-16) has collected as important features of postmodernity. It reflects discontinuity between economy, society and polity; the transfer to a post industrial, information and consumer economy, a reorganization of middle-class employment, income, expenditure and attitudes (especially to work and leisure), heightened conflict between private and public realms, culture reflecting plurality, mixed lifestyles based on immediate gratifications, fantasy, novelty, play, hedonism, consumption and affluence. There is also a dissatisfaction with modern politics; its sameness, customary allegiances, predictability, bureaucracy, discipline, authority and mechanical operation. Instead, postmodernity stresses difference, dealignment and realignment, unpredictability, freedom, delegitimization and distrust, power and spontaneity. There is a tendency towards reemergence of charisma and ideology and rhetoric, growing power of the media. Tolerance and freedom is flourishing in a new pluralistic and democratic politics by communitarian and democratic political activity.

One need not agree with Gibbins in every aspect of the above which clearly is not a consistent listing of features. Even if only some of those factors are becoming important, it is fairly obvious that this development defies our normal concepts for analysing social change; there are hardly any basic principles ordering our thoughts as we saw it in the discussion of modernity. For some, this is on the border of chaos. But it may be possible to create a little order by illustrating postmodernism on the basis of three features of fragmentation: individualism, internationalization, and organizational segmentation.

Paradoxically, the gain in *individualism* owes a great deal to the modern society which raised the level of income for many people and thus reduced their dependency on family, patrons and so on. Those who have few working skills and/or are suffering from deficiencies are now supported by the welfare state at levels that were unthinkable before World War II. Poverty certainly has not disappeared but, across the board, the security of most people is very high compared with the conditions when Weber and Durkheim analysed the advent of the modern society. Understood in that perspective one can say that, particularly in Western Europe with its social security systems, individual choice is possible in new ways. The individual is not bound to use all his or her energy to secure basic needs of survival, and the traditional links to the wider family for subsistence are severed.

The individual should be perceived from new bases of understanding; the research results of the science of the modern society are being challenged. The gender gap is reduced for the successful individual, linked to the general spread of higher education and women staying in the labor force after marriage. The bases for the class-divisions of the modern society are being undermined, as several factors indicate: the differences between blue-collar workers and white-collar employees are becoming blurred, the traditional petty bourgeois group of self-employed people like shop owners is dwindling (except among first-generation immigrants), and trade union membership is declining in most countries. The traditional political parties have declining membership, the left-right ideology differences are becoming obscure, political rhetoric increasingly centers on the importance of personalities (and the lack thereof in many politicians!), and there is less emphasis on the larger picture or conditions for politics. Furthermore, many political decisions are really made in a complex interaction between organizations - particularly interest organizations and public bureaucracies which function in an elaborate network of continuing negotiation relationships. Under these conditions it is no wonder that the strong individual tends not to turn to political parties or trade unions for assistance in general, but rather prefers to act *ad hoc* and to use the channel appropriate for each specific situation, as he or she sees fit. One side of this development may be the growth in protest movements - which have in many cases matured into social movements of different kinds which do not just protest, but act in order to change things into something better.

Another side of this individualism is a reinforcement of the drive towards market solutions rather than standardized government provision of a number of services. If individual tastes are to reign, there is no general desire to let governmental bodies produce goods and services because they do not conform well to heterogeneity. Therefore, the trend towards diversity has several consequences. One may be that private markets take over, and individuals have to pay the price for services rendered. Another may be that public organizations are explicitly asked to diversify and compete on a quasi-market, where poor performance sooner or later will lead to organizational decline and eventually to termination. An intermediate form may be found by letting individuals have access to publicly financed vouchers for certain services; the vouchers, once turned over to a service producer, can be exchanged for real money at the treasury. Both public and private producers can accept such vouchers.

Modernity and postmodern conditions co-exist. The successful postmodern individual, then, is well informed, influenced by an international spirit in the arts and TV and has easy access to any information available on the Internet. By contrast, others are left in the world of the modern society and its standardized responses to social problems, maybe enrolled in some standardized workfare program to keep the poor from ending up in the streets. In between, we have a large number of people working within the industrial and bureaucratic organizations of modernity. They follow the routines of such organizations but at the same time they feel some of the attractions of postmodern conditions towards more freedom and at the same time a larger responsibility for their own affairs. Consequently, they are in the middle of social tensions between different logics, creating some turbulence in the workplace, in attempted moves towards contested change.

Internationalization plays quite a role in the above description of individualism. The autonomy of the national state is being broken down, and *loci* of authority moved to international fora; some with federal elements like the EU, some with weak confederal elements like the UN, and some with *ad hoc* understandings and treaties like the World Trade Organization. International laws like the declaration of human rights increasingly present states with claims to change normal procedures and institutions. The UN struggles to get recognition with police authority in peace keeping. National borders are being weakened, a very visible problem is the large number of refugees of varying status who are moving from North Africa to the Mediterranean European countries or from Eastern Europe to West European countries - all in spite of tougher immigration laws in those countries. Economically, multinational firms are working together across virtually every national state border, and the flow of international capital is staggering, reflected in the growth of the large international stock exchanges in Frankfurt, London, New York and Tokyo; the national banks of both small and large countries are without the powers they had when the borders were better sealed. The growth of the Internet and other international communication channels indicates how information is accessible regardless of physical location.

In one way, internationalization could be seen as a centralization rather than a fragmentation: International organizations are organized as bureaucracies and use bureaucratic instruments, like regulation, to be implemented by the national states which are now forced to take the new institutional regime into account. But seen from the individual states the overall result is a fragmentation because there are many loci of international authority, some of them competing for legitimacy. Internationalization, then, does not imply one world government or authority, and consequently it may correspond to fragmentation.

The third element of fragmentation is *organizational segregation*. One aspect is horizontal *segmentation* where the state apparatus is specialized to a large extent, not only by new state offices proper, but also by involvement of new bodies of interest representation in administrative and advisory councils or commissions. Thus, even though the administration may formally be under the responsibility of a cabinet minister, the actual organizational form does not permit the political leadership to be in command. Furthermore, a complex pattern of interaction arises among the many separate organizations in order to promote coordination, in effect creating a continuing system of negotiation (Marin and Mayntz eds. 1991) (Pedersen and Nielsen 1988) where it is difficult to determine which organization, if any, is in charge. In a way it is the logic of a continued trend towards corporatism, but to an extent that prevents control from a few centers.

Another aspect of segregation is *decentralization*. The modern society saw centralization: in production in the form of large plants and financial crystal palaces, while in the public sector there was the state which organized public action in an elaborate division of labor. Under postmodern conditions there is still large-scale mass production, but new forms of niche production, home production, and cooperatives abound, in a complex web of contractors and sub-contractors. A well known example is flexible specialization (Piore and Sabel 1984) where companies based on modern technologies can adapt to changes in demand very quickly. In the public sector, a complex pattern of an increasing number of public and quasi-public organizations is established with an overarching principle of getting the actions as close to the user as possible. This means decentralizing public powers - in some cases to local governments which in turn may decentralize their powers to service delivery organizations of various sorts - in other cases to new forms of state-owned, user-run organizations. Within organizations, there is heavy reliance on the lower echelons of the work force and an emphasis on the ability to adapt to the demands of the users or customers.

This means new forms of organization, more forms of organization, and many organizations which interact in a complex web of market relationships, or contractual relationships, or continuing relations of negotiation and so on. The modern conception of organizations as clear entities with discernible boundaries is replaced by complex interaction networks across formal organizations and shifting responsibilities for the actors involved. Management becomes a complex affair of keeping oneself informed about developments within networks rather than being kept informed about the actions of subordinates; the important administrative skill is to keep processes moving towards a target that is not well understood by any of the participants.

Consequently, the systems of neo-corporatism that were built up by the West European welfare states are being undermined and replaced, increasingly by more local negotiations between a number of actors that is not predetermined by institutionalized procedures. Some observers see the development as one towards chaos. At least, there is agreement that the future becomes less and less predictable. Recognized sub-divisions of the society related to class, gender, age groups, occupation and so on become less relevant as do their corresponding groups of organizations like political parties, trade unions and particular interest groups.

CONTRASTING MODERNITY AND POSTMODERN CONDITIONS

To summarize the differences between modern society and the postmodern conditions, the following pairs may highlight quite typical, but yet contested contrasts which we consequently cannot substantiate by hard data. The discussion covers only the societies of the Western hemisphere, not developing countries. And there is no contention that a total change has taken place - we are discussing trends towards something new. The only general characteristics we can employ are the global and visionary *rationalization* of the modern society and the local and practical *reasoning* for postmodern conditions; the contrast of the search for absolute, scientific truth versus the *ad hoc* presentation of circumstantial or particularized evidence. The "binary" discussion below is summarized in Table 2.1.

In the economic sphere, the problematics change from understanding the system of *production* to understanding the pattern of *consumption*. The development of technology makes ordinary production of goods a technical problem with little involvement of human beings, and therefore the demand side comes into focus to direct that production system according to the needs of the consumers. Consumption certainly is at the center of human thinking. For human beings in general we see a move from a concern for covering *basic needs* to a maximization of the *quality of life*. The general level of wealth is so high that previous problems of getting bread and shelter have become a non-issue, and the new issues are linked to improving luxury assets, vacation time and so on. Therefore, the concern of working people has moved from securing *working conditions* (providing the material basis for the basic needs) to securing a proper use of *leisure time* - sports, cultural affairs, TV, and a second home. There is a broader and intensified interest in cultural affairs, in an increasing differentiation among many tastes and new symbolic values. Satellite communication channels make obsolete the idea that performance is location-bound.

Table 2.1 Modern society and postmodern conditions

Modern Rationalization	Postmodern Reasoning
Global visions	Particular interests
Production	Consumption
Basic needs	Quality of life
Conditions of work	Leisure time
Mass production	Flexible specialization
Production society	Information society
Class society	Pluralistic society
Integration	Differentiation
National culture	International images
National state	International regimes
Party politics	Personality politics
Politics of consensus	Politics of persuasion
Planning	Spontaneity
Reason	Imagination
Interest organizations	Social movements
Centralization	Decentralization
Wholes	Fragments

In the production sphere, standardized *mass production* is being replaced by production in a pattern of *flexible specialization* having little demand for storage of final goods waiting to become shipped to retail stores. Instead, the production follows immediate changes in tastes of consumers, as communicated to a decentralized system of producers able to retool their machine equipment overnight and then produce for immediate sale in the region. Consumers thus have great influence on what is being produced. In effect, the society changes from a *production society* where in the short and intermediate run the producers decide what to make and how, to an *information society* where demands are communicated easily from consumers to producers, often via intermediaries that digest impressions from various sources into more manageable principles for production. It it the handling of data and information that is decisive, not the ability to produce in a narrow sense of the word.

Given the change from production to consumption, notions of the *class* society must yield in favor of a *pluralistic* society with a highly differentiated pattern of humans pursuing their particular ideas. The ideas of strong *integration* via interest organizations and of a common symbolic world must give room for a *differentiated* and non-mass organized system of interests. Previous concern among social researchers for identifying material structural patterns, largely thought to determine the conditions of life for those fitting the patterns, must yield to concern for cultural ideas and symbols of ideas which are not tied to particular material groups but attract followers of the situation. Here the information society plays a strong role in disseminating cultural ideas by television and computer networks. The *national culture*, so important in creating faithful followers of a common goal by referring to ancestors of enduring importance within music, literature, paintings and so on, is challenged by *international images* linked to televised virtual realities, supported by the pop music of the day.

This cultural internationalization is paralleled by the opening up of the *national state*; national powers increasingly are circumvented by the powers of *international regimes* which do not permit parochial demands to intimidate minorities. Increasingly there is a demand for national legislation to comply with the minimum acceptable standards of the "international community".

Within the political spheres, changes are quite dramatic. First of all, *traditional party politics* based on class divisions recede as the class basis of the society is eroded, and is replaced by *politics of personalities*, reinforced by the information society with televised sessions of talks replacing the face-to-face meetings in the localities organized by the local party branch. The ability of party leaders to attract mass loyalty based on a televised image becomes more and more important, as does the ability to treat members of the press. Given such an empowerment of the leadership, a *politics of persuasion* replaces a *politics of consensus*, stressing the ability of the leaders to present their ideas to a large public and get immediate reactions, based on the techniques of the information society, telling them and their political opponents of the preferences of the situational majority. Thus the deliberations for compromises with other parties retract in favor of direct appeal and applause, which the political opponents must then accept as the will of the public. It also follows that careful *planning* of an integrated package of state interventions must recede in favor of more *spontaneity* to adapt political ideas to the situational vogues. Furthermore, the ability to build up decisions based on *reason* as understood in the rational decision-making process is replaced by constructive use of the *imagination* which follows the signals received from a multitude of sources.

Interest organizations, for many years the tokens for perseverance and endurance within many policy fields, building their influence pattern on the ability to continue past conversations and on the control of members, are increasingly challenged by *new social movements* which have no other resources than their present followers and an ability to use the media of the information society in a strategic way. Within the trade unions, there is increasing revolt against the organizational top, demands for more local autonomy and threats of giving up memberships. More workers are hired *ad hoc* and specialized staff members increasingly work as project consultants, roles for which unions have little expertise.

Apart from the politics of the *centralized* personality, more and more political activities take shape as *decentralization* to the localities, permitting differences between the many individualized ideas to be played out. Local governments in some cases take over more responsibilities, but one also sees new forms of detached governing bodies which function in new forms of public-private partnerships or new forms of user-controlled service organizations. The politics of the *whole*, the grand visions, changes into a politics of *fragmentation*, the local interests, where differences are acceptable - within limits - and even encouraged to make sure that the different preferences of people are satisfied. The great narratives of the modern societies are replaced by local stories.

Still, the internationalization of a number of themes goes against a total fragmentation. Problems of ecology, human rights and "policing" of areas of ethnic unrest are becoming concerns for which international regimes make institutional settings to counterweigh problems created by local action or inaction. Consequently, the modern state gets squeezed between supranational and local initiatives.

Modern and postmodern conditions co-exist and indicate a number of conflicts. So while some strive for independence from conditions around them, there are at the same time some basic interdependences among most people within societies, and some of those relations may be intensifying. And these are some of the reasons for collective action.

Socially, there is an interdependence in institutional and organizational settings and it may be understood as a growing need for coordination of social actors despite differentiation in language, systems of meaning, and identities. The society has not disappeared altogether, in spite of desires of individuals to perform on their own terms. The postmodern fragmentation in such an understanding, then, creates problems regarding collective solutions, but some actors try to overcome such problems - for instance, by collective action, as we shall see.

Materially, there is interdependence from externalities and dependence related to common resources to be used by social actors; this is often addressed out of ecological concerns. The problem then becomes how to organize in such a way that the material interdependence does not become problematic; this could be done by actively addressing the problems of how to organize for collective action. In the postmodern development this kind of interdependence may very well be neglected by actors not used to having concern for a proper resource base of collective action. There is then a need for someone to help develop understandings of how to take necessary interdependences into account.

Time also creates interdependence, in so far as interaction requires some understanding of how to communicate. The more the organizational setup becomes fragmented, the more each actor will try to neglect such interdependence in favor of creating their own autonomy, and if they follow their own rhythms only, strong discrepancies may occur. But this is precisely where actors realizing their need for collective action will set in.

Spatial interdependences should be understood in terms of geographical and/or ecological spread of externalities. This is where international regimes in particular take up the challenge of coordinating collective action, most visibly within environmental protection. But also infrastructural investments and maintenance are requirements for interaction and thus are tasks for collective action.

POSTMODERN CONDITIONS VERSUS POSTMODERN VALUES

The discussion above contrasted the modern society with postmodern conditions. The discussion is meant as an approximation to descriptions of what is happening in the Western societies. It is not a subscription to particular values inherent in postmodernism. A number of dilemmas in social science

theories are presented, meant to enhance our understanding of the development of society and, therefore, there is no intention of making the postmodern conditions look especially desirable. We must simply take note that
such changes seem to be under way, and then discuss to what degree modern
theories do or do not adequately grasp the aspects of changes we want to
analyse in the Western societies.

So there is no contention of "the end of history" (Fukuyama 1992) in the
sense that we have approached a perfect society and hence put a stop to new
values. And there is no idea of less need for ideologies now communism has
been fought successfully in Eastern Europe. We are hardly approaching an
idyllic and calm society where marginal problems are negotiated peacefully
between representatives of different social spheres. But ideologies may
change into less coherent thought constructs, if postmodern conditions
prevail. If so, we should reflect upon such change instead of denying that it
is taking place.

Furthermore, as indicated several times, modernity and postmodern conditions co-exist. The Western societies are not closed entities. This means,
first, that there is a steady inflow of people coming from areas of unrest,
many of whom certainly are in no ways postmodern in their orientation.
Second, it means that there is room for exchanges of differing political views
and interests, which create tensions between modern and postmodern principles; tensions that will be "fought out" in yet undetermined discourses. The
point, then, is that there is no absolute theoretical foundation upon which we
can build our understanding of these developments - at least not in the sense
that modernists would do it. It does not really matter whether or not we like
this, what matters is that a substantial number of people act along such lines,
and as researchers we must build up an understanding of how and why.

The ideas about a bottom-up approach to be discussed later, are not
meant as vehicles for promoting postmodern conditions - they are only to be
seen as possible vehicles for understanding and analysing such conditions.
Nor are they to be understood as mirrors of a special enthusiasm for postmodern thinking like "all ideas of common bonds are obsolete" and thus
legitimizing attempts to withdraw from any collective action. And finally,
there is no intent to promote nihilism or the idea that any value is as good as
any other and that, consequently, we cannot judge the actions of other
people. Judge we can and must, but we have to specify the value basis we
use.

STATE THEORY AND THE PUBLIC POWER

Above we went through some of the characteristics of postmodern conditions and some of their consequences for the organization of society. We discussed a development towards stronger individualism and at the same time an internationalization. The state, however, is important in many types of collective action, particularly in Western welfare states. So if it is undergoing change, what does this mean for our understanding of collective action?

Both trends can be seen as creating problems for the understanding of the state as the largest collective within the nation (sociology), and as an autonomous entity (political science). Again, it should be stressed that we speak of dispositions towards change, not absolute and *ex post facto* indisputable evidence. We speak of societies where modern and postmodern ingredients are present simultaneously; figuratively speaking they compete for the attention of researchers and people alike.

Conceptually, the national state is an entity closely linked to the notion of the modern society. Increasingly, and in accordance with the trends towards postmodern conditions, that form of state as a concept has come under fire regarding usefulness in analysing the present society (Fox and Miller 1995). Several questions have been raised: Is the state an entity, autonomous or not, or is it a hybrid, basically run by individuals or by relatively autonomous groups of people? Are we interested only in the state as such, as an organization, or do we have an interest in the role of the state in society, generally or in specific contexts? Furthermore, are we interested in the political struggles related to those roles, as they unfold based on aspirations to conquer positions reinforced by state power - or as struggles between incumbents of such positions? The answer increasingly lies suggested in the second half of the sentences above.

The concept of the state is well established in the social sciences. It is of interest to all disciplines, but for varying reasons. In actual research interests, the disciplines overlap to a considerable degree (in many German universities, political science is part of the sociology department), but one might nonetheless venture the following categorization. In political science, the state is the authoritative allocator of benefits, and important research questions concern how actors come into power positions related to that allocation. In sociology, the state is the largest collective within the nation, and important research questions relate to the symbolic role and the integrative forces in the society, led by the state. In economics, the state is the authoritative moderator between buyer and seller, that is, of contractual relations, and important research questions go into how the allocative efficiency in the society fares under various types of state intervention.

We shall not pursue a comprehensive discussion of state theory and how it fares; this would demand a book-length manuscript (like Hoffman 1995). We will approach the state from the perspective of political science and sociology, combining thinking across the disciplines. The main question is: In what capacity is the state of interest to individuals and groups involved in collective action under postmodern conditions? As in the rest of the book, the discussion relates to states of the Western type.

Regarding the problems of understanding the state as the largest collective phenomenon, only authoritarian states (many of which have disappeared after a while) have been able to uphold the impression that one center can secure the best interest of all citizens. In all democratic societies, there have been continuing efforts to infuse diversity into the processes linked to state activities. This does not mean that large-scale diversification comes about automatically; on the contrary, the research on neo-corporatism - and other versions of the theme of interest organizations and the state - has shown that powers may be quite centralized, but not only to the state, more likely to a network of centralized agents of diverse interests (Marin and Mayntz eds. 1991). Within the state apparatus, there is ample evidence that, over time, more entities are created, and trends towards decentralization to local governments and/or special self-administering units are strong (Bogason ed. 1996).

Regarding the autonomy of the state, the development indicated above in itself challenges the idea of a unit making its decision without much interference from the outside. International regimes also undermine autonomy. Nonetheless, autonomy seems to be extremely important in the political rhetoric; no politician wants to concede publicly that the elected top is not really in charge. It is then quite another question whether the diversification of the state apparatus means new forms of autonomy to the sub-systems, as Willke (1992:126), among others, would maintain with theoretical roots in Luhmann and autopoiesis. Analysing that theme is beyond the scope of this book.

This section is subdivided so that we discuss first one of the most influential theorists of the modern state, Weber, whose ideas about the strong and bureaucratic state have been quoted time and again by political scientists and sociologists. We then go on to new facets that have crept into the analyses of the contemporary state formations: less interest in the structural sides, more interest in the processes; less interest in resources, more in power relations. Finally, constitutions have very much come into analytical focus; no wonder given developments in Eastern Europe. We are interested in constitutions, not as legal constructs but in their role as creating legitimate powers for action, but not necessarily linked to a specific state apparatus.

Weber and State Theory

Most state theorists use Weber's (1978) ideas of the state as having monopoly on the legitimate use of force within a territory. Understanding the definition then means understanding the meaning of monopoly, legitimacy, force and territory. No in-depth analysis of those concepts will be carried out (see, for example, Hoffman 1995:33-47), but some brief comments may be in order.

The historical context of the definition should be made clear. Weber wrote in a period of time when the great nation-states proved their capability of integrating millions of people in large machines of war and letting them fight one another with only a few incidents of error understood as defection from the common goal of fighting the enemy. Until the breakdown of the German Reich in 1918, there were very few mutinies in the military branches. Furthermore, the civil population of the countries involved made great sacrifices in the work for the industrial war production. Organizing both the military and the war production was a large-scale operation requiring a capacity of control which was implemented as a bureaucratic capability, and the bureaucracies of that time had the opportunity to operate to perfection. On all counts, those processes may be interpreted as the perfection of the modern society and the national state - rationalization by industrialization and bureaucratization.

Accordingly, the monopoly was necessary since no state could afford to be challenged or even doubted in its role of organizing whatever was neces sary to reach the ultimate goal of winning over the enemy. On the other hand, it was clear that it would be necessary to have the population accept the measures taken by the state, hence the need for legitimate action, obtained by democratic procedures in the election of the leadership. The revolutions in Russia proved the message. Force is the ultimate means of control, and therefore it is reserved for the state; Weber did not mean that force was an instrument to be used every day. But during the war the capability certainly was demonstrated, and not only on the battlefield. The main proof of the capability was in fact within the normal boundaries of the territory where the state showed its capability to maintain order. The territory indicates the limits for state action with normal means; outside, the state can only act by resorting to force - or by the threat of the use of force unless the opponent complies.

These capabilities, then, are closely linked to the operations of the archetype of the modern state which had its golden age in the first half of the 20th century. But as we saw above, modernity is undergoing change, and so is the modern state. The traditional views of the state are linked to a number of factors which have increasingly been challenged.

The *sovereignty* of the national state is a classic feature in national and international politics, seeing armies, navies and border patrols zealously guarding the borders of the nation in order to protect it from intruders wanting to impose their will upon the national decision-makers by force. This understanding of the national state is being undermined by international cooperation in general, first of all by federative arrangements like the EU, but also by international agreements like the WTO and the Human Rights convention, as we saw above. Lawyers and middlemen take over where military force had the potential; new regimes (Rittberger ed. 1993) determine the scope for action. Furthermore, the transactions by multinational firms which can move their profits to the countries with the most lenient tax codes show that there are more subtle ways of undermining the principles of the sovereign state; the same goes for international cooperation among trade unions. Partly as a consequence of these tendencies, it is difficult to keep up the importance of the national territory as a distinguishing factor for the state, although certain groups like refugees may still find it hard to cross certain boundaries. It is also questionable whether the state has control over the movement of goods and persons in most Western societies of today. The internationalization and liberalization after the Second World War makes such control less and less likely to succeed.

If we turn to public administration, the idea of sovereignty has also played some role. The political leaders were seen as the only ones who could legitimately take decisions of national importance. Such a view does not square with the consultative character of the political processes of today where many interest organizations are asked in advance to confirm the decision to be taken (Marin and Mayntz eds. 1991). It is hard to maintain that the state is characterized by a *formally centralized structure of offices*; on the contrary, more and more offices are being created far from the apex of power in most states; in particular by transferring powers from the central administration to local governments, Britain being one noteworthy exception (Page and Goldsmith eds. 1987). Furthermore, the state lets third parties like interest organizations and non-profit organizations administer many tasks (Hood and Schuppert eds. 1987, Streeck and Schmitter eds. 1985).

The old doctrine of public administration concerned the separation of politics from administration; in such an understanding the public employees only serve to find the means for the politically given goals. It follows from the above that it is increasingly difficult to assert that such political strategies are made by the top, for example by ministers or even the prime minister; strategies are rather conglomerates based on inputs from vastly different elements of a dispersed system of offices, networks and so on. Consequently, there is hardly any *one distinctive state interest*; rather a number of interests are found which may even compete with one another in searching for the support of other important interests, and they may compete with one another for primacy in influencing the development of the society. Seen from a theoretical perspective of the organization, the metaphor of the pyramid (hierarchy) has been replaced by the metaphor of the circle where the situation defines where authority may be located (Hummel 1990).

The idea of different loci of influence also penetrates the understanding of how public organizations are to interact with their environment. There is a rich literature on networks of organizations working in different types of configurations of relations (Marin and Mayntz 1991). Indeed, there are cases where observers see interest organizations and firms defining the agenda and process of public decision-making (Pedersen and Nielsen 1988).

Some state theorists have stressed the separating line between the state and the rest of society, the state being a particular structure operating on its own logic. Such *differentiation of the state from civil society* becomes difficult to sustain as more and more interest organizations are involved in preparing and implementing the state policies for the future. One example is the monopoly of coercion, which is one that most state apparatuses keep reserved for their purposes, but increasingly not as part of a unified, internally consistent hierarchy. And in some nations, one sees formal private organizations performing the roles of authority in private police forces and prisons. It seems, however, that the implementation role is kept distinctly "public" by means of, for instance, an oath procedure where officers are sworn in as representatives of the general public.

Although the state concept(s) are thus being challenged, the state is certainly still a topic in the social sciences. Maybe it was mainly political science of the mainstream American type that for a time forgot the state in favor of the political system and similar concepts, while in continental Europe the concept of the state was hovering in the background most of the time. In the US the book *Bringing the State Back In* (Evans, Rueschemeyer and Skocpol eds. 1985) triggered off a round of discussion on the usefulness of the state concept; while in Europe Marxists developed their ideas about the state into much more refined versions than were seen in the 1970s and early 1980s (see for example Birnbaum 1988).

The interest in analysis of the state has over time narrowed to analyses of bureaucracy as the main agent of the state. Just to give one recent example we may quote a definition like Birnbaum's conception of the state as

the historical completion of a process of differentiation with respect to a set of social, religious, ethnic and other peripheries. This differentiation implies the institutionalization of the state, the formation of a tightly knit bureaucratic apparatus which is both meritocratic and closed-off to various external intrusions, an administrative law and a secular approach - all of which are barriers marking off the boundaries of the space of the state. (Birnbaum 1988:6)

Birnbaum does not directly use Weber and resort to the use of force, but the ideas of Weber on the role of bureaucracy and its closed nature are important in Birnbaum's writing.

Since Weber, most definitions of the state have been related to his concepts as we saw above. As political scientists have expanded their interests in research to local governments, quangos, para-state organizations and other fields of study, they have had problems with relating the specific subject to the general umbrella of monopoly on the legitimate use of force within a territory. A possible interpretation is that one should not really see this as a problem for the *concept* of the state, but as a problem for political scientists struggling to define their subject and trying to put it into a context. If that is so, one might expect to see older political scientists criticizing the younger for having re-invented the wheel - everything has been seen at least once before. This is precisely what happened in the American discussion of bringing the state back in. The debate started by Evans *et al.* (1985) had a reply by Almond (1988) asserting that there is nothing inherently new in the "new statist" approach - American mainstream political scientists have always to some degree taken the powers of the state apparatus into account. Fabbrini commented (1988:894) from the sideline that mainstream political scientists may not have neglected the institutional components entirely, but they have undervalued their importance. That goes particularly for a great number of analyses of American politics; internationally there has been more emphasis on the governmental apparatus - in developing countries, in Eastern Europe and in international politics.

Based on the observations above on postmodern conditions, one may take the discussion a little further. The facets outlined above - the loss of sovereignty of the national state, the reduction in the strength of the state hierarchy, the intermingling of the state and civil society, the increase of actors desiring to participate in the use of the public power and so on - point to an undermining of the received view of the state. The state as a product of modern society clearly is facing trouble in cases where not only modernity but also postmodern conditions form the valid context.

Given the problems of state theory outlined above, it would hardly make sense to seek an integrated and institutionalized concept. Instead, a number of aspects will be discussed; first, the state as a relation and second, a restriction of that relation, to the public power.

The Relational Aspects of the State

Wittrock and Wagner (1990) discuss several aspects of the developments in state theory. First, the conceptualization of the state tends to be constellational rather than unitary: the state is not seen as a monolith, but as a constellation of institutions, be they municipalities of the 19th century fighting poverty, or semi-corporatist networks promoting industrial innovation. Second, analyses of state developments are relational rather than directional. One aspect is a focus on relations between state institutions and the society rather than a focus on specific events like the role of the state in the outbreak of wars, revolutions and the like. Another aspect of relations is the rejection of the notion of the state as a unified entity commanding things to happen in society; this notion is unable to capture what the American state of the 19th century was about; the dichotomy between state and civil society thus is blurring important bases for understanding the relationships. Third, Wittrock and Wagner challenge the notion of an evolutionary view of societal transformation, understood as a generalized unilinear sequence which more or less can be found in all societies. Thus they reject the understanding that there are possibilities for initializing processes leading to a constant improvement of society, for example, by adopting a liberal system of democracy.

This is roughly equal to saying that there is no general model of the state, that *the* state does not exist but a number of organizations and networks furnished with public power can be found, and that no particular desirable model of the state exists waiting to be adopted by "developing" societies - or any other society for that matter - to enhance their standard of living or cultural life.

Some "new statists" went even further by mainly discussing the roles of public administrators, managers, professionals and so on, and their motivations for action in and on behalf of the state. The preferences of the state are not identical to those of its officials, but represent an amalgamation; the officials' resource-weighted preferences result in a state preference after being aggregated in a conflictual or conciliatory manner (Nordlinger 1988:882). The state gets autonomy *vis-à-vis* the society by a number of strategies. If it enjoys general support, it solidifies it and if there are differences of opinion, the public officials persuade or bargain with those having other views to change them. Officials may also deter opponents from using their resources, by accepting protests and such like but without changing their decisions, or even by using coercive powers to threaten and repress opponents (Nordlinger 1988:883). This was not to suggest that the state has always a greater impact on society than the other way round; but Nordlinger tried to balance internal as well as external interests and powers instead of just seeing the state as a system balancing powers outside the political system proper.

Jessop (1989) also stressed the relational character of the state, rejecting both the "state-centered" theorists giving the state a force in its own right and the "society-centered" theorists seeing the state only as reflecting powers in the society. As the state grows, its unity and distinctive identity are diminished as it becomes more complex internally; its powers are fragmented and it becomes dependent on cooperation from forces in society for its successful intervention into that very society. This means that one research problem to be pursued is that of (state) power. For example: in what distinctive ways does the specific institutional and organizational ensemble under scrutiny - identified as the state - condense and materialize social power relations? Furthermore: how is the political "imaginary", in which ideas about the state play a crucial orienting role, articulated, how does it mobilize social forces around specific projects, and how does it find expression in the terrain of the state?

These questions are quite fundamental, and they do away with the unified concept of the state. State powers can be executed, but in specific contexts by specific actors, and how and with what outcome is an open question until one specifies the conditions for action. One example of such an analysis was made by Atkinson and Coleman (1989) comparing the policy networks of industrial policies in a number of countries. They derived the strength of the state by distinguishing between networks where the state structure has a) high autonomy and is highly concentrated b) low autonomy and high concentration, c) high autonomy and low concentration, and finally d) low scores on both accounts. They then related these four structural characteristics to the degree of mobilization of business within the sector in question (high and low) - leaving them logically with eight types of network ranging from state-directed networks, where the state is in control, to industry-dominant pressure pluralism, where business controls politics.

If one follows the results and theories above, an important corollary is that, perceived in terms of networks, one cannot speak of any *one* "strong" or "weak" state; the strength varies with types of bureaucratic structures and the organizational patterns of business and other social actors *within* the nation (Bogason 1992).

Fragmentation and the Public Power

We have adopted a view of the state that stresses some degree of fragmentation, de-emphasizing the Weberian hierarchical notion without totally doing away with the possibility that such a hierarchy can exist and act through its staff. This perception is congruent with the discussion of postmodern conditions and the fragmentation of society without denying that modernity still prevails in many situations. Politics and policy are still linked to some common resource, the use of which is contested in an ongoing process between interested parties. The contest, however, is not necessarily bound to the modern state apparatus.

Some observers see a development process towards a shrinking or even minimal state (Crook, Pakulski and Waters 1992:102-104). But it may not necessarily be so. We see inclinations towards marketization and privatization, but the pattern is strongest in common-law countries like Great Britain and the USA; in other Western countries the picture is more ambiguous. And even in cases of organizational privatization, there may be less deregulation than political rhetoric indicates (Christensen 1988), meaning that the state keeps some means of influence over market allocation.

Regarding the power patterns, one may see the state as intertwined with society and vice versa, not as a closed entity directing social actors. Above, Birnbaum was quoted regarding an integrated state concept. Birnbaum himself has troubles with the strong state, noting (Birnbaum 1988:188) that the strongest state of all, France, has been showing signs since 1981 of an opening up of the bureaucratic apparatus which is the characterizing factor of the strong state. So, even though one may agree with Birnbaum (1988:189) that collective action depends on the type of state in relation to which it is constituted, there could be more than one *organizational* type of state within the same nation, dependent on different constitutional points of departure. Each one implements different qualities of the public power which then in turn gives those who want to act collectively different things to relate to. The monopolistic side of the traditional state concept, as well as the territorial aspects of that monopoly, are thus challenged.

It is reasonable to say that the state, thus conceptualized, under postmodern conditions is on retreat, but hardly minimized. And there is reason to reconsider such a concept of the state in order to create a new platform for analysing the emergent forms of networks between social actors wanting to pursue some degree of collective action. They do so by pooling resources for action, and the public power may be an important vehicle for this by providing resources such as legitimacy for action, money and expertise. So even if one uses a network approach to analyse collective action linked to the state, any network *per se* does not qualify. In the de-unified or dispersed view of the state it is analytically true that many subsystems are found, but their capacity to act in a state role is nonetheless in the last resort *linked to a formal public power*. This power either can be empirically identified in one document or another, or it can be derived or deducted in other ways from a constitutional principle of the state or an international regime.

For example, the incentive for interest organizations to participate in "iron triangles" or similar constructs often lies in the wish to influence a decision to be implemented later by public authorities - or to prevent such a decision from being made. Similarly, local governments form interest associations in order to be able to influence future decisions to be made formally by the (national) state. The organizations of professionals often do all the work linked to the licensing of their members, even though the license is a legal state document; their power in this capacity then can be traced back to a formal power. Even social movements can use the public power for their purposes, as a "political opportunity structure" (Tarrow 1994:62) where skilled actors can use part of the state apparatus for their purposes - while other parts might still be perceived as hostile and hence constraints. Thus environmentalists may find support among the professionals of a Ministry of Environment, while police forces will still object to environmental activism infringing on private property.

These powers can be followed back through a chain of decisions to some sort of constitutional construct. The networks are given legitimacy on the basis of that constitution, which may itself be legitimized in several ways; in nation states by the sanctioning through elections and so on, in international relations by explicit agreements between the actors involved; in local matters by a mix of agreements and elective arrangements. By referring to a constitutional theory of public action one need not specifically support the normative views that may be raised pro and contra the roles of constitutions in the policy process (see Elster and Slagstad eds. 1988). There are consequences of constitutions which may serve politically conservative interests, but they also serve to protect minorities from sudden change due to the whims of the majority, or to prevent an eager state bureaucrat from using his discretion to solve a problem that should or must be solved by (party) political rather than professional means. In this context, however, we are not particularly interested in such consequences; our aim is only to find a suitable research tool for identifying and conceptualizing our topic.

A constitution may determine the range of activities for which the use of the institutionalized power is valid. This, of course, goes for the traditional modern national state where a constitution - in a written version or created over time as common (law) understanding among actors - forms the rock bottom of what is permitted and required from actors. But interestingly enough, constitutions of new sorts are increasingly being used in those international regimes which tend to undermine the sovereignty of the modern state; they are often called charters (for example the UN) and serve the same purpose as a constitution: to determine the validity of the norms and institutional arrangements constraining and empowering present and future actors.

Constitutions, power and institutional arrangements are important elements in an understanding of the circumstances under which the state conceptualized as the public power may come to work. But if we take a look at contemporary actions, there is no reason to restrict this understanding to the concept of the state. Following Weber there has been a general agreement among social scientists that the state is the only construct having the right to legitimately use physical force. But in international relations, there are cases where this authority has been given to an international organization, namely the UN. And within the state territory we see some states contracting out traditional police powers to private firms. But one should be careful in observing what is going on in those cases. In each and every case, great care is taken to ensure that the specific circumstances or validity of the actions are spelled out. Thus in international relations the use of force is usually restricted in a document determining the range of possible actions, and in the relations to sub-contractors there are likewise clear limits as to what actions the contractor may take.

If we follow this line of thought through, it is possible to sort out networks of activities based on constitutions (charters and such like) that determine the validity of institutions and the scope of actions possible, based on that constitution. The important feature in our context is that in order to speak of a public power, it must be possible to trace that power back to some type of constitution. Empirically, action may then be based on the provisions of a constitution of *national state*, or the rules of an *international regime* like the declaration of human rights, or a clause of the EU. Furthermore, one may identify more localized special networks of interaction based on a constitutional setting for a limited group of people like a municipality, a township or even a public elementary school. From those there can be traced a connection back to the constitutional setting of the state or some international regime.

There are some reservations, however. Most state theorists stress the role of a hierarchy of rules and norms. Such hierarchical understanding of the state definition may increasingly be out of step with the empirical reality of the Western democracies, at least if the hierarchy is understood as an incontestable one. Whereas Weber's classic concept of the state is founded on the legitimate use of physical force to carry out the will of the political holders of power (and independent of society), and whereas the classic Marxist position is that the state is nothing but the mirror of the economic order (and thus dependent on society), theorists have come to the conclusion that neither position is fruitful.

Therefore, the state could be a dynamic concept; processes of relations between actors which are often in a position to challenge one another regarding the other party's authority. In periods of uncontested interaction, there may be established hierarchical relations, but there is no notion of definite links based on hierarchy. Furthermore, as indicated above, the public power is not restricted to being a power based on a national state constitution. There may be several constitutions that apply: nationally as well as internationally based.

Some may see the link to constitutionalism as building in an inherently conservative bias in the analysis, linking the (American) understanding to Rohr (Rohr 1986) or his like (Fox and Miller 1995). But it should be stressed that the link drawn above is not intended to be normative; there is no claim that a particular constitution is the only and right document to direct one's life, nor any demand that such a document be interpreted in an absolute way. So there is no particular connection to features like American constitutionalism and the legal battles on the provisions of that constitution for equal rights, right to life and so forth, and the interpretations by the Supreme Court. Rather, the legitimation of the use of the public must somehow be dependent on some constitutional form, but precisely how is constantly up for interpretation by the actors involved.

In this setting, *institutional arrangements* become of interest, because they couple the discussion of the actor involvement and the freedom of the actors to perform within the limits of a structure. In Chapter 3 we shall discuss the somewhat abstract dispute concerning the relations between actor and structure in political science and sociology. The main analytic problem is the inability of researchers to decide what is "in the last instance" decisive - is it the actor who can then form the structures in which he operates, or is it the structure, putting such strong limits on the actor that is not possible for him to change the conditions for action? Our answer to this problem is that the distinction is not fruitful; one must understand the world from the perspective of an ongoing process where actors perform roles under given constraints, but in doing so they change those very constraints step by step and may even be able to turn constraints into assets.

The institutionalistic approach of the Ostroms is a case in point. The important connection is not the specific interpretations of the American constitution (Ostrom 1991), but their understanding of systems of control at several levels of generality is of extreme importance (as expressed in Kiser and Ostrom 1982). In that understanding, constitutions are *rules about rules*, that is to say a system determining mainly who may, must or must not interact with whom under specified circumstances. The significance of this will be elaborated on in Chapter 4 on institutional theory.

The important facets, then, of state theories in analysing policy under postmodern conditions are the resources - legitimacy, money and expertise - linked to the uses of public powers derived ultimately from a constitutional construction, and the interaction of interests in the society trying to use those resources for their purposes. Lacking the visions of modernity to substantiate particular claims, the parties instead must follow procedures that make their decisions acceptable. In such an understanding of *the state as a relation*, the state may still be very important to collective action and hence public policy. But such an understanding of the state invites new ways of analysing policies - how they come about and what consequences they have. This is addressed in the following chapters.

3. Collective Action in Networks

In Western democracies, experience shows that people cooperate to achieve common goals. Collective action takes place whenever individuals cooperate in the face of a common goal. It may happen because they are members of an organization, but it may also happen across formal organizational boundaries, in sub-sections of organizations or between individuals who do not have formal organizational ties in relation to the particular problem they jointly want to solve. In other words, the organizational structures and ties are not given.

This chapter sets the parameters for the rest of the book in two ways. First, a discussion of collective action. Why act in unison with other people? We shall go through some of the large amount of literature addressing collective action. Some of it examines why in principle it is not possible to cooperate, some evidence notwithstanding; other parts of that literature have more positive reflections on cooperative behavior. Second, it discusses a meta-theoretical problem - the actor and structure puzzle which has been an important theme for many years in the social sciences. It is particularly pertinent in problems of collective action and, in order to reach a workable compromise between them, we proceed by relaxing some of the preconditions of non-cooperative theory, thereby permitting the individual actor to let preferences be dynamically influenced by the action situations. Third, by linking collective action to the public power discussed in Chapter 2, we shall get an understanding of collective *public* action.

THE PROBLEM OF COLLECTIVE ACTION

Collective action is a heading used for many kinds of analysis, and in order to restrict a potentially large perspective, we need to clarify the links to two directions of research; the workers' movement and new social movements. In some nations, the important type of collective action is understood as restricted to the workers' movement, emphasizing the importance of strikes, demonstrations and revolutions or, more peacefully, organizing workers into labor unions. One example is Birnbaum (1988), examining the influence of the structure of the state and the élite linked to it upon the formation of such types of collective action and the strategies they pursue. The second is collective action as "social movements", meaning movements of protest, *ad hoc* rallies for action, temporary groupings for influencing particular questions in the locality and so on. (see for example Rucht ed. 1991).

Neither of these approaches is our primary interest, even though some postmodernists see social movements as the most interesting feature of these times, but they may be within our scope of concern, depending on the special features of the action situation which we will not define *a priori*. The approach below to collective action is rather general, but later on we shall restrict our interest to collective *public* action. In the first steps, we include any kind of action involving more than one individual interested in achieving the same goal without competing with one another or dominating each other. Since our main interest concerns providing one or a few common good(s) of interest to a collectivity, it is the definition of such goods that determines whether or not the subject falls within our sphere of interest. Those which do, we analyse as decision-making entities, understood as institutional arrangements aimed at easing the process of collective decision-making.

Collective action can also be approached less directly by looking, for instance, at some consequences of collective action. Elster (1989:17) refers to the *problem* of free riding or the *problem* of voluntary provision of public goods, where the rational self-interests of individuals lead them to behave in ways that are collectively disastrous (see Taylor 1982:1). This is a theoretical, behavioral way of stating it; one could also refer to substantive problems like avoiding pollution of the environment, preserving fisheries or common grazing fields, or preventing the deterioration of a neighborhood.

Such substantial problems, however, can only be solved if a certain amount of cooperation among people takes place. Hence the question: how is it possible to make people cooperate? Theories of collective action are found within several disciplines and, therefore, as one might expect, the answers differ, depending on the perspective and research tradition. The general answer to the problem, however, is either that people do *not* voluntarily cooperate by means of collective action, or that they cooperate because they are induced to do so by forces outside the control of the individual. We shall discuss those answers and come up with some qualifications to such general accounts of human behavior.

The discussion below is divided into three main clusters: theories based on individualism, generally negating the possibility of cooperation, particularly over time; theories based on individualism and institutional constraints; and theories discussing organizational factors that make actors more positive about collaboration.

Collaboration hardly possible

The first example of difficulties in cooperation is based on game theory. The original game theory builds on the rational, self-interested actor determined to maximize his material welfare regardless of the costs for others.

The classic game is "prisoner's dilemma" (Hardin 1982) where two individuals suspected of armed burglary are questioned separately by the state attorney. They did not know each other until they agreed this one coup. The police lacks clear evidence to convict them, and therefore the attorney offers a lenient sentence to each of them if he confesses and thus becomes the state's witness against the other one who will then get a sentence as the main culprit. If neither confesses, they can only be convicted for illegal possession of firearms. If both confess, they will get an intermediate sentence. For each individual, the options are clear: Be silent and risk a maximum sentence, or squeal and be assured that you will only get an intermediate term in prison. For the observer it is easy to reckon that both should adhere to a Kantian principle and do what each would prefer the other to do to oneself, but neither trusts the other, and the collective result therefore is suboptimal to both of them, to say the least, but on the other hand, it is not the worst possible outcome.

A crucial aspect of this kind of game theory is that the game is noncooperative, that is, the players make their decisions independently of one another (though not necessarily at the same time); there are no external mechanisms for enforcing commitments or promises, the players cannot make binding commitments (Rasmusen 1994:18). The players do not communicate about the preferences behind their choices, there is no idea of particular properties of the process leading to the choice and hence the players cannot, for instance, agree on side-payments. So the terms of noncooperative and cooperative are not referring to the amount of conflict involved in the game.

Mancur Olson's (1965) basic argument is fairly simple: There is no incentive for rational individuals to join forces in large groups in order to act in their common interest. The reason is theoretically derived, based on an analogy between individuals and firms in a perfectly competitive market: it is not rational for the individual to assume the costs of, for instance, lobbying on behalf of a large number of co-interested people because the costs to do so exceed the expected benefits; furthermore, the rational individual knows that the organization would not feel the difference if one member (oneself) withdrew, and therefore one will withdraw; this the more so because one is convinced that the benefits obtained by the organization are collective goods in the sense that they cannot but benefit members and nonmembers alike (Olson 1965:11-14). Since everybody reasons like this, the collective good will not be provided on a voluntary basis; there must be some degree of coercion or side benefits to persuade people to join.

The core idea, then, is that everybody prefers to take a free ride, but the consequence is that no one actually will ride because there is no one to provide the necessary vehicle. The limitations of the theory should be clear: Olson addresses the problems of large groups, and only to some degree of small groups (Olson 1965:2):

> Indeed, unless the number of individuals in a group is quite small, or unless there is coercion or some other special device to make individuals act in their common interest, *rational, self-interested individuals will not act to achieve their common or group interest.* (Italics in original)

In small groups where the contributions of each member are identifiable and discernible, both for each contributor and for the other members, and where the contribution is considered to be worth the costs, the matter is different. That observation is helpful when one wants to understand how it is possible to mobilize individuals to collective action and keep them mobilized under conditions where there is continuing and active social control by members *vis-à-vis* one another. Olson has a short discussion of "intermediate" groups, that is, groups of such a size where there is no incentive for individual members of the group to provide the collective good themselves, and at the same time any contribution (or lack of contribution) will be noticed by the other members of the group. Olson concludes that the collective good may or may not be provided (Olson 1965:50) - not a terribly exact statement.

Furthermore, Olson does not really address anything but a situation of continuing theoretical interaction as in the perfectly competitive market; how that continuing situation could come about is not discussed; in other words, Olson does not ask how (large) groups are formed and how they grow. His theory is static, he only says that groups cannot persist solely in their public good capacity if they are large.

Collaboration may be possible

The general conclusion of the lack of cooperation has been challenged, based on the characteristics of the game. Prisoner's Dilemma is a highly restricted theoretical construct. The players do not know one another except for one short incidence (crime) which failed; they do not expect to see one another again; they cannot communicate during their process of choice. In other words, they have no past obligations to fulfill, they do not expect to be confronted for their particular choice in the future, and they have no way of influencing one another by indicating solidarity or similar norms. No wonder, then, that they choose the solution that is less beneficial for them than if they had both chosen not to confess. Their calculus is only directed towards the immediate future: if one stays silent and the other squeals, the silent one is the sucker and must spend a long-term sentence in prison. If both squeal, there will only be a medium-term to spend. So play safe and squeal.

Changing the pay-off matrices may have strong implications. For instance, consider the "battle of the sexes" where the situation is that a married couple faces the choice of spending the evening together, which they would like to do, but one prefers to go to the theater, the other one to the movie. Or, a quite common situation among modern two-income families, the couple must consider a number of offers for jobs in different cities, where typically each city offers fine opportunities for only one of them, while the other one must take a less satisfactory job if they move there. Such a problem can be solved by expectations of the future, but much to the detriment of one of the parties, or it can be solved by taking the joint benefits into account. The married couple thus takes the past commitment to honor and love each other as an incentive to find the solution that gives maximum joint benefit regardless of the distribution between the parties (Scharpf 1988:37).

Elster (1989:24) states a collective action problem as a n-person non-cooperative game, meaning that the players make their choices independently of each other. He defines this as a *problem* because the players do not cooperate except under very specific circumstances. But collective action can be found; explaining such a success is Elster's concern, and he explores bargaining as the means to overcome the difficulties. Axelrod has refined the game to be iterated a few and many times (Axelrod 1984). Repetitive games change the whole structure of the perceptions of pay-off for the participants, the most successful strategy appearing to be to cooperate unless the other actor defects; in that case one should also defect in order to punish the other actor, thus indicating what is the only proper way of action - the name of that game is "tit for tat".

Hardin (1982:158) has shown that under dynamic conditions, the general conclusion of non-cooperative behavior in the game does not apply; analytically he shows that there may exist a contract by convention, that is, social contracts sustained by moral obligations, tacit consent or fair play. This indicates that the general model of the economic, rational actor may not always apply. In a later analysis, Hardin (1995) has kept the rational actor model and shown that individuals may have an incentive to join groups, namely a need to be together with people who think and act likewise; such feelings have had little importance in prior rational actor models.

Based on a discussion of the dynamics of a prisoner's dilemma game, Taylor (1987:168-75) argues that the presence of the state makes positive altruism and voluntary cooperative behavior atrophy. The more the state intervenes in matters of providing public goods, the more "necessary" it becomes: the state is like an addictive drug on which we become dependent (Taylor 1987:168-169):

> In the presence of a strong state, the individual may cease to care for, or even think about, those in his community who need help; he may cease to have any desire to make a direct contribution to the resolution of local problems, ... The state releases the individual from the responsibility or need to cooperate with others directly; it guarantees him a secure environment in which he may safely pursue his private goals, unhampered by all those collective concerns which it is supposed to take care of itself.

There is no particularly theoretical argument behind this assertion other than (based on Titmuss' (1970) discussion of blood giving) altruism creates altruism, and when the state reduces the need for altruism, it will die out as a social relationship. Taylor criticizes mainstream theories on individual behavior for being static in that human nature is taken as given. For instance, with reference to preference structures, he suggests (Taylor 1987:176) that a combination of egoism and altruism forming the utility function of an individual will alter over time in a way which depends on the player's choices in previous games and on whether these choices were made voluntarily or as a result of the presence of state sanctions.

This contention is a version of the general thesis that structure influences the actions of individuals, but also that individuals are able to change the structures over time. This line of thinking has been followed by theorists discussing the human uses of natural resources. Some of them took game theory as their point of departure. The "tragedy of the commons" was coined by Garrett Hardin (1968). Crudely stated, his theory is that people who act rationally and in a self-interested way will exploit common-pool natural resources - that is, natural resources that no one can restrict the use of by, for instance, claiming property rights with no regard to the consequences for other people and/or the physical environment. Consequently, if sufficient numbers of actors use the resource, they will continue to do so until it deteriorates. Peasants having common grazing fields will add cows even though they see that there is not enough grass for all the cows to eat well; fishermen will continue fishing even though they realize that the fishing results in fewer and fewer fish, industries will continue polluting the air even though they may realize that the result may be a destruction of the ozone layer, and so on.

The rationale behind this collectively self-destructive behavior is that the individual actor has no incentive to refrain from using the common-pool natural resource. If he retires a few cows, this merely gives an incentive for his neighbor to put a few cows more on the field; if the fisherman stays home two days a week, there are better fishing opportunities for his competitive colleagues; and the individual industrialist sees no reason to change his energy sources to more expensive ones as long as his competitors are using cheap coal burners.

Common sense seems to call for central government interventions into such problems. The EU Commission allocates fishing quotas to the fishermen of Denmark, Great Britain, the Netherlands, Belgium and Germany to regulate the fishing in the North Sea. Governmental agencies determine the amounts of sulfur dioxide that industries may emit. Another standard recommendation for stopping overuse has been the development of property rights allocated to the individual users so that each and every one by personal responsibility for the use of the resource can find the optimal level of use.

But research has shown (Ostrom 1990) that there are other options; it is possible for people to set up their own institutions for collective action which successfully regulate the uses of common-pool natural resources so that they do not dry out, become emptied of fish or are not changed into a desert. Local people may cooperate for mutual benefit without initiatives coerced by external agents - but often with help from external agents, called upon by the locals themselves. Alternatively, the interested parties may be able to change the system of rules within an existing institution regulating the use of a common-pool resource, often by first closing the access to the resource so that any new user must be subject to such rules (Gardner, Ostrom and Walker 1990).

The experience is clearly based on a perception of individuals actively involved in a continuing process of making an institution work, not by fixed rules but by flexible means, ready to revise any strategy that does not yield the expected outcome. Participation in such an institution is thus a demanding endeavor and, by saying that, it is also indicated what may make such an institution collapse. Such individuals do not fit into the general model of rational, self-interested economic man; for he is interested in immediate maximum material gain, which cooperation with such an institution will not yield. On the other hand, it may also generate gains in the future, but that is precisely the kind of calculus that is seldom seen in game theory.

At the same time, however, it is clear that survival is not just contingent on the continuous involvement of individuals. The institutional rules and to a certain degree the relations of the user organization to the larger community also play a critical role. Rules must be of a character that is simple and at the same time nearly self-enforcing so that any break of the rules is sanctioned.

Factors promoting Cooperation

The discussion above has been based on individuals and their choices founded on preferences. What do those following a more organizational research design have to say on these matters? What about choices made by organizations? And what about actions where actors are difficult to identify?

Organization theory may be helpful in identifying mechanisms that keep people from leaving the group. Among economists, Albert Hirschman's (1970) ideas about *voice* and *loyalty* have turned out to be concepts of considerable interest in accounting for such behavior. Sociologists and political scientists ought to be able to come up with a more refined vocabulary.

Indeed, Lindblom (1965:66-84) has given us quite a range of concepts to analyse mutual adjustment among actors. Since the book was published before Hirschman's, he could not of course reflect upon it. There is a definite parallel to situations of *voice* where the actors do not just express an opinion, but induce reactions from one or more other actors, as is Hirschman's case:

> Voice is here defined as any attempt at all to change, rather than escape from, an objectionable state of affairs, whether through individual or collective petition to the management directly in charge, through appeal to a higher authority ... or through various types of actions and protests ... (Hirschman 1970:30)

In other words, we are analysing situations where action is part of a strategy. Hirschman assumes some degree of hierarchy, but we may nonetheless posit that the parties involved are to some degree in a relatively symmetric relationship so that neither can unconditionally alter the situation for the other one. And even if they formally could do so, it would not be a feasible option for whatever reason. In Hirschman's case it is unwise not to listen, even for the management, because those voicing concern convey the message that there is a risk of exit of customers, voters and/or other supporters, unless new forms of action are taken. Therefore, this is a situation of *negotiation*, not just a voicing of preferences.

Since the desire from those using voice is to get a response from other decision-makers, we are within what Lindblom (1965:33-34) calls *manipulated adjustment*. First, the negotiation, the situation where the idea simply is to induce a response from the other party. There are, however, several special cases of negotiation: the *partisan discussion* where the parties exchange points of view on the possible "objective" consequences of various forms of action, the *bargaining* where responses are provoked by conditional threats and promises, the *bargained compensation* where the parties make conditional promises to one another, and the *reciprocity* where the parties induce responses by calling in an existing obligation or acknowledge a new one.

The "minimal" strategy probably would be the partisan discussion where information simply is put forward about the problems in hand, that is, what the consequences are of proposed or factual actions - and the "maximum" strategy is where the parties can make bargained compensation so that all parties see themselves as gaining from the interaction. The minimal strategy also includes situations where the other party does not - as assumed by those starting the process - react; the statements then serve the purpose of making clear to other observers what is wrong, according to the opinion of the actor making the statement, and thus legitimize later action (including an *exit*, the statement then is "slamming the door").

A further strategy is *indirect manipulation* where one party uses some of the strategies above to induce a third party to affect the second party to reach the desired decision. This probably is a very common strategy among seasoned bargainers - why face "the enemy" directly if you can make someone else do the hard work!

To sum up, the mechanisms discussed above may indeed be useful in analysing some of those cases where collective action does take place, particularly as a reaction to what is seen as harmful to certain interests. The categories suggested by Lindblom serve the purpose of distinguishing between different types of communication between the parties involved, and differentiate between types of situation that deserve a better fate than being brought together under the heading of *voice* (Hirschman 1970). This is not to criticize Hirschman's book, but rather to challenge the lack of imagination of political scientists using Hirschman.

Analysts of social movements pose the question of how the birth of an enthusiastic group of people working intensely towards some common idealistic goal may turn into a more organized, coherent venture - or die a quiet death. Is there some sort of common dynamic? Tarrow (1994:118-134) discusses a number of ways to, first, *frame* collective action in some common cultural bonds, ensuring that symbols form a continuing and visible element of the mobilizing process, and second, to ensure further progress towards *strategic* action by forming consensus and then by using the media for communicating the strategies to a wider audience. The next step towards endurance is to get organized, which according to Tarrow (1994:135-136) consists of three stages: to set up some degree of formal organization to implement the goals of the movement, to organize for common action demonstrating the basic ideas of the movement, and to mobilize structures linking the work in the field with some kind of overarching leadership to coordinate action. Of these, only the second, demonstration, is visible to the public, it being the basic activity binding participants emotionally to one another, but the first and third are those most important if the movement is to survive beyond the very first stages.

In other words, even the most "wild" outbursts of human reaction must infuse some elements of rational organization if they are to live on. Given the special character of its basis, protesters and so forth, such organizational endeavors require quite sophisticated skills by a determined leadership to make the organization robust in the face of opponents, but still flexible to satisfy the changing demands of the members (Tarrow 1994:136). By saying this I do not mean to imply that social movements must necessarily organize, or that such organization is desirable in any particular way. I just report on factors important *in those cases* where participants want to continue their efforts.

Organizing processes, then, are crucial to the continued existence of collective action. What attributes of the organization and its processes may one then point to as important? McCarthy and Zald (1987) point to the crucial role of resources which must be mobilized in support of the organization - from media, authorities and other parties, and by interacting with other organized movements. Resource mobilization theory thus moves the focus of the analysis away from a preoccupation with the resources of the direct participants in favor of a broader array of possible assets outside those working directly for the cause. Furthermore, some strategic actions to secure resources beyond the immediate need of the cause are taken into account, including winning the support of a broader mass public and media for the cause, and introducing some flexibility in the targets set for the collective action. Finally, the existing codes for organizing embedded in the traditions of society may be used more efficiently, including making use of the professional capabilities of members, their access channels to institutional centers, their working conditions giving them opportunities that an assembly line worker would never experience, and so on (McCarthy and Zald 1987:19-20).

As Klandermans (1991:30) notes, the resource mobilization approach does not take into account mediating processes making people attribute meaning to events and interpret situations - the original approach may be subsumed under the rational actor approach. But when in use, one can hardly neglect the fact that resources are not just accrued in an empty space for their own sake, but in a social context; resource mobilization thus should not be studied for its own sake but in relation to the target of the collective action and the meaning ascribed to it by the participants and by opponents as well.

We may now leave the special insights of the social movements behind and ask how organizational responses to the concept of meaning can be analysed. There are several reactions in the literature as to how to analyse them; one is to stick to structural analysis, the other is more actor oriented.

Among the first, some models stress the role of routines and standard operating procedures, in the extreme case being applied to any new problem whether they fit the problem or not. In such extremes, there is no preference formation or organizational analysis of the problem; action is taken as it was done yesterday and by using the concepts available in the organization rather than those that are related to the problem in hand. One such example is given by Olsen (1991) where the Norwegian central administration in the 1970s applied the standards for merchant ships to the new concept of oil rigs, disregarding some of the particular facets of such "vessels". Thus standard ways of thinking dominate new problems; this is one aspect of what March and Olsen (1989) call the logic of appropriateness, very much parallel to concepts like organizational culture, prescribing the members of the organization the proper conduct in particular situations. Thus, the structure and its mediating channels (culture) determine action. It is in a way interesting that the fathers of the garbage can model have turned to a structural model where the original garbage can was much more process oriented.

The second, more actor-oriented version leaves actors with more choice. One crucial element is the cognition of institutional factors and the ensuing active use in reinforcing the organizational basis for action by resource mobilization or the like. In the instrumental understanding of the organization described in the previous section, the relationship between goals and means is crucial. But there are other organizational factors of importance which expand the ideas of meaning. People acting within the organization reinforce and change practices over time, and one can follow their actions empirically. Activities do not just happen, but are part of the work procedures employees put to use. In many cases, they do not make any particular analysis of goal-means relations, but simply act as they see fit, sometimes changing the process incrementally to adapt to (minor) unusual occurrences. These observable and conscious defections from standard responses are important as indications of change, maybe permanent, maybe just for that particular case. Consequently,

> structure exists, as time-space presence, only in its instantiations in such practices and as memory traces orienting the conduct of knowledgeable human agents. (Giddens 1984:17)

which means that the organizing factors of an organization only work as long as they are accepted to do so. We may conclude that the more organizations remove themselves from a rule-oriented system towards an *ad hoc* working entity dealing increasingly with problems of risk in, for example, environmental affairs and with links to probabilities like in addressing problems of unemployment, the less rules of appropriateness may apply. Instead, we encounter strategies seeking to accommodate individual problematics of the organization (environmental affairs) or the individual (unemployment). This also may mean transcending the organizational boundary and cooperating with other public or private agents who happen to be relevant to the particular case.

THE ACTOR-STRUCTURE DISCUSSION

How do we delineate the scope for collective action? This is greatly contested in the literature. Two opposite poles in the scientific literature have been the *actor* approach versus the *structural* approach, and we saw examples of the differences in the discussion above. It is a highly complex theoretical field which will not be reviewed in full; see for example Lundquist (1987) and Fielding (ed. 1988). But the discussion indicated some overlap rather than irreconcilable differences. We want to pursue that at a more theoretical level.

The aim is to question the dichotomy of individualism versus collectivism in social science, by drawing on some of the participants in the theoretical debate of methodological individualism and on opponents to that theoretical position. So, individualism versus collectivism may from some vantage points be misleading labels, but they are applied only with the aim of illustrating two positions in a very general way. This is to show that one may compromise between the two schools of thought, especially regarding the role of individuals and their possibilities within structural constraints.

Individualism

Two of the most prominent scholars among individual methodologists are Hayek and Popper. There is a basic difference between Hayek who applies the term to a methodological principle, and Popper who applies the term to an epistemological principle (Scott 1973:215-216). Hayek discusses the methods and data to employ: they are to refer to the relationships between individual minds which we directly know. The start of a scientific inquiry should thus be termed by the concepts guiding individuals in their action.

The social sciences should constitute the wholes by constructing them from the elements. Thus, Hayek's principle is synthetic. Popper's principle is analytic. He insists that whatever methods we use, we should never be satisfied by an explanation in terms of the so-called "collective" - states, nations, races and so on. Popper thus tells us how to finish our inquiries, namely by reducing them to the behavior and actions of human individuals - institutions must be analysed in individualistic terms.

In his discussion of these meta-scientific principles Lukes (1973:121) starts out with Hayek's basic doctrine of methodological individualism:

> There is no other way toward an understanding of social phenomena but through our understanding of individual actions directed toward other people and guided by their expected behavior.

Thus, according to methodological individualism theorists, no purported explanations of social phenomena are to be considered explanations unless they are couched wholly in terms of facts about individuals. These "facts about individuals" may mean several things for the researcher who bases explanations on methodological individualism, from physiological over psychological to social aspects of the individual (Lukes 1973:124-126). Some use genetic make-ups and brain-states; examples would be Eysenck's classification of political attitudes along two dimensions: the Radical/Conservative and the tough-minded/tender-minded and his explanation of attitudes in terms of the central nervous system. Others use states of consciousness like aggression and gratification; examples would include Hobbes' appeal to appetites and aversions and Freudian theories that explain certain social actions as subsequent results of a sexual activity pattern.

So individual methodologists may use an array of ways to explain individual behavior, but the explanation is preferably based on general laws or specifications of particular circumstances (like structural constraints) which then influence the behavior of individuals[1]. This leads us towards questions of basic scientific principles: can we deduce behavior from theories or must we induce theories from behavioral observations?

In his guide to the politics of rational choice Laver (1981) has an important distinction between inductive and deductive theories. Inductive theories attempt to explain what is actually going on, and the ability to predict what will happen in the future is often used as a criterion to judge

---

1. In Lukes' opinion it is not possible to maintain that explanations can only be phrased in terms of individuals. As demonstrated by the four types of facts of individuals, they are difficult to conceptualize by referring only to the individual him(her)self. We very quickly have to take relationships among individuals into account.

them. In contrast to this, deductive theories are used to tell us what would go on under certain, specified circumstances. Their primary function is to expand our understanding of the possibilities, rather than to explain events (Laver 1981:11).

As a consequence of this distinction, Laver comes to the conclusion that the inductive explanation in the last analysis more or less says that the world is as it is because that is how it is, and therefore much emphasis is put on empirical evidence. The deductive explanation tells us how the world might be, when the world might be a number of things, and empirical observation is then of limited value. Laver chooses to use a set of *a priori* individual motivational assumptions which are then used for deductive reasoning (Laver 1981:15). This is his basis for methodological individualism, a conscious choice which has some drawbacks in terms of empirical reality, but has heuristic advantages in terms of rigor and coherence.

From such a starting point of scientific work it is extremely important that the analyst does not fall into the trap of mixing inductive and deductive types of analysis. Laver blames some rational choice theorists for first following a line of deductive reasoning and then, when the resulting analysis becomes glaringly unrealistic, modifying their *a prioris* by inductive reasoning in such a way that they can deduct the observed reality; they then go on deducting analytically as if nothing had happened (Laver 1981:16). A true deductionist, then, carries the analysis to the extreme. In the light of those results, the starting points may be modified, but not before. Of course, Laver is perfectly aware that any starting point for deductions will, to some extent, be influenced by observations made previously by the analyst himself or by those theorists the analyst draws on. Thus, the distinction between deduction and induction is probably never perfectly clean-cut.

There is, however, one school of thought that has gone far in the direction of deductive theory: public choice. In a discussion of the appropriateness of methodological individualism in inter-organizational relationships Vincent Ostrom (1986) argues that because individuals are ultimately the only ones that can be held to account for actions, individuals should be the basic unit of analysis. It is often asked which is prior - individuals or societies. Some may see the problem as one of chicken-and-egg

> ...where individuals function in structured situations, but it is in those structured situations where the socialization, acculturation, education and learning of individuals occur (Ostrom 1986:6).

This analytic problem may be solved by postulating actors who are individuals in some defined and nested set of relationships that can be specified as a structure of a situation (Ostrom 1986:2). In order to explore relationships, the analyst should stick to individuals and their roles in such relationships.

> There may be circumstances where it is unnecessary within the context of some specific problem that may be unraveled at an organizational of interorganizational level of analysis. But such a mode of inquiry may not reveal the source of the problem or offer a sufficient explanation. In that case we are required to use methodological individualism to unravel the nexus of relationships. (Ostrom 1986:8)

This Ostrom supposes to hold true within an analysis of "self-governing societies", that is, situations of collective choice with some degree of autonomy. If individuals cannot be held to account, it is not possible to speak of self-government, for such people are not capable of managing their own affairs, and hence are not able to interact constructively - such interaction is necessary to set up local associations, that is, local government arrangements. This principle of accountability may be one of the strongest normative bases for methodological individualists.

Collectivism

It is quite difficult to put the opponents of methodological individualism under the same hat, because they are united mainly in their opposition to methodological individualism. So there are limits to a generalized discussion about these scholars.

Collectivists maintain that the whole is more and in some cases logically something other than the sum of the parts. An example can be drawn from economics: the aggregate performance of a national economy cannot be determined by analysing the strategies of individuals acting in that economy. For instance, the reaction of individuals to an economic recession might be to put more money in the bank in order to save for a possible period of unemployment. But if many people react like that, the possibility for unemployment will become higher because the aggregate demand in the economy will be reduced. This is an unexpected or counterintuitive outcome seen from the rational individual, and cannot be analysed properly in individualistic terms. What must be understood is a number of structural variables on which Keynes, among others, built his theory: income, saving and investment functions (O'Neill 1973:15). The example probably becomes even more clear if we analyse what happens when income is being redistributed among people in different income classes: if low-income groups get more income, most of it will be spent on consumer goods, if high income groups get more income, chances are high that the money will in the first step go to investment goods. Thus, the aggregate demand in the economy will be different, depending on which group is being favored.

In other words, in the collectivist version there are certain characteristics about behavior which methodological individualism cannot grasp - be it the historical, legal and institutional preconditions of such individualism. And some preconditions like the distribution of power among individuals tend to be neglected. So, even though individual methodology tends to "demystify" the power of institutions by calling attention to the actions of people (O'Neill 1973:16), the resulting explanation obscures how the unintended or counter-intuitive *outcomes* of individual actions came about. The explanation is a sort of first level understanding, giving us little clue as to why much went wrong in spite of all good intentions on part of the actors.

Above we saw Ostrom's arguments for maintaining individuals as basic elements of analysis even in intergovernmental relations. Concerning the analysis of federal systems, Franz sets up an alternative approach to the one based on public choice. It is based on the structural properties of the inter-organizational arrangement and the strategies of the people involved in its organizations (Franz 1986:480). The formal structure of the federal system is determined by constitutional law. There are differences among nations - in the USA, the federal government can administer some programs itself, in The Federal Republic of Germany, the federal government must administer by delegating responsibilities to the Länder and localities. In Germany, then, there is a notion of partnership rather than center/agent relations[2]. The notion of power to the federal government is not completely denied an existence, but most coordination is contingent on interorganizational arrangements.

In order to analyse this system, the unit of analysis must be large-scale pluralistic systems consisting of formally autonomous, functionally inter-dependent organizations (Franz 1986:483). The institutional arrangements are defined by their interrelations, based on organizational theory rather than economic or other relations.

Organizations are important elements, and they are conceptually defined as open systems which act depending on the behavior of its individual members, which in turn is determined by the conditions of membership, career structures and formalized tasks. Individuals are not denied existence, but their behavior is structured by those factors. The actions of the organiza-tion, in turn, are restricted by other organizations operating in its environ-

2. Franz does not, then, take into account that a number of US federal programs are, as a matter of fact, implemented by states and localities.

ment. In an interorganizational perspective, organizations quickly become dependent on one another - interdependent - and the process results in a complexity where it is not easy to distinguish between strategic decisions made by individual organizations, as they are dependent on the resources of other organizations, like the capacity to make laws, to monopolize information and to perform and to finance certain public policies. The organizations therefore try to negotiate their environment, thus reducing the uncertainties they would otherwise face.

An extremely important corollary is that the interorganizational network may be constituted by relationships that cannot be derived from the components' actions. Coordinated action is not predictable on the basis of constitutional law, but results from the interorganizational bargaining among representatives of the organizations of the network and is contingent on the constraints and opportunities that the network offers (Franz 1986:487).

The difference is that the individualist approach will refer outcomes to strategies while the Franz approach stresses that individual strategies may lose importance in the process where several levels of networks interact towards a result that is not predictable.

Differences and Resemblances

In formal theory, there is a great deal of difference between the individualistic and the collectivistic approaches to analysis of collective action.

Among public choice theorists, Laver maintains the differences by sticking to deductive theory and then in effect denying that empirical verification is desirable. The predicting power of the model, then, is of greater interest than the exact one-to-one empirical match. Other public choice theorists have prepared the ground for empirical discussion of the principles and have left the individual as the sole actor, but they appear to maintain the basic tenet of the approach for normative reasons.

The first position is questionable because the predictions of the model may be circumstantial rather than due to the model. The relaxation of the demands on actors - as including organizations under specific conditions - makes more sense to those who have been involved in empirical research beyond the laboratory setting.

A major theoretical question regards the consequences of action. Collective approaches contend that the consequences of actions are not readily foreseeable because the properties of the networks that emerge are qualitatively different from the individual actions made by the participating organizations. But followers of the individualistic public choice approach also contend some unpredictability, namely that outcomes of individual action are not predictable. For instance, individuals might invest expecting a profit, but market forces will turn that profit into a consumer surplus, rendering little profit to the entrepreneur.

The two schools of thought actually converge on these points, though they are phrased differently: what we see is not what happens. The point is that, as individual observers, we can only see part of what goes on, and only from one perspective. It takes an overview, impossible to get for one individual at the time of action, to understand the complex forces at work and to grasp their interplay. Indeed, a basic rationale for doing research.

A Compromise: Actor-cum-Structure

It should be possible to reconcile the extremes of individualism and collectivism, not within the approaches themselves, of course, but as a compromise between ideals, with the explicit purpose of doing qualitative empirical research in collective action.

First, however, we need to see that in frameworks for empirical research there is some convergence, particularly regarding the role of institutional arrangements. The Kiser-Ostrom framework (Kiser and Ostrom 1982) is a micro approach, starting with the individual as a basic unit of analysis to explain and predict individual behavior and the resulting aggregate outcomes (Kiser and Ostrom 1982:181-182). These individuals, however, make choices within the confines of decision rules, and the analyst can make predictions about, first, the strategies that individuals will follow in specific situations and second, about the aggregated consequences in the society of those individual choices. The analyst is free to make assumptions about the individual, there is no *a priori* reason why, for example, the individual should be an extremely rational economic man type of actor. This, however, is often the model chosen by the analyst in public choice analyses.

The analyst must make assumptions about the individual's level of information, his preferences regarding outcomes of decisions and his way of ranking alternative actions. Furthermore, the analyst must know a number of attributes of the decision situation, like how many decision makers are involved, alternative choices that are available, relations between actions and results in the society, complexity, repetitiveness, communication possibilities among actors and so on (Kiser and Ostrom 1982:184-188).

Several of these aspects can be conceptualized by the rules of institutional arrangements which we shall see further developed in Chapter 4 on institutional theory: how many actors are allowed, what results can be authorized, what changes can be made in the decision-making process, and how specific decision situations are linked to other decision situations (Kiser and Ostrom 1982:191). This way of thinking is based on the division of decision-making logics into levels of abstraction, first conceptualized by Buchanan and Tullock in their *Calculus of Consent*, which in some observers' opinion used too much of economic man in its orientation (Buchanan and Tullock 1962). The general idea has been developed for both political science and economic analysis (Kiser and Ostrom 1982). These rules can be thought of as nested levels so that although any rule can be changed at some point in time, some can only be changed in the intermediate or long run; and those that govern the general principles of the decisions (like a specific type of democracy) are particularly difficult to change. On the other hand, such rules that are difficult to change increase the capabilities of the actors to predict.

Clearly, one of the most viable criticisms of methodological individualism, namely that individuals are treated as if they existed in a structural vacuum, is met by this approach. Individuals are constrained in their action by several factors, and they may use institutional rules as assets in their strategies.

Other theorists have an eye for institutional elements. Blackler (1992:278) calls for an approach to the analysis of organizations in the post-modern era linking cognition with social contexts and thus seeks something linking properties of an actor and aspects of institutions. The central theoretical task is to

> focus on the processes that link cognitions with social contexts, the ways in which taken-for-granted assumptions influence social imaginations, and the opportunities that can be created to manage significant infrastructural changes.

Blackler does so by combining theories of human agency (Roberto Unger) and cognitive theory (Lev Vygotsky). Unger's theory sets up a general framework of a *formative context* which provides an implicit model of how social life should be led. *Institutional* aspects define the institutional arrangements that define the rules for action, and *imaginative* aspects reflect the myths of relevant action scope that are in the minds of (most) actors within the institutional setup. Thus institutional aspects define, among others, the rules of powers within the polity, the judiciary, the bureaucracy and labor organization. Imaginary aspects tell the degree of acceptability relating to political passivity, inequalities in personal incomes and wealth distribution, differences in social rights and other phenomena (Blackler 1992:179-182).

The principles of the formative context thus systematize conditions under which we act, and give the analyst the opportunity to relate an empirical world to theories of particular types of action (like bureaucracy, representative democracy and so on). The theory of activity systems provides the analyst with concepts to systematize the elements of performing an act that may conform with or modify the formative context.

If we think of the formative context as something rather near to institutional arrangements, we can discuss some of the various versions of "new institutionalism" (March and Olsen 1989, Ostrom *et al.* 1994) which do, despite their differences, help us grasp *systems of interaction across formal barriers*. March and Olsen basically recommend a collective approach, Ostrom *et al.* an individualistic approach. March and Olsen fully realize the differences between the two basic ways of analysing politics (March and Olsen 1994:3-5), but apparently they are not willing to acknowledge the progress made by researchers of the individualistic approach within the last decade or more. March and Olsen see the differences as individuals behaving rationally, acting to maximize their preferences in an atomistic political community on the one hand, and a socially constructed actor taking institutions for granted and acting within its rules and practices on the other.

But none of these alternatives is viable; from an empirical point of view one can show that individual action can be of importance, and from a theoretical point of view the problem is raised as to how change comes about if actors always adapt.

March and Olsen tend to reify the institution which could instead be considered a concept:

> ... in the struggle to survive, institutions transform themselves ... Surviving institutions seem to stabilize their norms, rules, and meanings so that procedures and forms adopted at birth have surprising durability. (March and Olsen 1994:18)

On the other hand,

> Institutions change as individuals learn the culture (or fail to), forget (parts of) it, revolt against it, modify or reinterpret it. (March and Olsen 1994:19)

These formulations are a little bewildering. In so far as we can see changes towards postmodern social conditions, the institutional context may increasingly *not* be taken for granted the way it is in the modernity. Consequently, it makes sense to develop theoretical approaches attuned to

individual action linked to institutions rather than to behavior determined by
institutions.

A reconciliation of the approaches, then, should be an attempt to keep the
notion of people seeking to act strategically, also to their own benefit, but
realizing that they act within institutional constraints. This we shall call
actor-in-structure, found in the more traditional individualistic approaches
like public choice and game analysis. Another version is one of individuals
pursuing some kind of goal, but realizing that there is a potential in working
with the constraints and resources that are institutionally determined. This
we shall call *actor-cum-structure*, found in the recent new institutionalism
based on individualism.

An *actor-in-structure* realizes the limits of possible action and does his
best to exploit the course of possible action within those constraints. This is
the course taken by many "economistic" analysts; a special line of research
(for example game theory) goes into analysing how different institutional
settings might shape the behavior of a rational actor. But one could also say
that March and Olsen pursue such a line:

> Insofar as political actors act by making choices, they act within the definitions of
> alternatives, consequences, preferences (interests), and strategic options that are
> strongly affected by the institutional context in which they find themselves.
> (March and Olsen 1994:8)

Of course, the first eight words indicate that the political actor may not
make any choice at all; still the characterization of actor-in-structure seems
appropriate. The actor validates action under the rules of the institution, not
unlike a process of interpreting the law (March and Olsen 1994:10).

An *actor-cum-structure*, on the other hand, is a socialized individual who
realizes the limitations of institutional rules. Still he may act within those
constraints to change the content of or the standard interpretation of such
rules to allow for new courses of action. This may take place in interaction
with other actors where the process of mutual influencing is pivotal for an
understanding of how the outcome in terms of institutional rules is
determined. So institutions are not only understood as limitations for action,
they may also serve as resources for action.

The difference from March and Olsen becomes clear in the goals for
action. March and Olsen claim that people act in order to fulfill the ideas and
principles of the institution:

> In the institutional story, people act, think, feel and organize themselves on the
> basis of exemplary or authoritative ... rules derived from socially constructed

identities, belongings and roles. Institutions organize hopes, dreams, and fears, as well as purposeful actions. (March and Olsen 1994:5)

While there is no reason to doubt that institutions play a significant role in people's lives, there is reason to believe that people do act within an institution with ideas of getting some purposes, which they at least think are their own, fulfilled. Simon discusses this (with the purpose of crushing Becker's use of economic rationality in all social matters):

> Everyone agrees that people have reasons for what they do. They have motivations, and they use reason (well or badly to respond to these motivations and reach their goals. (Simon 1987:25)

It is then an analytic question how to conceptualize this; Simon's purpose was to do away with the substantial rationality of neoclassical economics in favor of a more procedural rationality. The disagreement between the more individualistic and the more collectivistic versions of the new institutionalism is not on the adaption of the substantial rationality - one of the most outstanding representatives of the individualistic version uses bounded rationality (Ostrom 1990). So we need to gain an understanding of the formation of preferences if we are to solve - or rather shed light on - the disagreement.

This may at least in part be seen as a process of cognition. Scott (1995) has found that cognition is an important facet in the new institutionalism in sociology:

> Symbols .. have their effect by shaping the meanings we attribute to objects and activities. Meanings arise in interaction and are maintained - and transformed - as they are employed to make sense of the ongoing stream of happenings .... To understand or explain any action, the analyst must take into account not only the objective conditions but the actor's subjective interpretation of them. (Scott 1995:40)

One may add that factors other than symbols may be treated in the same way, broadening the world of cognition for the actor. This may be done by developing the *individual-cum-structure* understanding; this avoids the problems of lonely maximizer on the market, and defies the structural dope who has no capacity for change. So we need research tools tracing the actions of individuals and helping us organize those actions in an analytic way. Here the ideas of structuration theory may be helpful, and we shall return to these in Chapter 4.

(RE)CONCEPTUALIZING COLLECTIVE ACTION

We have seen that there are theoretical arguments for the lack of collective action, based on methodological individualism, where the topic is cooperation among individuals linked to one another by a non-binding relationship. Within collective approaches, cooperation is more taken for granted; the topic is cooperation among individuals linked to one another through some minimum of common organizational relationship. Within methodological individualism, the analysis is founded on individuals' self-interested reasons for (not) cooperating; within the collective approach, there is a conception that individuals have an inherent willingness to cooperate.

The collectivists would argue that the rational individual, choosing freely, does not exist and that people can only be understood in their social, cultural and historical contexts. The response from individualists is that people cooperate if they see it is to their personal advantage to do so, and this utilitarian perspective is the correct one from which to grasp human behavior. One may also engage in a normative discourse on these points, the collectivists holding that there are intrinsic values in maintaining relations with our fellow members of the community, and hence an obligation to cooperate to a certain limit. Some of the individualists would concede that there is a certain need for individuals to have a community to identify with, or that the community may not be totally alien to individual thought; nonetheless, this does not mean that one can deviate from the priority of liberties - rights may not be pushed aside for the sake of any idea of the common good.

Neither position is held here. Methodologically, the discussion below leads to something like the stance the collectivists hold - that people can only be understood in their social, cultural and historical contexts - but that does not mean acceptance of any and all of the particular normative demands that may be found regarding the moral standards of people's behavior in the locality. In particular, one should have the right to act otherwise than the majority and the right to be passive in a number of relations (see Fox and Miller 1995:36-39). In line with this discussion, we try to find a middle ground for analysis.

Even within the methodological individualistic approaches, we have seen examples that people do cooperate under certain circumstances, first of all through the realization of some self-interest in doing so. This may be a result of some degree of coercion or a threat of coercion, in general due to some degree of state regulation. So cooperation may be obtained by centralization of power, for example to an outside (state) agency to regulate the behavior.

But there also is a possibility that people cooperate if they themselves can set up the conditions for that cooperation, and if they can themselves monitor that cooperative institution. In addition, one can conceive of decentralized groups nested into a larger network of institutional mechanisms for solving problems that cannot be solved locally, that is, as a sort of safety valve (Ostrom 1990).

Elster's (1989:15) answer to the collective action problem is that when collaborative endeavors fail, it is because bargaining breaks down. So institutional arrangements facilitating cooperation between individuals are important for collective action. The rest of this book will discuss such institutional arrangements and methodological problems in studying them. We need not at this point go into a concise discussion of the incentives encouraging individuals to start collective action.

The real issue of the literature, then, is not individualism versus collectivism, but *the degree to which the researcher's assumptions concerning the actor include engagement in cooperative behavior.* Not that these actors must engage in consensual relations; it only means that they can exchange points of view and *amend their principles* - preferences - in the light of this information. In other words, social dynamics come into the development of the relationships and the points of view of the actors are no longer fixed in the analysis, but are allowed to change during it. As long as there is such a non-cooperative foundation of the interaction process, there are few dynamics involved. As soon as a possibility of cooperation is introduced, the whole analysis is changed.

At stake, then, is the basic concept of rationality. Rational actors maximize their benefits and take nothing else into account. It is easy to act rationally in a number of situations where trading is the theme, like in computerized dealing of bonds or other assets. The main factor is using available information as price signals and acting accordingly. No individual contact is necessary to trade, as long as the necessary elements of trust or security are there to let each dealer enter the system of trading. The dealers do not interact about other themes and consequently act rationally. Similar understandings can be upheld for international politics as long as the actors, the statesmen, restrain themselves to sending signals of policy to the adversary and do not become involved in personal communication. So one may signal warnings by moving troops, by declaring intents, limits for acceptance and so on, and thus stay rational. Likewise, production plants stay rational by not informing the public about the composition of the emissions from their smokestacks, as long as nobody knows about it, there is no basis for interaction, that is, intervention by outsiders, and hence profitability can be optimized.

Social interaction changes these preconditions. When individuals become involved in personal communication, a number of factors other than the rationalized signals become important. Businessmen invite one another to lunch, to their homes, they get to know each others' families and so on. The same goes for statesmen. Many steps are taken precisely to create personal ties between actors to establish personal bases for trust and understanding. At the same time, of course, a basis for deception is created if one of the actors breaks the underlying rules which the other party would expect to be followed - the Habermasian ideals of being sincere, attentive, and contributing in substance to the solution of common problems (Fox and Miller 1995: 120-127).

Whether or not the actors follow such particular rules of the game is not important here. The point is that social interaction changes the basis for analysis into something more complex, from a fairly simple and computer-ready simulation of a non-cooperative game into a wholly other understanding of social life.

In the discussion of organizations above, we saw that organizational procedures may help actors to approach the rational ideal in that internal processes aim at building up priorities for the organization which the actors representing it *vis-à-vis* other organizations have to follow. But there is also evidence that such rationality cannot always be obtained, as indicated by garbage can analyses.

These reflections point back to the discussion above leading to the concept of the *actor-cum-structure*, where structure is a mediating element for influencing actors who, in turn, over time may change structural elements. Important was an understanding of the cognitive processes indicating how individuals understand the world around them, and how they react, not passively as structural dopes, but actively reflecting over their experience with other actors.

For the purposes of the remainder of this book we may now (re)define the concept of collective action:

> By collective action we mean a process where actors organize for joint decision-making for one or more purposes and, in doing so, give up some of their autonomy and give up their freedom of action in favor of the joint decisions regarding that purpose.

The purpose may be mainly *action-oriented* such as security against intruders or running a day-care center. It may also mainly be *symbolic* such as being a member of the "Moral Majority", but only in so far as the collectivity does in fact make joint decisions in order to use the symbolic action for a purpose. Purposes may also be mixed as in membership of a political party where both activism and symbolism prevail. In theory, the number of purposes is unlimited - at some maximum we approach the idea of the (welfare) state. The important point is that the members share an interest and want to pursue it in collaboration with one another. In other words, the conception is not limited to the public good as defined by the economist, where jointness of supply and impossibility of exclusion are the determining factors (Hardin 1982:17). When we speak of collective action, it is because people take joint decisions regardless of what any kind of theory has to say on the subject they choose to organize around.

The *loss* of some degree of *autonomy* is an important requirement. This creates tensions among individuals, and in cases of disagreement one must either follow the decision of the majority, or one must leave the group, once the possibilities to deliberate on the subject are exhausted. Consequently, political dissidents leave the party, dissatisfied tournament players find another club and so on. Citizens accept the laws until they manage to organize for the law to be changed. One subtle point is whether one wants to be part of the "game" (Hardin 1982:30); in other words, what options does an individual have not to accept what other members perceive as prerequisites? Is there an option for workers not to join the union? If formal demands do not exist, are the informal pressures then strong? Such questions are not open to citizens; once you have opted for citizenship in a particular state, all burdens and benefits are equally shared.

Decisions are taken *jointly*. This does not mean that every individual has to sanction each and every step in the process, it may mean that some take decisions on behalf of the others, or that decisions are taken by anyone entering specified situations, *according to the rules of the institutional arrangements covering that situation.*

Therefore, it is important to understand the significance of institutions for collective action. In this book we are interested in the state because it may have important implications for collective action. One may assert that it is the most potent form of collective action - the national state acting on behalf of its citizens indeed has shown a capability for action second to none. Given the fact that all Western societies have large public sectors, and given the fact that the citizens cannot escape membership of that public sector - which is parceled out in various ways according to the political organizational pattern of that society - it is clear that it is collective action on a grand scale. We need a discussion of the relationship between public sector collective action and more voluntary collective action. It follows below.

COLLECTIVE ACTION USING THE PUBLIC POWER

Chapter 2 discussed how to understand the state under changing conditions. We have not done away with the state, but we have broadened the scope of public action to being linked not only to a state constitution, but also to other regimes that enjoy legitimacy usually contingent upon the state. Our conception comprises networks linked to formal public powers in various ways, and this perception is at odds with the traditional views of the state as something rather integrated, unified, hierarchical, top-heavy and so on. This disaggregate view of public action is one increasingly being discussed by social science researchers, but it has yet to win broad acceptance.

What evidence is there of a widespread interest in collective public action under postmodern conditions? Some might predict that since the individual is so important under postmodern conditions there is no need for collective action. This is hardly a tenable position. The individual no doubt will pursue his or her own strategies, but few probably have all the resources necessary to go ahead solely on their own. The tasks taken care of by the advanced welfare state within education, day care and other functions still will be done by collective endeavor to some degree, but maybe not in the form of a public professional organization. And we might mention other tasks from the advanced Western urbanized world where forces are joined to make the co-existence of many people within a limited area endurable.

In order to proceed, we must identify the key elements for an empirical analysis of collective public action, that is, where the public power is of some importance as a resource basis for action. These key elements therefore must be linked to the notion of the *public power* as the basic distinguishing factor of the publicness for collective action. We ask the question: who may use the public power to act, how may they do it, and with what resources?

This leads into questions concerning *actors* (who?), *organization* (how?), and *resources* - our task is to determine how they can be related to the above understanding of the public power and its use in collective action. Much of the discussion may resemble a general state theory analysis, but at the end of each section the perspective will be broadened as much as possible. Basically, the idea is as follows: The public power is discernible as a number of possible resources for action; however, these will not be worth much without some organization as a platform for action. Both resources and organization are available as public entities, but may be used by other actors as well.

Resources

Given our definition, resources are central to a discussion of public action - resources are so to speak direct vehicles for the public power. Here, we shall restrict the discussion to a fairly general level, leaving a number of concrete resources out.

First, there is the basic public power which may be made operational in two ways: *law* and *money*. The state can create rules that determine what is to be accomplished, how and if necessary when; these rules form one backbone for state action and regulation of the conduct of other actors. In addition, the state can extract money from those who are subject to its rules and redirect that money to whatever purpose it has the power to accomplish.

Second, there is a resource of *knowledge* to be used for the conduct of running affairs and for new action. Such knowledge is linked to the staff due to their training, but also exists in rules, made in the past. It should be noted, though, that data in and by itself is not worth very much; it is the way that data is organized for use in action that determines whether the information is created and knowledge then can become useful - precisely as with statistical data: it is the manipulation of data by tables that conveys messages to us, not the data themselves. Consequently, files must be known and be accessible in the right situation, and individuals with expertise must be placed in the right positions. If not, the power of knowledge is a perpetually sleeping bear.

Third, there is the creation of an *identity* which makes people prone to follow directions, even though they may not agree in every detail. Some would call this the legitimacy of the state. It may call upon feelings like solidarity or, indeed with regard to other nations, the reverse. This power is socialized into people, but of course the strength varies among countries and within countries; not everybody is prone to follow any demand from the state, and some states seemingly have stronger national symbols than others.

At the concrete level we find numerous instruments available for collective public action. They can, however, be discussed under relatively few headings.

First, there are *rules for behavior*. Many such rules are material rules: requirements, permissions and prohibitions setting the standards for the policy field under examination. Here it is indicated what must be done, what may be done and what is not permitted to be done. There is a rich literature on rules in public administration (Lundquist 1987), but often very much geared towards the specific national sets of rules. International comparisons are mostly found within specific sectors.

A particular behavioral set of rules concerns procedures; these rules indicate who should or must interact with whom under specified conditions, more or less in connection with the rules for behavior. There seems to be a tendency towards more procedural rules and fewer material rules set by parliamentary laws. This means that the output and desired impact of the policy rules are to be set as part of a negotiating process involving the interested parties.

Second, we find an *infrastructure* providing physical facilities for those who need them for transport and so on. This is the typical state instrument: facilitating a few basic needs for the citizens. This is often done without discussing the particular ways the infrastructure is being used, but in some cases, like in the implementation of town planning by zoning, rules may restrict the use of the infrastructure.

Third, there can be *in-kind services or money transfers* to facilitate the access to certain services. Only human fantasy limits the range of services than can be made available by public provision of services (Heidenheimer, Heclo and Adams 1989). Most of them are related to the growth of the welfare state where more and more spheres of family life are being made part of the public responsibility. Money transfers are given to firms or individuals in order to reduce the costs borne by them in regard to some aim. Transfers can be direct, as money paid out for the recipient to use as he or she sees fit, or indirect by reducing the fees for using a particular public service.

Some of these instruments can be used alone or in combination, and their exact content can be developed over a series of interactions between actors by the extended use of procedures or bargaining; therefore the precision with which they are formulated may be of some importance for the way they work. There is the possibility that the instruments are developed in a long series of interactions and thus when they are formulated as a standard or another measure, they function well because all parties involved have agreed to that content.

Types of Actor

We have defined collective action as a process where actors organize for joint decision-making for one or more purposes and, in doing so, give up some of their autonomy and give up their freedom of action in favor of the joint decisions regarding that purpose. What links can one think of to the public power?

We have seen that organizations can act alone or in cooperation, and similarly that individuals can act - on the basis of organizational belonging, however. Is the actor public bureaucracy or a private organization, or some mix of interaction between several organizations? It is not only single public hierarchies which carry out public powers. This can be done in cooperation with other organizations, public or private, or by private organizations alone or in cooperation, and it can be done by agreement or by tradition.

The question can be posed whether private firms in some cases have such a strong say in a bargaining relationship with public authorities that they in fact become main actors. One should be careful, however, to identify how this relationship develops rather than just saying that the private firms decide. There may, as in industrial and technology policies, be national champions, and the private sector may in the last resort have the strongest say, but precisely how and when are questions that should be answered if one wants to learn about how a state carries out tasks.

Our typology, then, does not in and by itself discriminate between actors because of their formal status as private or public. They all have tasks, resources, instruments and must by means of organization change the resources into capabilities for action. Therefore, it must be stressed that the discriminating factor is the *relationship between the public power and the development of these capabilities for intervention.* Private organizations or networks do not have the public power unless they have explicitly had it handed over, by written agreement or by common understanding. But under postmodern conditions, this happens increasingly, and the struggle between different actors to get this particular recognition is becoming more intense.

There is no fixed and common rationale among the actors for using the public power. In some cases there is a strong ideology contending the more normal views. Much action by the state may have no immediate or significant impact on the material life of people, but nonetheless it fuels heated disputes because some feel that the type of action is out of bounds or that it is at odds with their basic values. It is probably the latter sense which has received most interest from researchers and therefore there is a tendency to focus on the identity of individual actors.

Political institutions may create an interpretative order by shaping meaning, and the order provides continuity and a basis for understanding political behavior (March and Olsen 1989:52). Therefore, of course, their influence in such respects must be contested by those who do not see their ideas being confirmed by the existing or the dominating institutions. The influence of institutions goes beyond ideological discourses. Any more or less coherent set of ideas relating to more practical aspects of social life may be influenced by the way institutions channel them; therefore matters relating to the administrative organization of state intervention within any policy field are of interest here. In such an analysis, a distinction between state and society can hardly be upheld (Jessop 1990:303). An approach based on the state as relations of power is more sustainable, the powers being institutionally determined.

Organizational Forms

A third important element for understanding collective action using the public power is organization. Organization is critical for the task of changing resources into capabilities for action (Lundquist 1987). Instruments cannot be used unless there is some kind of organization to structure their use and back them up.

At the most general level, there must be authorities to sanction those who do not follow the rules that prohibit certain actions, linked to some kind of enforcement. These authorities are mostly hierarchies in one form or another. They may be actively oriented in that they perform the actions necessary for seeing that rules are followed, or they may be passive in that they only react in the case of someone bringing suitable information to their knowledge.

One determining variable distinguishing organizations could be the degree of freedom or discretion allowed to the members of the organization while keeping the notion of organization, for example by determining a certain degree of coordination between the members (Mintzberg 1981). Organizational theory has come further than discussing hierarchies; in general there are large numbers of organizational forms on a continuum ranging from a strict hierarchy to social interaction of individuals with no ties whatsoever attached to other individuals - in which case there is no organization as we normally understand the word, but there will be a market-like arrangement. Typical middle forms could be the professional organization where individuals act on the basis of shared knowledge or skills, or divisionalized organizations where the coordination of a number of subdivisions takes place at a certain level of management. In addition, there is the small organization where coordination is typically achieved by mutual adjustment of its members.

These organizational forms could also be used to discuss inter-organizational forms of action, where instead of individuals to be co-ordinated we discuss interaction between organizations. A typology here could be hierarchy, federation, bargaining and social choice indicating the range from a tight control system to no lasting interaction whatsoever (Lehmann 1969). Inter-organizational forms have become increasingly used by states for involving formally private actors in the policy processes. Concepts like corporatism, neo-corporatism and so on cover some of that reality which has helped to make obsolete the traditional, hierarchical conceptions of the state. So has the direct involvement of private actors in administering state rule systems and money transfers.

Over time, then, the theoretical understanding of the organization has moved from a relatively static concept like bureaucracy to a very volatile phenomenon like the network. The rationale has been changed from structure to process.

THE PUBLIC POWER IN NETWORKS

How are the concepts useful if one wants to understand changes in capabilities for collective public action? What has changed, how and when?

The trends towards postmodern conditions have consequences for the state, broadly construed, from unified hierarchical organization towards *networks of governance*. There is a pattern of change in the Scandinavian countries towards organizational fragmentation (Bogason ed. 1996). Denmark is the front runner in that respect. It has given many public service production organizations more autonomy with a user board of directors in charge. Furthermore, local governments may set up neighborhood councils. In addition, contracting out is becoming a widespread phenomenon. Finally, new forms of state grants enable local "entrepreneurs" to control local projects without much interference from the town hall. Sweden is experimenting with neighborhood councils, and service production is more and more organized as a version of contracting out, called the provider-producer model. Norway is experimenting with neighborhood councils and contracting out, but on a smaller scale than the two other countries.

This development means new channels of influence from below, both from private and from public organizations, all to some degree using the public power as part of a collective choice process. First, local organizations and groups will press for influence on matters related to their daily affairs. Consequently, to some extent local government will have to interact in a process of negotiation of terms for future interaction and substantial matters like regulations and budget or transfers. Second, local groups and organizations may get involved in creating links to counterparts in the locality; within other local government areas and/or to higher levels of government. The Scandinavian tradition for organizing for common interests is strong, and the local organizations may set up their own interest organization, both locally, in the region and at the center.

Consequently local government is challenged to engage in new forms of inter-organizational and inter-governmental relations. If the local organizations engage in large-scale links outside the municipality, the municipality council is more or less bypassed, facing strong pressures for change and demands for resources. At the same time, they are facing an increasingly fine-tuned or large-scale web of interest organizations nationally. A parallel development is found in the analyses of functional policy networks (see for example Kenis and Schneider 1991, Damgaard 1986) across levels of government. In intergovernmental terms, the issue is to what extent such networks *de facto* gain control. If a strong alliance of functional interests is being built, it may be extremely difficult to break.

In somewhat different theoretical terms, the postmodern discourse relates the above development of the society to tendencies towards compartmentalization. One version stems from general systems theory, an example is the *autopoiesis* thesis: the society is seen as a number of sub-systems which basically operate on their own; there is a whole language structure linked to each sub-system making it operate perfectly on its own, but on the other hand preventing it from communicating perfectly with other sub-systems (Willke 1992). This is a tendency that is visible most clearly within the academy: legal scholars may as such not understand the discourses of economists and biologists, unless they agree to transcend the normal boundaries for disciplinary communication. We are not going to pursue that line of theory because it operates at a level of abstraction that is too high for the analysis of collective public action in the locality.

Another version of the compartmentalization idea is found in the *flexible specialization* conception of industrial production (Piore and Sabel 1984). This means the end of large-scale production units tooled once a year for the next year's mass industrial production. Instead, a large number of local production units are found, linked to the international community by communication networks, able to adapt the production to new demands from design centers around the world. Physical distance ceases to be important because production can be made for local areas, adapted to local mores and tastes, within an overall general concept. Benetton is the archetype of such a production system.

A third version goes into the extreme *individualization*. This is particularly visible in analyses of communication. The technical development has made it possible for those who master some basic techniques - and who have access to adequate communication technology - to choose among many options in data and information bases, among mass communication channels, among individualized bulletin boards for exchange of personal experiences and learning and so on. What we see, then, is a world of unending choice for those who have the resources, intellectually and materially, to do so. This is not the end of the modern society with some large-scale mass production, with computerized large-scale bureaucratic management of trite social cases needing *ad hoc* social assistance, or computerized treatment of tax returns. The modern and postmodern in that respect go hand in hand. But the development within the public sector towards fragmentation reinforces the trends towards postmodern fragmentation described above.

Those theories, of course, are very different and we only want to point to their agreement as to the fragmentation under the postmodern condition. There may be several consequences for the analysis of collective public action. White and McSwain (1990:49-56) explicitly discuss the consequences of postmodern conditions for public administration in the USA. They see many random, conflicting inputs to the political system; this development creates a constant mood of change with many new programs and interferences based on shifting constituencies of policy with few shared principles. Public administrators face challenges to mediate and structure this overflow of demands. They see a need to maintain an institutional context creating meaning for action; to engage in "reconstructing society" by mediation and to let public organizations secure consistency and links between initiatives. These tasks stress the need for public administrators of great personal integrity and wisdom who are capable of understanding action as a continuing process of cooperation between individuals and organizations.

Such lines of thought indicate why the bureaucratic paradigm for organization is being undermined, as we saw in Chapter 2. There is less and less acceptance of a command system whose standardized decisions are becoming archaic in the light of the great variance of the population served. The bureaucracy is well tuned for standard problems with no time pressure, but does not fare well in a constantly changing world. The bureaucracy emphasizes the accountability to the managerial and political top, giving street bureaucrats little discretion; but the changing environment demands new decisions which a tight bureaucracy cannot deliver in time. The consequences can be understood in different ways; one example is the "post-bureaucratic" paradigm (Barzelay 1992:117-132):

- from public interest to results which citizens value
- from efficiency to quality and value
- from administration to production
- from control to winning adherence to norms
- from specifying functions, authority and structure to identifying mission, services, customers and outcomes
- from justifying costs to delivering value
- from enforcing responsibility to building accountability and strengthening working relationships
- from following rules and procedures to understanding and applying norms; identifying and solving problems; and continuously improving processes
- from operating administrative systems to separating service from control; building support for norms; expanding customer choice; encouraging collective action; providing incentives; measuring and analysing results; and enriching feedback.

The question is not whether this development is acceptable for specific groups in the society, the important thing is that the list is indicative of what is happening. So, the purpose here is not to discuss the precise relevance of each and every element of this particular paradigm, and it does not form a normative basis for this book; it is sufficient to understand it as a part of a movement challenging the received view of many people - particularly public employees - of how government should operate. Some observers may see it as an attempt only to infuse private sector management ideals into government but, apart from the "customer" concept, there is nothing inherently "private" in the list above. The values of people may be changing in directions that do not support a uni-dimensional understanding of a public interest, and hence a basic prerequisite of the public bureaucracy is being eroded. The problems of people are becoming very much diversified; hence the use of "customer" may be appropriate, not because customers create profits, but because customers are listened to. Delivery of "value" is to be understood in this context.

Our interest has mainly been to indicate some aspects linked to collective public action. The above discussion makes it clear that a normal organizational analysis of the uses of the public power does not make sense under a number of circumstances. In such cases, the analytical interest moves towards public organizations and private organizations, individuals and groups, that are working together across formal organizational boundaries in *networks* that defy traditional understandings of the phenomenon. Formal organization may be important, but it is not the only vehicle for analysing collective public action. Forces in the society may in extreme cases capture the state apparatus, but conversely it is conceivable that forces within the apparatus likewise may capture the most important power relations. In any case, there is competition to get recognition and hence the possibility of enjoying a part of the public power.

The development of political science in a way is indicative of this conundrum. Some typical topics of the political science literature of the 1970s and 1980s were planning (Friedmann 1967), implementation (Pressman and Wildawsky 1973), ungovernability (Rose 1979), privatization (Savas ed. 1977), (de)regulation (Graymer and Thompson 1982), third sector (Salamon 1981). This list can be seen as an indication of, originally, a strong interest in making the state control important aspects of the society (planning), and then a growing dissatisfaction with what the state actually did and how it did it (implementation and ungovernability). Then came the stream of alternatives to direct state control or state action (privatization, deregulation), and an interest in hybrid forms grew with the realization that we cannot speak of an either/or of public/private (third sector). What we increasingly see is a number of actors and organizations getting involved in action within networks.

It seems that the development within collective public action will take place within *networks based on hybrid forms of organization, backed to some degree by the public power.* Collective public action no longer takes place only in organizational forms defined by the public sector. Under postmodern conditions no one will accept such monopolies. There are clear indications of such a change of the state from being only the modern, rationalized agent into something new under postmodern conditions, with increasing differentiation, and this fits the postmodern conditions, the details of which we do not have to reiterate here. But there is still some interdependence, as we saw in Chapter 2.

In both cases of differentiation and interdependence, the questions of collective action and access to the public power may become important. First, the publicness in a discussion of Western states must at least mean constitutionality in the sense above, and researchers should take an interest in how social groups struggle for the support of or the control of powers that originate within the constitutional system. This struggle takes place much more broadly in organizational terms than is conceived by the modern understanding of the public sector. But second, the public power concept as understood here takes us away from discussing formal authority only; we can go into an understanding of how powers are developed from formal ones to more comprehensive instruments of influence on a broad scale, in processes of organizing that go beyond the public sector or an interaction between public and private.

This is where the renewed interest in local collective action sets in - there is a demand for research tools to analyse the fragmented society and its actors involving themselves in attempts at collective action. There is a growing literature on various versions of governance and networks, and the development has been reviewed in several journals and books, with somewhat differing perspectives - Bogason and Toonen (1998) on comparing networks, Kickert, Klijn, and Koppenjan (1997) on managing networks, and Rhodes (1997) on governance. What unifies this literature on networks is a general common understanding that rule from the top is waning and that large bureaucracies have severe difficulties in functioning as prescribed. Furthermore, since decentralization, privatization, contracting out and increasing involvement of third sector organizations is taking place in most policy fields, inter-organizational relationships are increasing. These are both vertical, that is, between levels of administration, and horizontal at each level, and thus the number of relationships is potentially large.

In his discussion of policy networks, Klijn (1997) shows how networks are discussed in comparable ways in political science, organization theory and policy science. Organization theory and policy science give up the rational autonomous actor, deal with boundedness for actor and organization, and find a need for a process perspective. Likewise, political science finds a need for addressing many actors that decide, not within a well defined system of power, but in a (mostly) loosely structured system of decision-making that may be more or less closed for other actors. The consequence of the development is a movement away from the understanding of government, to be replaced by an understanding of governance, from organization perspective to process perspective. In addition, this draws attention to the institutional context of the processes, that is, concern about the degree to which there is a stability in the relationships.

Bogason and Toonen (1998) find networks everywhere in the advanced literature on public administration, but they take note that this development is not exactly new. It is rooted in an academic process going in a way back to Simon's challenge in the 1940s to the traditional rational model of decision-making, and in the 1970s the change towards inter-organizational analysis gained momentum in many fields of analysis, more or less at the same time. The development since then is seen as a consequence of development towards technologically (in its broadest sense) more complex situations, and internationalization, and therefore they see no end to the need for better analytical instruments. These are, however, hardly to be found within just one discipline, but require inter-disciplinary approaches. And the demand is not so much for even more discussions of particular configurations and their special qualities, but for more substantial understandings of what is going on in the networks. Imaginative uses of game theory, resource dependency theory and communicative and discourse theories are examples of such desirable progression.

To sum up, we may say that many segments of society want a share of the public power. There is a development towards such shares being distributed by many types of networks of governance. These are, however, not processes of competition where anyone may get what they want if they apply sufficiently strong pressure. There are norms at play to indicate limits for the uses of the public poser, and there are specific organizations that care for those norms. Thus, there is a general concept of the "public good", indicating a special and *general* responsibility for actions on behalf of a presumed entity. This concept at least is an important element of the daily practice of many officials, and it would be an all too academic exercise to neglect that practice entirely. In the next chapter, we shall discuss a conceptualization that goes beyond the state and goes across the distinctions of public and private organizational forms operating in networks - the institution.

4. Institutional Theory

Under postmodern conditions, the strong organizations built up under modern society - the bureaucracy, the interest organizations and the political center - are under pressure. Their legitimacy is not automatically recognized, many social actors try to circumvent them, their representatives feel anxious and not well informed about the attitudes of their members, their leadership realizes that members are withdrawing their support and/or stop being active within the organization. But this may not mean that active individuals stop being active in social issues; they may develop new channels for exerting influence. If so, we need concepts to catch new forms of social interaction, favoring an understanding of processes and relationships rather than of formal organizations. In Chapter 3, we used the concept of network to indicate the change.

We shall see that some versions of institutional theory may provide us with a more advanced framework for analysis, integrating networks with substantive understandings of the processes. This chapter contains theoretical and conceptual discussions to indicate how institutional analysis is to be understood in analysing collective action in networks, creating public policies. So we understand it as a political phenomenon, but the distance to sociology in general and the sociology of organizations in particular is not great, nor is the distance to institutional economics - depending, of course, on what specific schools within those broad disciplinary groups we want to examine. The aim, then, is to reap the benefits of knowledge no matter what discipline it originates from, and accordingly the discussion is not intended to be carried out on the basis of some specific intra-disciplinary understanding. Various definitions of "institution" are discussed within three perspectives: micro, macro and a mix of those, conceptualized as structuration. This means a focus on processes of interaction, and a special perspective, bottom-up, is introduced, to be applied in the next chapter.

APPROACHING INSTITUTIONS

In Chapter 3, we distinguished between individualistic and collectivistic approaches to the analysis of collective action. Within institutional analysis, the same dividing line exists, and we shall explore it below. The discussion of institutions below aims at understanding political institutions, that is, institutions involved in collective public action. But as indicated, the borderline between the disciplines in this kind of analysis is thin, and this book is not intended to maintain a particular disciplinary stance. Nonetheless, a disciplinary background is difficult to ignore and impossible to uproot completely, so to some degree disciplines will influence what can be said.

One particular branch of political institutional analysis will be excluded from our interest: the version limiting the discussion to political institutions seen as organizations. Examples would be a parliament, a presidency, courts, local governments and so on; for instance, in a national context, Dye (1992:21-23), or in a comparative perspective, Weaver and Rockman (eds. 1993). The rationale for excluding such an understanding from this book is that it would be too narrow an understanding to equate institution with organization, thus excluding from the analysis all non-organizational factors. In this book, institutional analysis means analysing interrelations between actors, that is networks, irrespective of the organizational basis.

Some political scientists have broadened the organizational perspective a little to include systems of governance; Beyme (1987:56-58) finds that typical explanatory phenomena are coined as federalism, the autonomy of local government, decentralization of administration, differentiation of court systems - or debureaucratization, modernization and so on. While this certainly is a much more promising way to go, most empirical analyses are limited to the formal aspects of the political system. We shall give one empirical example, namely analysing "regionalism" which is a phrase used by many politicians to discuss new channels of influence within an EU committed to the principle of subsidiarity. Is the Scandinavian region, then, comparable with a French or an Italian region? It certainly depends. In the Scandinavian countries, a region equals a county for physical planning purposes; in the South, regions are much larger and structurally different. Comparisons based on such formal designations do not make much sense for political scientists. Formal entities with the same designations differ in size, powers, functions and political culture, and a comparison must be based on something other than "the regional level". Sharpe (ed. 1993) analyses the various versions of a level of government between the center and the locality in Western Europe and Poland and shows a host of rationales for setting up different systems of "meso" government, a phrase that at least captures one essence of such a governmental level, but which is of little help beyond the identifying phase of a research project. Thus, analysing an Italian region and a Scandinavian county as equivalents is at best a hazardous task.

Institutional analysis has solid roots within at least three of the social sciences: economics, sociology and political science. Each of those disciplines has distinct theorists working towards specific goals within the discipline, but nonetheless there are common traits. Historically, the period around the end of the 19th century was important (Scott 1995, Chap. 1). At that time, so many institutional systems were changed, particularly by creating formal, democratic constitutions. Most countries in Europe from then on drew on the role of (formal) law as an instrument not just for power holders, but also for citizens as an instrument of protection against a strong state. So it is no wonder that theorists of that time reacted and created new theoretical constructs to understand better what was going on.

Institutionally-oriented *economists* like Thorstein Veblen and later on John R. Commons went beyond the generally accepted approach based on individual preferences and choices and put emphasis on factors like habits and conventions derived from the institutional setting, or interaction (transactions) taking place within rules of conduct, or institutions. This was a way of conceptualizing the broader social setting for economic transactions. *Sociologists* like Durkheim and Weber were leading figures within institutional theory; Durkheim initially on an individualistic basis, but later he turned to emphasize the institutional setting external to the individual and backed by sanctions. Weber never explicitly discussed the term institution, but his analysis of administrative systems certainly must be regarded as institutional analysis; he is careful, however, (in opposition to, for example, Marx) to maintain that the individual has choices to make within those structures. In Europe, political science was not well developed at that time, but in the USA, a *political scientist* like Woodrow Wilson did careful examinations of the legal framework and administrative settings of national governments, emphasizing their roles as formal systems and evaluating them based on moral philosophy. In particular, constitutions were important objects of analysis, no wonder since this was a period which saw massive changes from élite systems to mass democracies, established by the processes of writing new constitutions.

Among the early institutionalists, then, the economists and the political scientists mainly resorted to collectivistic approaches, understanding the role of rule systems. The sociologists did similar analyses on the role of social systems (and thus also realized the importance of non-formalized rule systems), but included institutionalists in the more individualistic camp as well. Across the board, the topic was how individual behavior was embedded in institutional settings, inducing certain types of behavior and discouraging other forms. Within economics and political science the institutionalists did not fare well over time; from the 1930s one saw a benign neglect by the majority of theorists who were now busy developing behavioral models of the economy and the polity. If institutions mattered in political science, it was in a formal or organizational way, and the theme was not really explored, but reduced to a residual variable. Within sociology, there was more pluralism; Talcott Parsons and later Philip Selznick are examples of theorists with a firm grip of institutional theory (Selznick 1996).

The behavioral approach pushed institutional analysis of those kinds off most of the research agendas and university curricula after the second world war. Institutionalism returned to political science based on methodological individualism in the 1960s, but did not gain momentum until ten years later. It never really disappeared from sociology. It came to economics in the 1970s, but now based on individualism, and to political science collectivists from the mid-1980s.

Economist Oliver Williamson wrote his *Markets and Hierarchies* (Williamson 1975), based on transaction cost analysis, discussing under what circumstances firms might want to resort to market relations, and when they would prefer to internalize transactions to get better control over input factors to production. He also set up a number of forms of control for the managing segments of production: externally by contracting out and franchising, internally by divisionalizing the firm. These alternatives were used as metaphors in many other disciplines, in political science much to encourage alternatives to the bureaucratic organization. Terry Moe (1984) took an early leading position in refining the ideas for use in the analysis of public organizations. The economic neo-institutionalists have a special interest in analysing the regulative qualities of institutional rules (Scott 1995:35) and their behavior-shaping mechanisms of sanction - rewards as well as punishments. The main goal is to analyse the traditional economic concern for the economy: efficiency.

A few political scientists had re-introduced institutionalism somewhat earlier: Buchanan[3] and Tullock published their *Calculus of Consent* in 1962 (Buchanan and Tullock 1962), and Vincent Ostrom his *Intellectual Crisis in American Public Administration* some ten years later (Ostrom 1974). They analysed the consequences of various institutional settings for individual choice, they were firmly rooted in economic theory and methodological individualism, they shared the general interest in the regulative qualities and the ensuing efficiency of the institutional arrangements, and they formed the basis for the school of public choice which crosses the threshold between

3. One may, of course, object to my labeling Buchanan, a Nobel laureate in Economics, as a political scientist who persistently uses economic theory for his political analysis. Yet I consider his and Tullock's work to be political science as much as many other analyses.

economics and political science. Beyond this there are great differences which we need not go into here (Mitchell 1988). Niskanen (1971) and later Dunleavy (1991) developed public choice towards an understanding of various institutional settings and in particular their influence on bureaucratic decision-making. Elinor Ostrom (1990) developed it towards an understanding of self-governing associations controlling the use of natural resources.

The collectivistic branch of political scientists took up a discussion of the neo-institutionalistic approach from the early 1980s (March and Olsen 1983), and March and Olsen's 1989-volume *Rediscovering Institutions* has now become a classic. Parallel to their work regarding interest in institutional factors (but from a different perspective) was the group that wrote the book *Bringing the State Back In* (Evans, Rueschemeyer and Skocpol 1985) which pleaded for a better understanding of the role of the state and particularly the bureaucratic staff in political analysis. These political scientists initially were up against the behavioral "revolution" of the post-WW2 generation. The disagreements in the "state-back-in" seemed to some more apparent than real (Almond 1988, Nordlinger 1988, Fabbrini 1988), while March and Olsen's intended fight with the methodological individualists has not seen reconciliation yet. The collectivists shared an interest in the normative qualities (Scott 1995:37) of the institutions they took up for analysis. Where the individualists stress the (material) interests in using an institutional arrangement for individual purposes, the collectivists emphasize the obligatory character of institutional norms, more and more understood as culture which is reinforced by the activities of the participants. March and Olsen (1989) use the term *the logic of appropriateness* to indicate that this is a normative concern.

In sociology, there has also been a group of methodological individualists working much in parallel with their companions in economics and political science, first of all James Coleman who emphasizes that researchers using rational choice as a basis for analysis in sociology differentiate themselves from other sociologists by stressing the importance of analysing the optimizing behavior of actors at the individual level (Coleman and Fararo 1992:xi). Other sociologists analyse optimization at the system level, if at all. The collectivists, however, have had a much stronger general influence. Berger and Luckmann published their *Social Construction of Reality* in 1966, but the book was to some degree neglected during much of the Marxist analysis dominance in the 1970s and 1980s. However, it came back in the syllabi around 1990. It stressed the role of institutions and the human action reconstructing those institutions. Scott (1995:40) sees cognition as the main factor joining sociologists interested in neo-institutionalism;

this means that they see as the main driving force the individual's internal representation of the environment, creating a meaning for that individual to act in specific ways. Basically, there is not much difference from the normative group above, but where the normative school does have some difficulties in analysing change in institutions, the cognitive approach stresses the role of interaction in the development of institutional arrangements; people seeing their environment as socially constructed, but also acting to change things as they see fit. In other words, there is some link between the collectivists and the individualists in this approach, making dynamic analysis of the institution more likely. Anthony Giddens had parallel analyses, most strongly expressed in *The Constitution of Society* (Giddens 1984), to which we shall return below.

We may conclude this initial presentation of the neo-institutionalists by underscoring that they are not solely confined to their mother discipline. First of all, methodological individualists have scientific cooperation across disciplinary boundaries, to some degree paying tribute to *homo economicus*[4] and the rational paradigm in general (see, for example, Barry and Hardin 1982). But collectivists also collaborate outside their disciplines. Thus, Campbell, Hollingsworth and Lindberg (1991) edited their book with the explicit aim of confronting different versions of analyses within political science, sociology and economics with one another in order better to understand the institutional mechanisms within different sectors of the American economy - whether they operated as markets, hierarchies, clans, associations or other kinds of networks (see also Streeck and Schmitter eds. 1985). In the Scandinavian countries, researchers have cooperated across political science and economics to analyse the "negotiated economy" as an alternative to mainstream neoclassical economics and mainstream political science democracy at the macro level (Pedersen and Nielsen 1988, Nielsen and Pedersen eds. 1989).

Is there one definition of institution which we can use as a basis for further analysis? In the mid-1980s, the German political scientists set out to map the field of institutional analysis within political science. One result was the article by Göhler and Schmalz-Bruns (1988) presenting us with a literature review based on German and international books and articles. Somewhat discontented with the result, they approached a definition by relating the discussion to sociological understanding of norms and (German) Ordnungstheorie, theory of order. Hence their general definition of institution:

4. Many of the common strands across the three disciplines are analysed in a book with the timely title *Economic Imperialism. The Economic Approach Applied Outside the Field of Economics* (Radnitzky and Bernholz eds. 1987).

Institutions are patterns of recurrent acts structured in a manner conditioning the behavior within the institutions, shaping a particular value or set of values and projecting value(s) in the social system in terms of attitudes or acts. (Göhler and Schmalz-Bruns 1988:316)

This definition is a classical example of sociological determination through structured environment. DiMaggio and Powell (1983:148) also follow that tradition, discussing institutionalization within a specific (organizational) field as a process comprising several elements: an increase in the interaction among organizations in the field, where structures of domination and coalition have emerged, and where there is an increase in the information load with which the organizations must contend. Furthermore, there is a development of a mutual awareness among the participants that they are involved in a common enterprise. In other words, the institution is a network of organizations with special links and some common bonds, if not norms. These organizations tend to become similar in a number of aspects; this process is called isomorphism, a pressure towards becoming alike.

Thelen and Steinmo (1992:2) use Peter Hall's definition of institution as

The formal rules, compliance procedures, and standard operating practices that structure the relationship between individuals in various units of the polity and economy.

Here the individual enters with a clear role, where above it was (maybe) understood (Göhler and Schmalz-Bruns) or suppressed (DiMaggio and Powell).

As general phenomena, institutions, then, seem to be important entities governing facets of our lives. The examples above should suffice to conclude that the general features of institutions are

- a *structure* based on interaction between actors
- some degree of common understanding or *values* and
- a certain pressure to *conform.*

Actors are individuals or organizations - as we shall see below, there is quite a difference as to whether one stresses one or another of those features. So the elements above are only starting points for a more sophisticated understanding of institutions.

CONTEMPORARY INSTITUTIONAL RESEARCH

The approaches across disciplines, then, fall into three categories. The first, based on methodological individualism, has the consequences of strategies of actors under varying institutional constraints as its main focus. The second, based on collectivism, has mainly dealt with the various facets of institutions creating social order. The third category falls in between these main types because its focus is neither on actor nor structure, but on processes between actor and structure, pointing to human agency but at the same time stressing the role of institutional limits and capabilities in the short run.

Micro Behavior within Structural Settings

The bulk of theory in this group may be characterized as versions of rational choice, in some versions called social choice, in some public choice, based on the activities of some version of *rational man* (economic man, political man, depending on the aspects of the world the analyst is interested in) working towards an optimization of his or her gains or benefits, given a certain structure of individual preferences, and *given some institutional constraints*. We have, therefore, to discuss attributes of the actor representing the micro-level behavior, and attributes of the institutional arrangements.

In Scandinavian political science, Hernes (ed. 1978) has become a standard reference on the consequences for behavior of systems as market, democracy and bureaucracy. These are understood as generalized institutional arenas, forming incentive systems for individual behavior. In the *market*, individuals act on the basis of preferences for different goods, given a certain price structure. The ideal market which the individual cannot by himself affect in any direction functions as a system of control for the economic actor; the most important information is prices which the rational economic actor, maximizing his welfare, uses for ordering his options for trading, given a certain preference structure and given a certain disposable income. The rationality context is welfare maximizing in the short run which is foreseeable and stable.

Within *democracy*, one can paraphrase the seller and buyer in the market. Buyers are individuals acting as voters based on preferences regarding problems to be solved by the political system. Sellers are politicians maximizing their main goal or reelection. As a voter one can exercise support by voting and by membership of political parties; control mechanisms thus are votes and membership. Politicians are informed of the opinions of the voters from votes and the support by members of the political party. General policy principles are determined by the party based on the standpoints of its members. The rationality context then is vote maximizing and active membership in order to voice opinions.

Within the *bureaucracy*, individuals act on the basis of instructions, as conformity to superiors is an important parameter in maximizing a career. Crucial information is general rules for action, orders from superiors and feedback about the implementation of actions. In principle, all information is in writing and is recorded. Further basis for action is the expertise the bureaucrat has acquired and accumulated over the years in the organization. The rationality context is a known and perceptible system of career and a coherent system of solutions *vis-à-vis* the problems that the organization is supposed to handle. Decisions are predictable in so far as they can be related to prior decisions; bureaucracies are based on continuity. The accountability is based on the chain of command which secures the coordination of all actions.

Those three institutional arenas, then, have in common the existence of a coherent, generalized system of control regulating behavioral patterns - the specific features differ, though. Comparable analytic patterns are found in other articles and books discussing institutions. In general, the behavioral concepts of the control system can be coined as rules for action. Kiser and Ostrom (1982) have set up an elaborate system of rules on three levels of action; we shall return to those later. Here it is sufficient to note that such rules may be more or less difficult to change for the actor in the relative short run; some rules are to be regarded as basic and unalterable, others can be applied with flexibility as problems arise.

What about the actor? Hernes (1978) did not examine the attributes of the actor in depth - Kiser and Ostrom (1982) have done more, as analysts working with methodological individualism mostly do. One example is rational choice whose explanations of behavior are based on methodological individualism with actors attempting to maximize their utility by their actions. Typically, the rational model is employed by analysts by identifying a number of given preferences (goals), finding a number of alternatives for action leading to different satisfaction of the preferences, and expecting a choice of action maximizing the fulfillment of those preferences, realizing what opportunities are forgone by that specific course of action. This realization is important in that another action may be chosen, not because the gains by the chosen action change, but because the losses of not choosing other actions are given higher priority (Harsanyi 1986:86).

Harsanyi discusses the actor as such and choices based only on his preferences. The rational actor, however, will soon have to confront the world around him, and this means that there is no freedom to choose, but rather a number of constraining factors to review before action may be taken.

In so far as these constraints are not of a physical character, we may systematize them under the heading of institutional arrangements. Furthermore, there is the question of what resources the actor may control in situations of exchange - which will be a characteristic of most situations as soon as we have left the idea of man working for himself alone on a deserted island.

Within the micro-institutionalism there are several ways of defining the institution, among others equilibrium, norms and rules (Crawford and Ostrom 1995). Taking departure from Pareto-optimality, the basic idea of the first approach is to understand how rational individuals obtain *equilibrium* in interaction with other individuals; they keep changing behavior as a reaction to the actions of the other actors until the point has been reached where they expect no better outcome from their own actions. The parallel to neo-classical micro-economic theory should be obvious. Routinized patterns of action - an institution - thus are to be understood on the basis of the motivation of actors to create a particular equilibrium. One representative of this group is Andrew Schotter (1981). The second approach takes departure from *norms* regulating what individuals have as common perception of correct behavior under given circumstances, and thus form the foundation for an institution; a representative is James Coleman (1987). The third approach is based on *rules* where the cohesion of the institution is to be found in a common understanding that actions not complying with the rules prescribed will be sanctioned or nullified, if other actors endowed with the powers to do so get informed about it. Here Ostrom (1990) is a typical representative. The difference from Coleman is that norms may be expressed as rules, while not all rules may be considered solely as expressions of norms.

The third school seems to be the most common one. In particular, these analysts understand institutions as sets of rules constraining the options of the individual actor. We find the simplest examples in game theory where a simple set of rules define the payoffs of different choices by the actor who is then supposed to act accordingly, maximizing the gains or minimizing his losses by choices of action. But few institutional settings are confined to payoffs; most have a more complex structure, stating, for instance, whether a particular action is permitted, required or prohibited. It is, as a matter of fact, more typical of institutions discussed by rational actor analysts that they constrain the actor rather than condone or reward him. The individual is perceived as fallible, prone to shirking, wanting to defect from promises by cheating, and hence the actors need constant reminders of what proper conduct is supposed to be like within the institutional setting. If they do not adjust their behavior accordingly, sanctions will apply.

Within this understanding, then, an institution may be defined as a set of rules valid for (well-)defined aspects of human life, structuring information and delineating scope and time for action (Kiser and Ostrom 1982:179). The rules may be formal and informal, and they may be extended to moral sides of life.

Rational choice theorists have a special interest in how and why institutions are created. In other words, they see institutions as instruments for achieving purposes of utilitarian actors. Consequently, they have an interest in analysing the efficiency of alternative institutional arrangements in order to point to the best institution to obtain certain goals. It follows that the analytic aspiration of the analysts is to predict the behavior of the actors, and therefore the assumptions of the propensities of the actors to act must be quite strict - usually maximization of preferences which must therefore be presumed given and definite during the analysis. Therefore, rational choice theorists mostly analyse the setting up of institutional arrangements - what may prompt individuals to do so, what costs and benefits are associated with it, and how do various actors fare under new institutional conditions? Since many economists are involved in such institutional analysis, there is often a market allegory behind the approach (many players, full information, no reputation linked to players), and each game situation is treated as if one started from scratch; there is no personality-linked memory. Likewise, the preference structures of participants are set once and for all; there is no discussion of, for example, whether previous experience may have had an influence on the goals for action.

There is considerably less interest in analysing arrangements, unless the research interest is in how alternative institutional settings fare.

Institutions as Systems of Control

The second broad category of implicit and explicit definitions of institutions relates to systems of control, analysed not so much regarding the ways they affect individual conduct, but rather in a macro perspective where outcomes are assessed more broadly. Therefore, many organizational sociologists have had an interest in this type of institutionalism, particularly those analysing organizational behavior in a network perspective.

Göhler (1987:17-19) defines institution in general as internalized, persistent behavioral patterns and orientations of thought with a regulating social function. *Political* institutions, then, are rules for formulating and implementing decisions of a general binding character; often, but not necessarily, connected to organizations; in functional terms (that is, related to consequences for the society) unrelated to individuals but nonetheless determined by the behavior of identifiable individuals. Göhler then identifies the state and the government as a narrow conception and more broadly social organizations and rules of social behavior as institutional elements. The general idea of institutional analysis is, first - at a high level of abstraction - to have a broad institutional theory to develop concepts of explanation and normative justification existing for all institutions and, second - at a more concrete level - to have a theory of political institutions to develop its own particular concepts. We thus have several levels of analysis. When a political science analyst encounters a phenomenon that is addressed in other disciplines, he must sooner or later refer to the general institutional theory (Göhler 1987:37).

One of the most discussed works on political "new" institutionalism is March and Olsen's *Rediscovering Institutions*. They define political institutions as

> collections of interrelated rules and routines that define appropriate action in terms of a relation between a role and a situation. The process involves determining what the situation is, what role is being fulfilled, and what the obligations of that role in that situation are. (March and Olsen 1989:160)

An interesting feature of the book is the authors' persistent support of an understanding of the *logic of appropriateness* as a normative demand on the actor, and their criticism of the *logic of consequentiality*, the strategic actor of the rational choice type. To March and Olsen, institutions define what is appropriate, that is, institutions define much of the frame of reference for actors in almost any situation that may occur. A process goes on, determining what the situation is, defining what role is to be fulfilled, and what the obligations of that role in that situation are like. March and Olsen contrast the logic of appropriateness with the logic of consequentiality. The former is based on the fulfilling of the obligations linked to a role; action comes from the feeling of necessity, not individual preferences. The latter is the logic we use when we apply means to goals, expecting certain outcomes from such an action - and thus fulfilling the preferences that lie behind the goals. The former is the knowledgeable citizen who has been socialized, the latter is the rational calculating individual, as discussed in the previous section.

March and Olsen thus are close to Selznick's definition of an institution. Organizational structure is adaptive to environmental forces, and institutionalization refers to this process: to institutionalize is to infuse with values beyond the technical requirements of the task at hand (Selznick 1957:17). But they also come to claim that one must understand institutions as political actors:

The argument that institutions can be treated as political actors is a claim of institutional coherence and autonomy. ... the coherence of institutions varies but is sometimes substantial enough to justify viewing a collectivity as acting coherently. ... political institutions are more than simple mirrors of social forces. (March and Olsen 1989:17-18)

This is a decisive step away from the micro approach which would not allow for a perspective letting the individual actor out of sight - the micro approach would let individual actors represent the collective instead of making the collective a black box.

The difference is a matter of degree - the claim by March and Olsen is that individual personality, calculus of political costs and benefits, and expectations of the future are less important. Historical traditions and their interpretations, calculus of identity, and learning as recorded in history-dependent routines and norms are more important (March and Olsen 1989:38). In a subsequent book (March and Olsen 1995), it is made clear that a micro, that is, individual-oriented, approach may be feasible in some situations. But then the properties of such individual actors are important. Thus

Democratic governance ... involves ... organizing the processes of politics around discussion and respect in the service of a community of reasoning equal individuals, rather than around power and distrust in the service of selfishness and privilege. (March and Olsen 1995:180)

This can be seen as a support to the Habermasian individual of good faith and mutual trust, and a disapproval of the individual of the rational choice approach who is seen as promoting an acceptance of some degree of evil in the shape of selfishness. As a normative stance it is clear and understandable. Whether it creates problems for empirical analysis is, of course, to be determined by actual empirical research.

Institutions as systems of control are applicable to analyses at the state level. One such example is Ashford (1986) who treats institutions as a crucial analytic element in the development of the welfare state; he analyses the development by investigating the policy processes of five nations. By using the institutional definition of the state, Ashford wants to be in a position to detail with some precision what resources, methods and capabilities are attached to the exercise of authority in each political system. The operational aspects of the definition are found in the basic practices attached to the work of political executives, the organization and powers of the bureaucracy and the accepted methods for formulating, implementing and evaluating policies.

Institutions are the intervening variable between some ideal solution and the capabilities of government itself (Ashford 1986:6). An important part of the analysis is defining the dominant values which often work as limitations on the use of institutionalized or collective authority. This is not to say that such values are permanent independent variables that cannot be changed: the policy process is an interactive one, and the researcher must search for regularities in the institutional constraints and, in turn, examine how policies gradually change institutional constraints. Early decisions are precedents for solving later problems. In that logic, governmental capabilities, administrative organization and vested political interests were taking shape long before anyone imagined a welfare state, and it should be understood on that basis (Ashford 1986:17-20).

In such an understanding there is not room for much new in the short run. Institutions guarantee that change is slow and controllable. Yet abrupt changes do happen - as in Eastern Europe late in the very year when *Rediscovering Institutions* was published. Olsen's view of rapid change is that

> radical and swift transformations are likely to be a result of comprehensive external shocks and performance crises. ... The more inefficient (or obstructed) ordinary processes of adaptation are, the more likely that an institution or regime may collapse ... (Olsen 1992:16)

Otherwise, change happens because of step-by-step modifications of existing institutional interpretations. But how such alterations come about is beyond the explanatory power of the approach.

A Scandinavian example of organizational institutionalism is the theory of the negotiated economy (see, for example, Nielsen and Pedersen eds. 1989) which can be seen as a development of the systems of control set up by Hernes (1978), discussed above. But where Hernes analysed the problems of the individual actor (continued in Hernes 1983), Berrefjord, Nielsen and Pedersen (1989), however, emphasize the role of collective actors. They analyse the institutional arrangements set up by powerful organizational actors:

> ... decisions are made after institutionalized negotiations between involved interested actors, binding one another not through public or private legally binding concessions or contracts, but through discursive or political imperatives (Berrefjord, Nielsen and Pedersen 1989:20)

These imperatives are made, based on the interaction between autonomous actors; they cannot be enforced by legal means, and they are made by institutionalized negotiations where formation of meaning and influencing of preferences is decisive. Such a process must be understood as a historical phenomenon, and it must be analysed with the actor squarely in focus.

The way such an analysis is performed, actors are understood as organizations or collectives, not as individuals. It is typical that the processes under analysis are described in the passive, processes "happening" rather than actors "doing" (see, for example, Pedersen, Andersen, Kjær and Elberg 1992 and Andersen 1995). The aim of the analysis is to understand the resulting institutional web, rather than the actual contents of policies or the "winners and losers" of the political process taking place. In this sense, the analysis is oriented towards a description following Hernes' ideal types, which we identified above, not of the market, democracy or bureaucracy, but a description of the negotiated economy as an alternative to the received view of how decisions are made. Therefore, the precise mechanisms called for by Berrefjord *et al.* above - as to how preferences of the actors are changed along the processes - are not really unveiled in any rigorous way; they are indicated to exist and assumed to work as hypothesized. And consequently, there is no real theory of the actor - there is a theory of how actors may perform in a process of discourse; as with March and Olsen (1995) it is based on Habermas' communicative rationality, demanding actors to be worthy of credibility, to speak the truth and to speak in accordance with shared basic values (Berrefjord, Nielsen and Pedersen 1989:36).

Compromises Between Micro and Macro

In accordance with Berger and Luckmann (1966), the basic understanding in the third group of institutionalists is that the institutional environment defines and delimits social reality, but it is also reinforced or changed by *human agency*. What, then, is the nature and origin of social order? The main argument is that social order is based essentially on a shared social reality which is a human construction created in social interaction; that is, a *process* view. A variant sharing the basic ideas puts less emphasis on the *process* of institutionalization - organizations conform because they are rewarded for doing so through higher legitimacy, resources and survival capabilities. The analytic interest focuses on the *types* of processes that cause an organization to change its structure in ways that make it conform to an institutional pattern (DiMaggio and Powell 1983).

A parallel to this kind of institutionalism is pursued by those using the approach of "embeddedness", based on the argument that the behavior and institutions to be analysed are so constrained by ongoing social relations that to construe them as independent is a grievous misunderstanding. (Granovetter 1992:53)

Actually, Granovetter uses the concept of embeddedness in a less extreme way than the quote might indicate and reserves it as a middle road between structuralism and individualism. He does it as a challenge to Oliver Williamson's (1975) notions of economic efficiency in dealing with transactions. Instead, Granovetter targets the role of interpersonal relations within economic transactions, avoiding the idea of anonymous invisible hands of the market and eschewing the apparent clear and impersonal responsibility pattern of the organizational hierarchy. He favors the analysis of special power relations and long-term personal relations in the "market" and personal and shared understandings within the firm - these are ways of operationalizing the analytic principle of embeddedness.

The most comprehensive discussion of structure and agency is probably found in the literature by and on Giddens. His *duality of structure* is intended to overcome the analytic problem when the structural properties of social systems are both the medium and the outcome of the practices they organize; that is, when the properties do not exist outside of the action but are chronically implicated in its production and reproduction (Giddens 1984:374). Structuration is conceived by Giddens as:

> The structuring of social relations across time and space, in virtue of the duality of structure. (1984:376)

Giddens, however, is not terribly helpful in making his concept operational. His interest lies less in doing empirical research and more in developing a sociological approach, somewhat in the direction of a *grand theory*. We shall apply the notion of structuration in the light of the research interest behind this book.

First, there lies behind it an understanding of action as a basic tenet of the approach. Things do not just happen, and they are not inevitable, at least not in the particular form they take place in. This is a conscious choice by the actors, who "maintain a continuing 'theoretical understanding' of the grounds of their activity" (Giddens 1984:5). So things could have been otherwise at some level of analysis, even though an understanding like a *macro* economic balance based on Pareto optimality would not grasp the difference. On the other hand, nor does the analysis dig into the *micro* individual motivations for action in so far as this requires an understanding of some unconscious motifs; it stays with the conscious action. But the actions of people make a difference, and in that understanding the actors exercise power based on different types of resource.

Second, Giddens understands structuration as a continuing process of constituting and reconstituting conditions for action; this *duality of structure* is

> Structure as the medium and outcome of the conduct it recursively organizes; the structural properties of social systems do not exist outside of action but are chronically implicated in its production and reproduction. (Giddens 1984:374)

Structure is not a fixed constellation of relations between actors, but "rules and resources, recursively implicated in the reproduction of social systems" (Giddens 1984:377), something comprehended by the actors and used as constraints as well as resources in action. So structuration is a continuing process of actions by conscious actors whereby they may reinforce certain types of conduct or change them, depending on their interpretation of the situation in which action takes place.

The most important feature of this approach is its lack of determination which we find bound in the structure of most structural analysts. Giddens maintains the possibility of choice, of doing otherwise, where it is difficult to see such forms of "individuality" in a structural theory. This is done without being caught in the net of the opposite camp which understands individuality as voluntarism. Few, of course, believe in such freedom, but even the reconditioned model of individualism, subject to (structural) constraints, has serious limitations to it; primarily it is hard to see how those constraints could be changed. This is what Giddens offers possibilities for by the concept of structuration.

This understanding, however, is very abstract and needs further development for empirical research. In the following section we shall discuss consequences of interaction and the process perspective to get deeper into how structuration comes about.

CONSEQUENCES OF INTERACTION - THE PROCESS PERSPECTIVE

Analysing relations between actors means to some degree examining processes of interaction. There is no problem in analysing interaction with a clear purpose, this is mostly understood in terms of power and/or exchange-of-goods relations. But relations based less on maximizing or satisficing goals are more difficult to understand at the theoretical levels. A number of theorists argue that interaction creates some mutual obligations and hence leads to some degree of cohesion among the actors.

There are several lines of argument (Hirschman 1982). The first one, and the most common, simply says that the exchange of goods will create good relations between people - if nothing else because they become dependent on one another. This line of argument is found in the 18th-century literature and in any textbook on economics. It is also argued that, in and by itself,

> commerce drives forward the best sentiments of man who learns to deliberate, to be honest, to acquire manners, to be prudent and reserved both in talk and action (Samuel Richard, quoted by Hirschman 1982:1465).

Commerce, exchanging valuables, then, in this particular understanding, is an instrument not only for fulfilling wants, but also for a higher moral. We might with a certain risk of oversimplification extend the argument to saying that this is the effect of continued interaction with mutual non-hostile interests involved.

A second line of argument is found in Durkheim and contemporaries,

> ... we cooperate because we wanted to but our voluntary cooperation creates duties which we did not intend to assume ...;
> ... that our functional roles in the division of labor results in our finding ourselves caught in a network of obligations which we do not have the right to forsake ...;
> ... that the division of labor creates among men a comprehensive system of rights and duties which tie them to one another in a durable fashion (Durkheim, quoted by Hirschman 1982:1471)

There is no indication here of interests playing a role. The resulting solidarity is a moral element of social interaction. Interaction improves the likelihood that we will cooperate, and creates bonds that oblige us beyond the face-to-face relations which will always make deceit more difficult to carry through than it would be among strangers. Precisely how this solidarity is sustained - for instance whether interaction is necessary - is not made clear by Durkheim. Here is one reason why it is difficult to model his theory on the basis of methodological individualism. The collectivists will be more willing to accept this line of reasoning.

The methodological individualist will reason in terms of how the actor is affected, as in the Richard quotation above. Another case in point is Hirschman (1970) who discusses "loyalty" as an acting restraint for a generalized actor - it could concern the addicted customer of the local grocery store and the burned-out member of a socialist party alike. The loyalty is based on a general understanding of a penalty for exiting from the organization: the individual feels that leaving a certain group carries a price with it which he is not willing to pay, even though no direct sanction is imposed by the group. Another possibility is that the potential exiter (often an influential one) anticipates that an exit would leave the organization worse off than if he stayed (Hirschman 1970:98). What we see here is a force at work that does not at first sight square with the maximizer of own preferences: the potential exiter feels that he would continue to care about the decisions and subsequent actions of the organization. Hirschman refers this kind of action to a desire to avoid the consequences of hypothetical behavior (exit); this can be perceived as a benefit to the actor and hence an important incentive and part of preferences for loyalty.

Consequently, we cannot restrict the discussion to direct interaction between actors. We also have to identify possible norms that affect and restrict the behavior of actors or, more generally, the institutional set of arrangements that actors may perceive as constraints on and/or capabilities for action. This, however, cannot be done in a static way if we are to follow the principles of structuration; we need an analysis based on the understanding of processes. Understanding structuration as a process means that communication links are established between actors, enabling them to exchange[5] information about various facets of a problematic, often, but not necessarily always, removing apparent obstacles to reaching a solution that is acceptable to both (or more) parties.

Basically, the steps taken by actors should be understood as a process towards establishing a capacity to act, a capability *vis-à-vis* other actors (Lundquist 1987). We need not go into a discussion of what psychological mechanisms make individuals act; the body-subject must have some skills in perceiving himself and the environment and *understand* the situation that has arisen, he must have an ability to *make decisions* and some *preferences* as a basis for setting priorities between alternative ways of acting[6]. No actor can perform these skills to perfection in all situations, there are differences due to knowledge and intellect, and there may be different levels of trust and ideological accord. Furthermore, action may be dependent on material resources at the disposal of the actor: money, equipment, materials and so

5. Strictly speaking, there is no need in each particular instance to exchange information. One party may act based on the perceptions of what the opinions of the other party on a specific problematic would be. Those perceptions, however, must be based on previous information dissemination of some kind.
6. These three properties Lundquist (1987:43) names *understand, can* and *will*. They are odd linguistic constructs, they are verbs but are treated as nouns.

on. The individual actor may be put in a better position by education, both in general skills and in particular crafts related to specific tasks.

In relationships between individuals, then, progress related to action is made by mutual communication, whose significance depends on the way each actor works to build up some capability for action. If the actor behaves according to the rational model, he will maximize his preferences, so if they are known, the analyst can predict the decisions to be made. The demands for a rational action situation are very strict and therefore well suited for laboratory analysis, computer simulation and strict theoretical development (Ostrom, Gardner and Walker 1994:321). In the view of this author, empirical analysis of complex and uncertain series of interaction among shifting numbers of individuals is difficult with the strict version of rational choice. We will instead assume actors to be "bounded rational" and understand the process of acting as based on a series of communications between actors, each trying to affect the other's understanding of and scope for action, and modifying the institutional setting for the action along the road, based on heuristics and past experience.

Lundquist (1987:85-88) has extended the understanding of action processes between individuals to relations between collectives. The core concept is that of *organizing*, a process whereby *preferences* (goals, aims, ideas and so on) are changed into *priorities*, that is, directions for action, and where *resources* (money, employees, equipment and so on) are changed into *capabilities*, that is, instruments for action. Organizing is a decision-making process, and just as individuals have different personal and material preconditions for successful action, successful processes of organizing depend on the ways individuals (with different skills) and material resources are combined. This is not a passive process of reaction to management directives, individuals may apply a number of strategies in interaction to create what they perceive as the best fit.

Actions are made by individuals - even computerized tax returns are based on human programming of the machine. So narrowly understood, organizations cannot act. But individuals do act on behalf of organizations, and in doing so they take upon themselves tasks they might not have done otherwise. Furthermore, individuals do the setting of priorities and they are the mediators in creating capabilities. Individuals are also the bearers of the socialization taking place within the organization, often conceptualized as the organizational culture. The process of organizing individuals may be understood on the basis of four variables, modified from Leavitt: roles, procedures, structuring and culture (Lundquist 1987:98-102). The *roles* indicate the individual's scope of action, *procedures* regulate and coordinate the interaction between roles, *structuring* indicates the powers between roles, and *culture* is the (informal) norm binding the collective together.

These four variables constitute the basis for thinking about organizations; the important thing to understand from the perspective of this book is that the variables are not to be understood as structural fixations, but as elements in an ongoing process where the stake is a *series of choices concerning points of view on actions to be taken on a problematic*, where the actions are to be made by a collective. The organizing variables constitute the channels for converting preferences into priorities, and resources into capabilities. They may be understood as nested institutional levels where three layers of action scope are identified: the constitutional, the collective and the action levels, indicating differences in time horizons and in specificity of the instruments employed for action (Kiser and Ostrom 1982). Those principles also apply in a general sense in organizational action, but they are of course not limited to organizations; on the contrary they indicate how to understand inter-organizational relationships or the like.

ANALYSIS OF STRUCTURATION PROCESSES

To accept the contents of this chapter one must accept being eclectic in combining various elements of approaches to the analysis of processes of organizing, or structuration. We are interested in situated communication which at one level may be characterized by the use of roles, but which, after all, also takes place between body-subjects acting on behalf of their organizations. Both individuals and organizations have strategies for action, or projects they relate their actions to, and their communication is based on their understanding of strategies and projects. Communications may be grouped into patterns like policy networks, but not necessarily identified on the basis of formal policy definitions and understandings, and they often transcend formal organizational boundaries.

We can briefly touch upon the principles of analysing such communication; the detail of how to do this is the subject of the next chapter on bottom-up institutional analysis. We can compromise between the principles of methodological individualism and collectivism because both present us with unattractive and unrealistic preconditions for analysis. Individualism has a tendency to disregard the structural barriers that may hinder action as well as furnish the actor with capacities for action; the tendency to stick with the lonely individual maximizing his utility does not square well with observa
tions of people working together, disregarding their own immediate interests

and involving themselves in complicated non-zero-sum negotiations and tacit adaptation to the ideas of other members of such a group. Collectivism tends to neglect the individual and to see outcomes as predetermined by structural principles that are unchangeable within a fairly long time span. They thus cannot grasp that actors can and do make a difference under certain circumstances which it may not be possible to classify beforehand. The dynamics of the situation may be deciding on the particular actions that are taken, and such actions may change apparently unalterable structures.

Such analysis may be performed as *individual-cum-institution*. In Chapter 3 we discussed the *individual-cum-structure*, and that general idea is easy to transfer to an institutional setting: individuals (and groups) acting within an institutional arrangement, using rules as constraints as well as resources for action, and doing this in a dynamic way so that, over time, the arrangements themselves may be subject to change. What counts, then, is the practices of people, of body-subjects, not puppets acting in roles unalterable by themselves. These practices may also be analysed as representing the strategies of an organization. The data to observe are various forms of communication, but this certainly should not be restricted to documents believed by the analyst to be of particular importance because of their impressive binding or series number determined by an authorizing public entity. Such documents may be conspicuous, but they may also be deceiving and should be carefully put into perspective(s) based on other material. The apparent authority of documents should not be taken for granted. Basically the analyst should use a critical stance to any object just as historians use their supplemental insight to put any evidence they come across into a critical perspective. So other methods should be used. There may be lots of paperwork found in the archive, be they official ones or more private hidings of officials. Such documents indicate much about the actual practices taking place in the agency and in interaction between agencies. Furthermore, one may observe actual communication taking place, and one may interview people involved in previous communication situations, both about what they perceived took place, and what they understood in more tacit ways.

Thus one may use several methods to approach the problems of reconstructing the structuration processes linked to a problematic, seen as *individual-cum-institution*. In Chapter 5 we shall go into more detail about how to perform such an analysis; but first, we must discuss a particular perspective for such an analysis, namely the bottom-up approach.

TOP-DOWN AND BOTTOM-UP

The literature on policy implementation reflects on themes central for our understanding of how to do institutional policy analysis of collective public action - which may by some be called policy. For many years there has been a methodological debate going on in the political science and policy literature on how to structure empirical policy analysis: Should we take departure from the problems (goals) as stated by the top (the president, the parliament, the leader of the organization) or should we start out with the problems as perceived from the bottom (the client, the field worker)? There is no generally recognized answer to this question which may be understood as a provocation rather than a clear alternative. We shall review some of the arguments and then proceed to present an approach with a strong bent towards the bottom-uppers, but still to be considered a move towards a reconciliation with the top-down perspective.

Policy implementation research got its start as a distinct field in 1973 when Pressman and Wildawsky published their *Implementation*. Only a few years afterwards, policy implementation research had become a growth industry. Pressman and Wildawsky hit a broadly felt need for analysis to break the apparent analytic barrier between policy formation and policy execution, where political scientists had done most about the former and public administration researchers most about the latter. The empirical evidence from both lines of research, however, had tended to be based on actions of the offices of the organization without much interest in what actually happened out there; political scientists were interested in the making of law, public administration researchers were interested in how bureaux set up strategies. Implementation researchers broke the organizational barrier, doing inter-organizational and inter-governmental research to trace what actually happened in a sometimes long chain of actions by various actors involved in a continuing process of negotiating what should be done and what would be feasible to do.

The original implementation research was made *top-down*, that is, from the perspective of the decision-makers at the apex of the chain of actors. Typically these were legislatures writing a law or top bureaucrats or commissions setting out policy principles. How did the law or the policy fare? What happened to the ideas of the elected official or the orders barked out by the executive?

Richard Elmore has described the top-down perspective from the executive office as *forward mapping*:

> It begins at the top of the process, with as clear a statement as possible of the
> policy maker's intent, and proceeds through a sequence of increasingly more

specific steps to define what is expected of implementors at each level. At the bottom of the process one states ... what a satisfactory outcome would be, measured in terms of the original statement of intent. (Elmore 1979:602)

Policy implementation research followed the same pattern - what were the goals, how were they broken down to sub-goals and instruments? The new features of this approach to implementation research were the broadened perspective of the policy process and the tendency towards an intensified interest in substantial consequences or policy outcomes. The typical reaction was "what went wrong?", when the researchers found that as the distance to the top policy makers increased, the discrepancy between field actions and policy objectives increased, too. In other words, there was a tendency to phrase research questions in terms of organizational problems since the directions of the management of the organization did not accomplish what was intended. Implicitly, then, the cure was to strengthen managerial oversight and control instruments, a cure that disregarded the inter-organizational facets - over which managers do not have control, but must resort to negotiation (Franz 1986). In addition, it ignored the possibility that field workers may need some discretion in order to cope with variance not foreseen by the top (Lipsky 1980). Furthermore, the approach forced the researcher to accept the goal(s) of the policy as a given which in principle had to be followed because the legitimacy of the decisions of the top could not be questioned.

Soon a criticism of the top-down approach set in, already hinted at above. First of all, the approach was criticized for being unrealistic in focusing on the implementation of formal goals as formulated by law or executive order. This led the researcher to a focus on the chain of command established by the leadership and thus made the researcher run a risk of not encountering a number of activities that may be crucial in understanding the actual as opposed to the presumed network of actors involved. The formal perspective turns activities by actors who are not authorized to act into "noise" in an otherwise perfect and functioning world of correctly socialized individuals. In particular, the approach had problems in analysing interactions between organizations which all perform a role in the implementation process. Second, the criticism indicated that focus on formal tasks begged the question of relevance of those tasks to the formal goals and to the problems of those the public action would be supposed to help out. The researcher became the instrument of the political élite and would not be in a position to question the appropriateness of the perceptions of that élite and the way it links political aims to public action. This could be troublesome especially in cases where the goals were only indicated in a loose and imprecise way, giving actors some discretion to adapt to local circumstances. This is the case in many modern legislative initiatives, but it presents the researcher with a problem if the policy ideas as implied by the political élite are the only valid ones by which to evaluate ensuing local action.

Criticism was also voiced regarding the top-down perception of a policy process (Barrett and Fudge 1981), especially the lack of an understanding of the process as a negotiation process, and correspondingly a lack of understanding of the possibilities for implementing agencies to respond to prescribed goals and adapt them to local conditions. Both factors seem quite important in analysing implementation not as a technical problem, but as an inherently human concern.

An alternative is to do a bottom-up analysis. Richard Elmore has characterized the bottom-up perspective as *backward mapping* which

> begins not at the top of the implementation process but at the last possible stage, the point where administrative actions intersect private choices .... (and) begins not with a statement of intent but with a statement of the specific behavior at the lowest level of the implementation process that generates the need for policy. ..... Having established a relatively precise target at the lowest level ... the analysis backs up through the structure of implementing agencies asking ... what is the ability of this unit to affect the behavior that is the target of this policy? ... (Elmore 1979:604)

This means that the researcher must work systematically backwards from the pattern of allocation and along the chain of decisions to reconstruct the allocative process. Bottom-up implementation research, then, runs parallel to backward mapping, but in an investigative rather than a prescriptive manner. The trick is to take departure from a particular problematic, the *policy problem* (discussed in more detail in Chapter 5), which is addressed by collective action and thus, in so far as public actors are involved, becomes a part of a public policy concern. The aim of the researcher then is to reconstruct which actors are involved in the attempts to solve the policy problem, what their goals and resources are, and how they behave strategically. This is constructing what Hjern and Porter (1983) call the *implementation structure*: a number of activities whose common denominator is an interest and a stake in solving a policy problem. These activities are carried out by actors who often turn out to (but they don't have to!) belong to different organizations, in other words an interorganizational network coordinating the activities of parts of different organizations. We shall go deeper into this below.

The bottom-up approach was voiced in journals five to six years after the top-down approach hit the academic marketplace. A compromise or even synthesis was suggested only a few years later, and by both camps[7]. Sabatier (1986) has suggested an approach that starts out bottom-up with the policy problem and the strategies of actors across organizational boundaries and sectors (public/private), and how they form a network. These actions, however, must be put into perspective by the structuring forces of legal and socio-economic factors - where in particular the legal framework may be manipulated top-down; furthermore, one must take into account the causal factors affecting the policy problem, and how these are perceived by the actors. The network is conceptualized as an *advocacy coalition*, pursuing the common goals, acting under constraints and conditions for capabilities from the environment.

The reaction from Hjern and Hull (1987) was that this compromise was too much based on a top-down perspective with a local network approach added; for instance, Sabatier assumes that actors want to add their ideas to a governmental program whereas Hjern and associates have found that, by and large, they don't: they want to exploit any program for their purposes and don't bother to formalize their aims. Furthermore, Hjern and Hull suspected that the existing programs would eventually form the basis for such an analysis, all good intentions to do otherwise notwithstanding.

Instead, Hjern and Hull offered a three-stage research process: a *first* stage involving a local mapping of the implementation structure, a *second* stage (overlapping the first) involving the development of program typologies and indicators for policy performance (outreach, fit program/needs, substitution of public/private resources, performance indicators), and a *third* stage comprising successive rounds of interviews from the bottom to the top of the chain of command within each program, confronting those actors with the research results regarding the actual processes within "their" program, to get their reactions. The results of the empirical analysis then must be confronted with the prescribed implementation structure to assess whether or not the existing policy network makes sense.

We will now turn to a more in-depth discussion of the bottom-up approach as the basis for an adaptation to collective public action under post-modern conditions, to the type of society where decision-makers at the top may be even less in control than their colleagues in the modern society - who, as we saw above, assumed that they were in control and were thought to be so, but often were not. And if they are not, a bottom-up approach may be one instrument to analyse the processes as they have unfolded.

---

7. Publication dates may deceive. An journal article has usually been on its way for several years. The bottom-up perspective was really developed and reflected in conference papers from the mid-to-late 1970s, the synthesis from the early 1980s.

POLICY ANALYSIS BOTTOM-UP

The bottom-up approach was systematized by researchers investigating regional policies and labor market policies. The researchers were confronted with an apparent mess of organizations, public and private, which involved them in a regional or local network of interaction to solve problems as they were seen out there (rather than as seen by the fathers of the law). The researchers found a lack of theoretical and methodological sufficiency in the traditions of public administration and political science where constitutional mandates and closed organizational goals were dominant. There was a poor fit between theory and empirical evidence.

Maybe regional policy and labor market policy are fields that invite discrepancy between the views of the organizational top and actual policies as they unfold locally. Circumstances of such policies are difficult (Hjern and Lundmark 1979). There is little knowledge of causal theories to promote the aims of the policies, and there is correspondingly little knowledge of how problems have been solved at the local level. One might understand the cases as examples of a benign welfare state apparatus confronting problems which have hitherto been ruled by market forces, and giving a formal response based on a traditional bureaucratic formula rather than innovative behavior from the top. This, then, prompted *ad hoc* responses from the local actors making do incrementally as they confronted new problems.

There are several intellectual roots of the bottom-up approach (Hjern and Lundmark 1979), and by traditional standards they are somewhat conflicting: they come from both collectivists and methodological individualists.

The first type of challenge to traditional ideas came from political science research which wanted to conceptualize the systems of control within a mixed economy. Basically, the idea was that neither market principles nor traditional liberal democracy conceptions described the processes of controlling the society of the type "Scandinavia" well. Both the ideal market and the ideal democracy were perverted by the features instigated by increasingly aggressive interest organizations. In terms of the market they thwarted the mechanisms of free exchange by means of collective bargaining, and in terms of democracy they short-circuited the processes of linking politicians and citizens by dealing directly with the bureaucracy. These problems were analysed by the Norwegian Power Research Group in the mid-1970s. In terms of neo-corporatism and its meaning to the democratic processes, the analyses by Olsen (1978) and associates have had a lasting influence on Nordic political science. However, they did not invite an analysis of actual policy performance; their interest was with the policy formation processes.

The second, individualistic set of ideas were based on research challenging the hierarchic model of public administration and arguing for stronger market-like mechanisms in organizing the public sector (Ostrom 1974). The original bottom-up research had political programs in its focus, and therefore a market parallel did not seem appropriate, but the idea of administrative actors having some sort of socialized self-interest did ring a bell for researchers. New research found local and regional actors making *ad hoc* coalitions for more efficient uses of public means that did not perform well within the formal organizational structure set up by the parliament and central bureaucracy. The solution in theoretical terms was to give up the traditional ideas about hierarchy within organizations as the most important factor constituting public organization action, and instead to emphasize links of negotiations between individuals crossing the organizational barriers in inter-organizational relations.

Hjern and Hull (1984) have emphasized the apparent lack of consistency; metaphorically they let "Weber meet Durkheim". They confronted the individualism of Weber with the structuralism of Durkheim in the analysis of inter-organizational relations. The starting point of implementation research was to challenge the received view by most managers that policy performance had to be equal to policy goals, unless some more or less criminal activity intervened. Deviation was seen as a violation of rules and, since such misdeed was frowned upon, the management more or less presumed that so long as there were few violations, policy goals were accomplished[8]. The researchers evaluating regional and manpower policies found that deviation was the rule, not the exception, but they also found that the organizational top knew very little about what was really going on because most activities were not closely monitored.

The aim of the bottom-up researchers, then, was to reconstruct the group of individuals linking organizations, to map their network regarding the policy problem under scrutiny and to understand their rationales for action. This was to reconstruct the *implementation structure*, an analytic construct, not something found in the phone directory. According to Hjern and Hull (1984), such an analysis based on individual motives for participation links the Weberian understanding of the role of accountable individuals to the Durkheimian understanding of the role of a social element in an

---

8. This approach is comparable with that of auditing: have the rules been followed and money spent according to budgetary categories? If so, the auditors are satisfied. But it is noteworthy that there has been a fairly large OECD initiative in the PUMA group aimed at broadening the scope of auditing. It is called performance auditing, aimed at analysing the rationales for action rather than the legality of action. So even auditors seem to be breaking the bonds of tradition.

individualistic world. In Durkheim's case it was the organic solidarity reinforcing common values and goals in a society with organizations pursuing
separate goals. In implementation research cases it became some values (differing according to the type of policy problem) linking individuals to a more
or less common understanding of a policy problem, no matter what organization employed them.

One can say that the goal for the bottom-up analysis of an implementation structure or any other collective action network is to reconstruct the
institutional setting within which individuals perform activities. The
activities may in principle take place within an organization, or they may
cross formal organizational boundaries, based on one or several norms spanning the organizations, or they may be set up by the individuals through
interaction or tacit understanding, maybe contrary to the goals of the
organizations involved. This is what I called an *individual-cum-institution*
approach above: individuals acting within institutional parameters, changing,
where possible, constraints into capabilities, in these cases by making
alliances where they may be found, also across organizational boundaries,
and thus framing action with a common understanding (institutional norm)
of the policy problem.

These individuals cannot be reduced *only* to mavericks maximizing personal interests, they *may* act as responsible individuals, accountable to
accomplishing the best possible outcome for the (public) program they are
involved in - as employees, elected officials or in other roles of importance
for the network. They *may* also pursue personal interests and preferences in
such a process, but there is no reason to have the two perspectives - of pursuing personal interests and pursuing a common good - rule one another out
the way March and Olsen (1995:Chap. 1) do. They can be combined in an
interesting way.

Durkheim saw organizations (in particular trade unions) as intermediaries
between the population and the state, in that they became objects for state
regulation while they were knowledgeable about the wants of their members.
Such organizations and their interplay with other actors guaranteed the
sensible development of the society which might otherwise have lost a common purpose due to the specialization processes of the modern society. As a
parallel phenomenon, the institutionalization of (local) actors in a policy
network may, then, be hypothesized to guarantee that those affected by the
policy are better served than they would have been under "normal"
procedures directed from the organizational top. In the latter case, the
specialization of each organization may prevent a common cause from being
pursued (Hjern and Hull 1984).

This approach has some strengths and some weaknesses (Sabatier 1986:33-35). The concept of implementation structure is based on a "snowballing" methodology by interviewing key actors who then identify other actors they interact with; these in turn are interviewed and so on This procedure is reliable in reproducing the network. Furthermore, the idea of letting the actors reflect upon their perceptions of the policy problem puts the researcher in a position to evaluate the relative importance of various governmental programs for solving the policy problems, and the accomplishments of other actors as well. These are then evaluated on the basis of all local consequences, both intended and unintended, based on their strategic interaction over time. The bottom-up approach thus is well suited to a dynamic analysis, focusing on changes as they occur locally, rather than as some program manager wishes to initiate new facets of his program.

On the other hand, the bottom-up researcher may overemphasize the importance of local points of view, at least as long as there are no compensatory interviews with the top. Furthermore, they must be aware of the historical background for local action, including prior activities outside the public realm. These problems may, however, be overcome by a proper research design.

The final problem relates to the *a priori* lack of theory about the policy problem and factors affecting it. In one sense there may be a temptation to use *grounded theory* (Glaser and Strauss 1967), but on the other hand nothing prevents the researcher from using a relevant theory available beforehand. Of course, this is a choice to be made once one has selected the policy problem. How is the researcher then put in a position to systematize the perceptions of local actors? There may be several ways to answer these questions. We will do so by discussing in the next two chapters how a bottom-up institutional analysis could be carried out, and we will set up the option that the policy problem may be conceptualized in a social construction process between researcher and research objects.

5. Institutional Network Analysis Bottom-up

How can we analyse public collective action under postmodern conditions? Chapter 4 made the case for institutional analysis bottom-up, this chapter discusses important aspects of preparing such an analysis, based on the principles from the previous chapters.

So how can we conceptualize the policy problem some actors want to solve or reduce? What norms and rules may apply to an understanding of the action scope related to that policy problem? What positions get involved in an interaction network working towards solving the policy problem? And what kind of order emerges from the activities of the network, and how does that order relate to the understanding of the participants in the network? These are the basic questions we are going to pursue. We discuss how to approach a research design based on the principles of institutional analysis set out in Chapter 4.

There is no final and ready recipe for an empirical bottom-up analysis. Most bottom-up research is highly qualitative, requiring the individual researcher to adapt the general principles to the concrete situation, possibly in several steps of induction and deduction, and, given the probability of high variance in such circumstances, it is difficult to generalize.

A GENERAL APPROACH TO POLITICAL INSTITUTIONS

Our interest in this book concerns collective public action, and hence in some sense a political activity where goods and values, including the right to future action, are distributed among the participants. The action is an authoritative allocation of goods and values, authoritative in the sense that it is seen as binding for the participants in the collective action, but not authoritative in the sense of being forced on the participants. We would expect some degree of deliberation taking place as an important element of the collective public action, minimizing the degree of disagreement among the participants, and advancing general acceptance.

Among the three "schools" of institutional analysis discussed in Chapter 4, the third one compromising between actor and structure seems most suitable for doing non-formal, bottom-up institutional research in local collective public action. It has the potential for empirical analysis of strategies pursued by individuals within institutional constraints, but also using institutional features as resources. They do this not only as someone following given logics (of appropriateness), but also by having strategies for attaining goals.

In institutional analysis, the recurrent concepts discussed in the literature above were a) interaction, b) value, norm, culture, symbol, c) rule, order, structure, capabilities and d) shared perception, cognition, meaning. On that basis, we shall for the purposes of this book define a political institution as follows:

A political institution is an authoritative interaction network linked to a policy problem. Among the participants in the network one can identify a set of general norms for behavior and a set of positions with specified rules for behavior. The institution has a potential to help generate order in relation to the policy problem. It tends to induce a collective understanding of meaning among the participants.

This definition gives us a number of keys to the analysis: we can identify some actors, we can identify a number of rules of the game, and we can assume some general implications for the participants. The main points in relation to the other implicit and explicit definitions above are the following.

First, we are talking of *interaction networks*. We are not in disagreement with large parts of the organizational theory defining organization on the basis of the interaction patterns between individuals: those with a relatively high interaction frequency form an organization. But by excluding the concept of organization from the definition we put an end to any trace of doubt: formal organizations and institutions are not congruent in this version of the definition.

Second, we speak of *links* to a policy problem, not a dominance by a policy problem (for definition, see below). The policy problem may be material, but that does not prevent symbolic aspects from having importance for the institution. In other words, we do not want to imply a strict functional institutional setup.

Third, an attempt to *integrate micro and macro* perspectives is made through the use of norms and rules guiding the behavior as in the macro control systems above; here, however, a narrowing of the perspective has come about by using the facet of the policy problem which then determines the boundary of the phenomena under scrutiny. Thus the comprehensiveness or generality of the control systems is replaced by one or a few narrower aspects, but still without tying the micro perspective to an organization.

Fourth, *order* is a crucial concept. This implies a certain conservatism and consequently there is no basic expectation for institutions to function as scouts taking us to new and exciting places to be explored. They rather secure predictability and continuity within given boundaries. Under certain circumstances, however, they may be important vehicles in innovations, but precisely how this takes place we can only know if we can specify the situational variables.

The political aspect of the institution implies that individuals accepting the institution accept the decisions that are made, or prevented from being made, within the institutional framework. Those individuals may oppose a particular decision, they may work to have it come out differently, and they may try to have it changed once it is adopted, but nonetheless they will respect a particular content as long as it has the institutional link in order.

The definition is to be regarded as a set of propositions. If one can identify the elements, and if they work as described, they form an institution, an interaction network with positions and rules that help generate order in relation to a policy problem in a way that is meaningful to those involved. The research task then is to identify a *policy problem, positions, norms and rules, order and meaning*. We shall detail these elements below.

POLICY PROBLEMS

Institutionalized social relationships should be understood in relation to an activity or a problem (Burns and Flam 1987:36-42, 105); they can hardly be understood without a knowledge of the situational conditions. Hence the need for a discussion of a policy problem.

Principles of Analysis

A policy problem can be defined as a problem that in the view of some actors requires action to be taken by several actors or requires action by an actor on behalf of several other actors. The actors must agree, openly or tacitly, on some basic parameters for that action; those parameters form the core, that is, the intentions of the policy.

A *public* policy problem is here seen as a set of problems to be addressed authoritatively by one or more organizations, mostly public, but maybe private, as when licensed to perform as an authority under certain conditions. The point is that at a certain time, a decision to invoke public action has been made by a political body, and such a decision then forms the backbone of the policy[9]. However, the ensuing development and implementation process may take us to other places than the fathers of the policy had thought, as the implementation literature (for example, Hanf and Toonen eds. 1985) has clearly shown us.

We want to apply a bottom-up perspective on policy formation and implementation, hence it is not satisfying to use the perceptions of *public* policy-makers exclusively on policy problems. For instance, the policies of public organizations may affect a policy problem without the appreciation of those responsible and thus without their taking what has happened into account. Furthermore, organizations with a *public* policy responsibility may act without taking the consequences of the policies of other organizations into consideration. This has typically been the case in regional policies where the regional dimension is simply disregarded by public organizations specializing in public functions like health and schools, and which may consequently close their regional offices just as another public organization is trying to help set up public jobs in that very area. Thus, organizational efficiency and regional or local goals collide.

In a bottom-up perspective, then, we are interested in which *public* policies affect given policy problems, but we also have a keen interest in what *other* factors may affect the development of the problem. Two things seem critical in order to keep this perspective: language and technology.

First, it is crucial that actors share a common understanding of what the policy problem is about, or at least that the actors have a common language or frame of reference for discussing how to interpret the problems. As we saw above, regional policy may be an example of the lack of a common frame of reference: the public sector body acts on the basis of efficiency related only to its budget and an explicit or implicit understanding of economy of scale and transaction costs between the center and the organizations placed in the regions. The regional policy unit may not use such reasoning because its purpose is to help reduce adverse consequences of decisions by bodies that refer to rationales like the economy of scale. Regional and local perspectives, however, do not have much clout: A common complaint among comprehensive (for example, regional) planners is that specialized bodies are very influential in political and administrative inter-organizational processes (Bogason 1986).

Second, different technologies exist for solving problems. One example may be the solution of traffic congestion on the roads around a city in the rush hours. The "Department of Roads" would probably suggest that the

9. Consequently, we do not discuss the problems of non-decisions and other interesting aspects of political action and prevention of action. For now we are interested only in policies that can be traced using decision analysis.

existing roads be expanded or that alternative routes be established so that the cars are distributed more evenly on the inward bound roads. The "Department of Public Transportation", on the other hand, would probably suggest that more buses be timetabled with a higher frequency and covering the areas of the suburbs more extensively, maybe also at special fares so that car commuters would see an incentive in using public transport and hence reduce the pressure on the roads. These two paradigms are not quite incompatible, but it would probably make most sense mainly to follow only one, or the city would run a risk of over-investing. And neither paradigm questions the basic needs for transportation - an understanding that would be challenged by a communication paradigm involving the possibility that people communicate less by meetings (at the workplace) and more by electronic means, hence enabling them to work more at home at a computer terminal.

The problem of the researcher is to conceptualize and theorize so that the policy problem is described and analysed independently of the organization-bound views we saw above. Of course, such views are of great interest for the political scientist as indicators of how the world is actually interpreted by organizational actors. Such views are important in analyses of conflicts. But the researcher should also be in a position to analyse policy problems without being tied by such perceptions. The researcher cannot find a more "real" reality, but by explicating the basis for his analysis it is at least open for discussion; this is not the case with organizational views.

At the same time, however, the researcher must understand how such organizational conceptions may come about and dominate the discourse on the policy problem. The researcher does not have to accept those views, but if he does not understand their character, he will not be able to analyse the processes that base themselves on such an understanding.

Implementing the Principles

The way the researcher addresses the policy problem is crucial for the whole analysis. This is where the scope of the whole research project is decided: what is to be included, what is to be excluded in the data collection process - only those which are relevant for the policy problem. So if the policy problem is not adequately conceptualized, a coherent analysis cannot be accomplished. On the other hand, it is possible to re-conceptualize along the road if some major problems turn up, but only if one then goes back to the data collected earlier to re-analyse whether they fit the amended policy problem conceptualization.

Below we shall take a closer look at three conceptualizations to help in grasping the policy problem: externalities, professional knowledge and discourse analysis.

A *first* way of approaching the policy problem is based on the economists who have provided us with an excellent conceptual tool: externalities. Simply stated, the activities of an individual or organization may affect other actors; if they are positive, it will add to their welfare; if negative, they will reduce their welfare. In the case of negative externality, those who suffer should in economic terms be entitled to compensation, a factor which the producer must take into consideration, that is, add to the costs of the production. It may, however, be difficult for the victims to claim their compensation - what is the value of factory noise, and how may one persuade the owner to pay? In the case of a positive externality, the problem for the producer is logically the same: he cannot collect any fee because the externality comes whether or not the beneficiaries want it.

Setting the economists' problems aside, the concept of externality seems intuitively well suited to identifying actors relevant for a number of policy problems. A typical application concerns environmental affairs where it is rather easy to establish a causal link between the disposal of waste further up the river and poor water quality down the river, or a connection between smokestack emission and sulfur dioxide pollution of lakes to the leeward of the polluter. In such cases, the policy problem can be stated in terms of acceptable emission given a desire to maintain a particular quality for the recipient, and the relevant actors would primarily be those who are dependent on the activities of the polluter (jobs, economic activity) and on the quality of the recipient (fishermen, recreational purposes, aesthetic qualities for residents). Pollution and production are not, however, purely of local interest; there may be a larger community (which may even transcend the national borders) where interests can be at stake (for example, the ozone layer).

Policy problems concerning the uses of natural resources may also be approached by the use of externalities. Elinor Ostrom (1990) has analysed a number of cases regarding the use of fishing waters, forestry and agricultural fields where institutions have been set up to secure some degree of equal access to the resource. She has in particular addressed the problems linked to the "tragedy of the commons" where users overuse the resource and thus remove their very basis for making a living; she has shown that the tragedy is not inevitable, given the right institutional setting defining rules for use, penalties for violating the rules and efficient monitoring of the rules. The analysis is based on a classification of the good that one wishes to preserve, on the basis of two factors. The first is *exclusion*: is it possible to exclude a user by, for example, pricing the good? Basically, this is a question of claiming and enforcing property rights. The second factor is *subtractability*: if one makes use of the good, does it preclude anyone else from using it? Eating a fish is an irreversible process, and no one else can eat it, but anyone can use the lighthouse for orientation. Elinor Ostrom's particular interest is collective action relating to goods where it is difficult to exclude users, and subtractability is high - typical facets of the commons. The policy problem, then, is conceptualized as an *appropriation problem*: who should get access, where and when; and a *provision problem*: how to maintain the stock of the resource so that it does not deteriorate.

Finally, externalities lie behind the understanding of a service industry concept as used, for example, by Ostrom, Parks and Whitaker (1978), where response time for the police force is an important parameter in analysing service quality. The same goes for fire engines, ambulances and other rescue services. It is important, of course, to understand this as a generalization; if disaster strikes with hundreds of fires, no service system can handle all the demands. But the analysis of Ostrom and associates has been used to indicate that cooperative agreements between various service producers (like the police) can reduce the overall costs of the service, so that not every police department needs to have equipment (labs and so on) to take care of any conceivable event. The more specialized the service, the larger district it can serve. In terms of policy problems, such questions often lie behind the concerns of citizens - they want to preserve a local public hospital even though it is not in the view of the doctors capable of much because it has insufficient specialization.

The approach has been used to analyse the organizational pattern of local government in Metropolitan areas (ACIR 1987, 1988, 1992), by and large challenging the view that consolidated metropolitan government is more efficient than fragmented, multijurisdictional local government. There must, however, be some overarching coordinating body in the area, and there must be some redistribution of resources between affluent and poor areas to secure some equality in funding services.

A *second* approach to the policy problem is linked to a more formal understanding, based on the (public) organization of a field of intervention: health, social affairs, regional development policy and so on - in some countries conceptualized as "sectors". Often these are very broadly defined, in many countries the "health" sector includes hospitals (including the insane), GPs, and care for the elderly, and within these sub-fields there are many extra specializations. Furthermore, there may be an overlap between, for example, roles involving care for the elderly within the health and social services sectors, and they may differ between countries. This said, there may be some advantages in using the sector concept. They are often staffed by professionals who have a distinct theoretical understanding of their trade. Thus there is a sort of short cut to conceptualizing the policy problem by adapting the professional knowledge. On the other hand there may be conflicting schools within the professional field, meaning that the researcher will have to interpret any interviewing situation according to the organizational leading ideas. We saw an example of this above, two governmental departments clashing on different interpretations of the needs for rush hour transportation, both neglecting the possibilities of, for example, electronic communication. Furthermore, there may be distinctly different opinions between the professionals and local people as to what is important and what is not, and consequently there may be strong disagreements regarding, for example, the proper use of policy instruments.

More generally, the above may be conceptualized by policy networks, a common term in much analysis of inter-organizational policy research; an example would be Marin and Mayntz eds. (1991). Of interest here is not so much the Iron Triangles of Washington, DC, but rather the interaction patterns among a multitude of actors, most of them relating to a public program. They may, however, have differing opinions about the proper way to perform the program, and hence there is a constant exchange of views about how to interpret the goals and how to allocate means and use instruments within the sphere of interest the participants share. So even though the point of departure for understanding the activities comes close to the policy sector, the resulting network is less restrained. Much of the policy network literature has its intellectual roots in the theories of the organizational society; partly based on the "neo-corporate" understanding of the role of interest organizations in advanced, Western society (Streeck and Schmitter eds. 1985), partly based on the extension of organizational theory into inter-organizational theory (Jørgensen 1977), spurred by the realization that the organizational boundary is difficult to define once many members of staff spend more time interacting with people outside rather than inside the organization.

Furthermore, there is a broad agreement that hierarchical relations within the public sector often have poor validity; inter-governmental relations abound where negotiation skills are more important than an ability to phrase an order (Barrett and Fudge 1981). In the Nordic countries, law-making has increasingly been constructed as frame legislation where a number of general objectives may be stated, and some procedural requirements listed, but otherwise the implementation is a question of having the ministry or even local governments set up goals and means. Such laws may invite continuing processes of interaction between a ministry and regional and local actors, and involvement of actors not previously counted on, such as non-profit organizations.

We are approaching some parallels to certain elements of discourse analysis, but this is after all so distant from the above that we shall understand the following as a *third* approach. Professional knowledge forms a cluster of interpretations of the world and of human activities, with some prescriptive elements regarding how to approach problem-solving. We find strong elements of professional knowledge in the policy sector and in policy networks. Professional knowledge is explicitly based on scientific theories which are in this sense generally known and subject to agreement and disagreement; this in turn forms the basis for scientific advances. But there are other forms of knowledge guiding human behavior; some are based on science, most are probably not, at least not directly and not as a conscious choice by the individual. These other forms of knowledge may also be clustered according to use by specific groups. Fox and Miller (1995) use the concept of *energy field* to represent

> a gathering up of sedimented comportments in *this* situation for projection into the future. An energy field is composed of bundles of human intentions, enthusiasms, purposes, and motivations projected from within varying nows. ...
>
> Ideas are brought into "good currency" through interaction in a particular setting with others. The ideas that circulate among participants as they interact, along with ideas generated during antecedent processes, attract participation. (1995:106-107)

The energy field constitutes an arena for exchanging views on what to do regarding specific problems, and the process progresses as individuals or groups exchange interpretations of their environment and of other participants' interpretations. Precisely how policy problems are dealt with within such energy fields is up to the participants, and their scientific description hinges on the interaction between researcher and research objects, who construct a common understanding in a process of dialogue. There are no particular expectations of the use of scientific or professional knowledge; in a number of cases it might certainly be the opposite. Such individualized problem identification might come close to a "thick description" or grounded theory (Glaser and Strauss 1967), but it is important to emphasize that this concerns the perceptions of people involved in or affected by collective action, and hence their views of the problems are important. In particular, we thus avoid the problems of the policy network approach which runs the risk of linking the research to the formal interpretation of the policy problem instead of the problems as perceived by those having to live with the consequences of public action.

NORMS AND RULES

The starting point for this discussion is values (Morel 1986:23-40) which are here conceptualized as binding conceptions of a rank order, importance or desirability of individuals and/or things based on a certain perspective, for example beauty, ethics, applicability. Social values are patterns of thought referring to principles for what is right or seems sensible. Norms are derived from values and can be justified on the basis of values; norms can be defined as binding conceptions of how each member should behave. Values tell us something about importance, norms about directions for action.

Principles of Analysis

Norms are seldom fully operational; actors must perform a judgment in order to adapt to the circumstances. Norms therefore can be difficult to identify in an operational meaning, and this is one task for the researcher in an institutional analysis. This may be done by rephrasing vague norms into clearer rules for action while at the same time adding formal rules for action within the policy field.

One illustration can be found in the discussions on solidarity and reciprocity. Reciprocity means that the giver expects to receive something in return sooner or later. Solidarity has elements of altruism, loyalty and reciprocity (Hegner 1986:411-413) and hence does not necessarily imply any return in the foreseeable future. In the first perspective, one service merits a service in return - and if nothing is returned, the relationship will fairly quickly come to an end. So the rules for action are quite clear. In the second perspective, we are talking about a type of cohesion not tied to clearly identifiable services, and no balance between those involved is expected in the short run; rather the solidarity is a sort of general safety net under everyone involved. Operational rules for individual conduct are, then, more difficult to identify. It is probably quite crucial for the actors whether their relations are based on reciprocity or solidarity, and a specification of vague norms is necessary in order to assess actual behavior.

Rules can, however, be of several types. From our point of view, it is important to be in a position to analyse whether the rules are open for interpretation and whether they are might permit change. We may distinguish between three levels of rules (Kiser and Ostrom 1982). At the *level of action* we apply rules directly affecting concrete action; we can speak of standards (dimensions for roads, specification of emission from smokestacks) or rules of conduct (traffic code). Those regulated by such directions may often apply them to circumstances, and they do this more than their superiors maybe would like (see Lipsky 1980). At the *level of collective* action we define rules for future action. These are principles for smoke emission or desirable conditions in the community and are often called policies although they do not become actual policies until they are implemented, that is, transformed at the level of action. At the *level of the constitution* we discuss principles for future collective decision-making, democratic principles and so on. These constitutional rules are typically very difficult to change; collective decisions are somewhat easier to take up for revision, and action rules are frequently adapted as part of the process.

At a more specific level, working rules can be set up in a number of categories (adapted from E. Ostrom 1986:468)[10] - in our context, they only serve as examples of possible rules:

- Boundary rules set the entry, exit and domain conditions for participants.
- Scope rules specify which states of the world can be affected and set the range within which these can be affected.
- Position rules establish positions and assign participants to positions.
- Authority rules prescribe which positions can take which actions and how actions are ordered, processed and terminated.
- Information rules establish information channels, state the conditions when they are to be open or closed, create an official language and prescribe how evidence is to be processed.
- Aggregation rules prescribe formula for weighting individual choices and calculating collective choices at decision nodes.
- Payoff rules prescribe how benefits and costs are to be distributed to participants in positions given their actions and those of others.

These rules are related to the elements of the institution, as defined here: the scope rules concern the policy problem, authority and payoff rules relate to order and meaning, and the remaining four rules relate to positions and the network. The rules are mainly of constitutional or collective choice character, defining the basic rules of the game and some policy aspects, whereas the action rules will be an outcome of them. They are to be understood as

10. Somewhat similar sets of rules can be found in Burns and Flam (1987:102-108), determining: *who* may act, *why* - for what aims, *what action* can be taken, *how* can decisions be made, *what means* are available, *when* can activities take place and *where*?

examples only, they apply to the specific conditions that are described by Ostrom, and they must be adapted to specific circumstances by the researcher doing empirical analysis.

The most important aspect of the multi-layered institutional arrangement is the realization that in decision-making situations, different logics of rules apply, depending on what level it takes place on. Thus, an actor making daily decisions must be aware of the institutional roots of a decision, if he contemplates acting otherwise than standard operating procedures would prescribe. If the rule is contingent upon the collective choice level, it is difficult to change without breaking the basic logic of the institutional system. On the other hand, this depends on the precision of the language of the rule; it may be phrased so that in reality the working rule(s) are made at the operational level, and thus are possible to alter at that level. If then it is desirable to change a collective choice rule, this must be done in accordance with the rules about rules set at the constitutional level; this requires awareness of such information by the actor at the operational level, who then must initiate the proper procedure rather than take substantial initiatives. Likewise, actors at the collective and constitutional levels must realize their potentials and limitations regarding action at the operational level. Since we are talking about roles, the same individuals may act at several levels, but they must adapt their reasoning to whatever level their action situation is at.

Implementing the Principles

There are many instruments available for controlling the behavior of actors (Lundquist 1987:140-168), but several are not directly relevant for institutional analysis. In this section, focus is on norms and rules, which are two sides of the same coin, namely prescriptions for human behavior.

Norms we understand as general principles for human action like "thou shalt not kill thy neighbor" as a doctrine to prevent people from behaving like animals or in a Hobbesian nightmare, or "don't be prejudiced against people from another race" as a principle facilitating human interaction in general. *Rules* are explicitly formulated prescriptions about what to do or what not to do under specified circumstances, and they are mostly based on sanctions that apply due to a monitoring procedure if the rules are not followed. Some norms have been translated into rules; the first norm above is obviously a basic element of any country's national legislation, but it is also then modified with operational exemptions so that under given circumstances, one may kill another person and not be punished. The second norm of not prejudicing has been made operational at a somewhat different level of abstraction, subsumed under, for example, the declaration of human rights, preventing employers from discriminating due to race. At the general level, the norm may be challenged by another norm; we know that racists do exist, believing that separating the races would be better for mankind. However, few of them would kill to obtain their purpose, so the first norm is under normal circumstances stronger than the second one, which is subject to interpretation in ways the first one is not.

In this framework of analysis, norms summarize something close to what Ostrom (1990) calls attributes of the community. Norms are important for the analysis, especially in a comparative project, because they form a general background for the phenomenon under scrutiny. Norms differ among communities, regions and nations, and they set different spheres of understanding for the policy problems. Thus there will probably be different norms in an urban and a rural setting concerning involvement in the affairs of neighbors who for some reason get into trouble. Family ties are mostly stronger, and generally speaking, the family is more involved in common production in rural areas. Social control is stronger, too.

Norms, then, are important elements of social control, but they belong to the more informal sides of human life. Since rules are explicit and have sanctions linked to them, those acting under the rules must be qualified to understand and follow them, or they are unfair. Rules may be categorized in several ways.

A first division categorizes rules according to substance or procedure. If the rule concerns *substance*, some material measures are used to indicate a desired output or outcome. *Output* measures are the easiest to specify: in environmental protection, for instance, the quantity of carbondioxide emerging from each smokestack may be specified; in fishery regulation the amounts of specified types of fish to be caught by each fishing boat can be prescribed. These measures are often called *standards*. They may be expressed as absolutes, maxima or minima, depending on the purpose of the rule. *Outcome* measures concern the material end-state of some object. In environmental protection, one may specify a maximum allowable amount of carbondioxide emission within a particular geographic area ("a bubble"), in fisheries one may specify a minimum density of certain types of fish to be found within an area. Outcome measures are difficult to use because of the need to specify action and then communicate it if the condition is met; in certain metropolitan areas, a smog-alarm may immediately affect the right of citizens to drive, based, for example, on certain characteristics on their license plate (for example, odd/even numbers) - but one must make sure that those citizens are given fair warning. The difficulties are also partly due to limited knowledge about the causal links between human behavior and the actual state of the environment; intervention based on a certain condition may be seen as arbitrary.

If the rule concerns *procedure*, actors are told with whom to communicate (or not communicate), possibly with specification of frequency and duration, agenda themes, level of participation or attendance for the procedure to be valid, and mechanisms for resolving disputes among the participants. This is an alternative to formulating standards, under the presumption that if actors who have interests in the matter are mandated to interact regarding the subject, they will be able to discuss the matter and sort out the differences; if no compromise can be reached, the rules on the procedure indicate how to decide - by vote, by mediation, by resort to a higher level of administration and so on.

In terms of contents and desired action, a rule system often states whether a particular action is permitted, required or prohibited; of these, only the first one concedes the actor some discretion since it opens up an opportunity but does not mandate the actor to do anything. The other two types leave the actor with no particular degree of choice: once the preconditions are met, the actor either must or must not act as specified. Requirements and prohibitions are normally followed by sanctions to make the desired behavior more probable.

Rules are formulated in a language, and since few languages are capable of describing the world in unambiguous terms, they are subject to interpretation before they are applied. The ambiguity may be put into the rules on purpose in order to make possible adaptation to local conditions, or in order to make room for changes in interpretation over time. It may also be due to lack of knowledge as to causal links between the factors covered by the rules; often ambiguous rules are followed by procedural rules to make sure that the right actors are involved before the decisions are made. Ambiguity also means that there may be disagreements among individuals in their particular interpretations of the rule, and ultimately, there might be a need for a body without substantial interest in the matter to resolve disputes between parties; this may be done by mediation or by a ruling (as in a court).

Norms and rules determine the basic code of conduct for individuals within an institutional setting. Analysis of institutions is often based on noncooperative game theory (Ostrom, Gardner and Walker 1994) where the actors do not exchange points of view during the game. This is only applicable to some rather restricted situations, and Ostrom *et al.* call for more dynamic analysis and the incorporation of dynamic factors making interaction between the actors possible as the situation develops. The need for development is particularly pertinent in cases where the number of participants is limited, and consequences of action are fairly visible to other actors. In large-scale problematics like ocean fisheries, the assumption that people behave like the "rational actor" is fairly valid. There are no possibilities of interacting with other actors, and consequently, we see overfishing and fishermen breaking rules (quotas) whenever possible. The textbook reaction is defection since there are no ties to other individuals, and the perceived gain from following the rules is negligible. The result is often detrimental to the common resource, so the tragedy of the commons may occur, but it *may* also be avoided if the institutional design follows recommendations by Ostrom (1990).

In small-scale problematics like fishing in a lake area, conditions may be altered dramatically. As indicated above, rules are mostly ambiguous, and actors need to discuss their application or even adaptation as the processes unfold, and this is what they do as soon as they perceive the situation as negotiable. This is where the analytic principles of non-cooperative games become less realistic. People have face-to-face relationships, they have knowledge about the other individuals that goes beyond the particular issue at hand, they know that they can discuss problems with other people, as the problems become visible.

Fox and Miller (1995:120-127) discuss how to approach such situations where "real" people interact to form a policy - an *authentic discourse*. They require four conditions to be fulfilled to obtain what they see as the ideal policy discourse. First, trust is required, and this presupposes that speakers at least strive to be sincere; a purely tactical game is out of bounds. Second, the intentions of the participants must regard a relevant problematic, or a policy problem, and it should be addressed from a higher level of abstraction than that of a utility-maximizing individual; some degree of a public purpose should be involved. Third, the discourse is an exchange of views, so participants must be willing to listen to other points of view. Finally, solutions offered must contribute substantively to the policy problem or to the highlighting of how the problem would be understood, or as a special understanding of the situation the negotiation takes place in. In other words, the discourse must be enriched; the individual taking part is not supposed to participate just to patronize the group.

These demands may sound a bit unrealistic. But they are not a far cry from what is known among skilled negotiators and participants in settings where the status of the participants is fairly equal, as in university faculty discussions. Insincere, circumventing, self-aggrandizing monologues are not readily accepted in such groups. This is not to say that every oral intervention is a clearly formulated substantial bid for a solution that benefits everyone equally, but it is expected that participants during the exchange of points of view do add to the common understanding of the group regarding the policy problem. There is no need to strive for something like a scientific understanding of the problem. As Lindblom has stressed repeatedly (Lindblom and Cohen 1979), the interaction of interested individuals may produce as much relevant information as may a research investigation.

POSITIONS AND NETWORKS

Within the parameters of policy problems and rules one will be able to identify a number of positions in relation to scope of action, including the formulation of rules. Individuals may have different positions in several settings.

Principles of Analysis

By means of interaction, positions and rules will form a network; a structure which can be identified analytically and separated from other networks so that the character of the institution can be discussed: its pattern of influence, exchange forms, typical instruments and so on.

If one uses the typology from above as an example (E. Ostrom 1986), rules will define the *boundary*: the basis for membership must be clarified; who can join and who cannot? Next, *position* rules clarify which roles different members can play in different situations. How decisions are made and where is clarified by *aggregation* rules. And finally *information* rules define what may be used as evidence in different situations.

Often formal powers can have great importance but, as organizational researchers know, formal powers are not sufficient in all situations; there is often a large network of informal roles and judgments of role incumbents which could turn upside down the impression one gained from the formal organization chart. Similarly in politics, it is not enough to read the constitution of a country to understand policy - one of the achievements of political science is precisely to help us understand how and why policies are actually made. For instance, corporate structures are not part of the Danish constitution, nonetheless, some researchers do not hesitate to label some of the interaction patterns in Danish politics corporate (Damgaard and Eliassen 1978).

In institutional analysis, both organizations and individuals may be used as units of analysis. Analytically, one must distinguish between individuals, organizations and inter-organizational entities and relate the interaction accordingly. There is, however, no *a priori* limitation on the perspective, no hypotheses about the significance of different types of actors. Sweeping generalizations like "human activity is hierarchically organized" (Burns and Flam 1987:49) seem meaningless as a starting point for analysis - whereas that would probably be true under specific circumstances. It is crucial, then, to specify circumstances, and that is the very task of the researcher. The circumstances indicate how roles may be understood in particular institutional settings, but the researcher must have a non-formal approach in mind; the role of the organization is to be regarded as a hypothesis, not as a given.

Implementing the Principles

The indispensable norm behind a bottom-up analysis is that the importance of formal organization in implementation - and in any other activity, for that matter - is to be regarded as a hypothesis. Thus, the organization vested with the formal responsibility for implementation *may* play the role implied by statute, but this is not to be regarded as a fact until that fact has been established by empirical research. One way of examining this is to use a "snowballing" technique (Hjern and Hull 1987) where a presumed actor is identified, interviewed as to his actual role in a defined problem field, and asked about his contacts with other actors in fulfilling that role. Those thus identified are then interviewed, and likewise asked for contact persons. Soon a network of people will unfold, and the implementation structure thus identified empirically from below.

A crucial question, then, is how to identify the first individual to be interviewed. This is done on the basis of the researcher's conceptualization of the policy problem and a first educated guess about which actors may be active in the last links of a policy implementation chain, if such can be identified. Such an actor has a position in an implementation network. Furthermore, one may structure the envisaged local policy processes in terms of planning, resource mobilization, effectuation and evaluation (Hjern and Hull 1987) - or any other sequence that fits the processes studied.

Positions are very much like roles: a cluster of expectations about relevant behavior in specified situations. Given that we want to analyse dynamic social processes, it is understood that positions are socially constructed and reconstructed over time as people interact, giving (or amending) any position its concrete contents and thereby reinforcing or weakening the first expectations.

Some positions - like the mayor, a section chief or any other member of a formal organization - are based on formal rules. Those rules mostly are on paper and constitute some of the most important elements of the formal organization, visualized by the organization chart and often reinforced by the formal behavior of the members of the organization. Subordinates pay tribute to the supervisor, and supervisors (hopefully) show respect for the work done by the employees. But there are also informal rules linked to the position, and these rules differ by organization. They are the sum of the experiences of the members of the organization over time.

In institutional analysis, the positions studied may be found in an organization. But there are other possibilities, and our interest may only be marginal as to their particular role within that organization. On the contrary, the importance of the formal organization is constantly being questioned by institutional analysts. Positions will somehow be interlinked, but often the links will be found across formal organizational boundaries. This is where the concept of network becomes important. Basically, the network is the sum of the communication links between positions and, together with them, it configures the institution if one wants to make the equivalent of an organiza tional chart. But, as the discussion of this framework shows, the configura-tion of an institution is nothing but the shape of some aspects of it; it does not equal the institution.

The world as we see it is populated by individuals with whom we inter-act, not with roles. The objects we can do research on are composed of *body-subjects* (Fox and Miller 1995:79-84). The researchers tend to disregard this when they interview individuals about other individuals. Those are real persons whom the interviewed person reflects on as individuals, not solely as holders of positions. Few are able to think in the abstract about roles, but everyone can comment on individual A and his particular merits and demerits. These are not only the actual performance in terms of decisions and exchanges of points of view, but also the signals that are not directly part of the spoken (or written) language; class, gender, personality may be important in the concrete situations, as are the locations and the time; with Giddens (1984), one can say that there is a time-space situationing which is important to grasp.

This said, it is still important to realize that individual participants may take different positions over time, depending on how the policy problems develop, and depending on changes in the participants' expectations of their own behavior and of the behavior of others. And sometimes it is difficult for other actors to accept an apparent change of principles due to a new setting. Porter (1990) introduces the concept of *structural pose* to cope with the problem in empirical research where he found that individuals assumed different roles with relative ease, together with values and scopes for action in different action situations; an observation that Porter found created great difficulties in linking them to institutions which apparently were constantly shifting. Structural pose stresses that individuals relate to different institutions in different situations. Thus a professional may in one context follow the principles set up by his community of peers, while in other instances, as a director of a service organization, he may comply with a mandate from the political leadership, even though it may violate the rules of thumb derived from professional research results. Structural pose may, for instance, be useful in implementation structure analysis where it highlights the major institutions involved in implementation and facilitates an analysis of their structures, values and personnel (Porter 1990:25).

The snowballing technique has been discussed at length in several contexts. An important question is whether this is just a technique or whether it really constitutes a norm for policy implementation. It is one thing to take field workers as our point of departure, it is another to make the assumption that the field workers are always right. Are we talking methodology and technique or is this really a (normative) theory?

Basically, this is a technique, and it has the important quality of being replicable. Any other researcher can test the validity of the positions and network by repeating the interviews. An important question is whether each and every researcher would start at the same point, but given the snowballing idea, the chances are relatively great that if just one of any of the actors having a position is "hit" as a starting point, the rest of the network will be detected.

There may, however, also be norms ascribed to the implementation structure that is found. Hjern and Hull (1982) ask for an *empirical constitutionalism*, to challenge the top-down version of constitutionalism based on the involvement of formal organizations. The actual actors, then, in this perspective define the "constitution" for the policy analysed. But how can we determine whether they are right? How do we evaluate their doings - which may be wrongdoings? Hjern and Hull comment:

> If implementation research is to fulfill its remit of empirical constitutionalism it needs to analyse the polity using organizational and methodological constructs which are agnostic to those of the formal constitution. (Hjern and Hull 1984)

This at the very least means that the formal constitution may spur unwarranted action. Hjern and Hull then proceed to get analytic support from Weber, by treating

actors as individually accountable for the alternative courses of action which they
take. In this view, action which, in some strict sense, is unconstitutional need be
lacking neither in accountability nor in subjection to democratic controls. (ibid)

This stance means that we require the actors in the implementation structure to work with a high personal moral standard. Such an understanding is
not uncontested. Linder and Peters (1987, 462-467) stress that even though it
may be true that the top-down perspective may lead to the faulty conception
that the leadership is fully in charge, it may be equally problematic to use an
empirical difficulty (lack of control) to put forward a normative statement
and use it as the sole basis for the analysis of complex organizational and
political problems. The suggestions of Fox and Miller (1995) to fulfill the
requirements of their *authentic discourse*, discussed above, may be seen as
one step towards solving the problem of democratic accountability if the
actors are behaving as bottom-uppers. The demands, then, are that actors
must be sincere, pursue a public purpose, be attentive to other views, and
contribute to the substance of the policy problem. Such actors are accountable and subject to democratic controls.

However, in a world apparently filled with strategic and tactical
behavior, not least within public administration, these demands may seem
somewhat unrealistic. The Habermasian world of free speech does not have a
fertile ground within the political realm precisely because so much is at stake
in the welfare state of the late 20th century. When the political systems of
democracy were established in the 18th and 19th centuries, the regimes were
night-watchmen states with few responsibilities beyond peace, order, and
establishing a system of property rights for commerce. Free speech concerning those issues was, in hindsight, not so difficult after all to establish,
though as history shows, there certainly was resistance from the ruling élite
of that time. But in contemporary societies there is much more at stake,
viewed from the top, and hence many potential dangers even to established
policies. Consequently, the top does not want to relinquish control of the
organizational set, and sees dangers to the course which was set if subordinates are conceded "too much" discretion.

On the other hand, the knowledge we have from implementation research
indicates that, indeed, there is a large number of actors in implementation
structures that do take their remit very seriously. In so far as this is the case,
and in so far as there is a gap between the formal principles of the policy and
the actual policy constructed by the implementation structure, standards must
be set up to evaluate that policy - on the basis of the needs of the target
population.

Hjern (1992) has come so far that he is willing to see the center's - in his case the Swedish state's - policies as illegitimate. Laws are implemented by experts who do not really spot the problems of the communities; they stick to the juridical definitions which probably coincide with their own understanding of policy problems, since experts - professionals - tend to be involved when laws are written in the national capital. One may argue with Hjern how far the repercussions regarding empirical constitutionalism are to be taken. Are we to encourage civil disobedience, as he seems to imply? Maybe that is to go too far, especially since he indicates no means of discriminating between types of disobedience. Surely he would not support the disobedient activities of some Nazi skinheads. Instead, one might recommend that discrepancies between the ideals of the center and the actions in the locality should be understood as signs of warning requiring closer investigation, but one should not *a priori* deem any of the parties illegitimate, nor should one transfer research results in that direction to a general theory. There is a need for a discussion of the moral and ethical consequences of empirical constitutionalism, not unlike the discussion of the uses of policy frames (Schön and Rein 1994).

ORDER AND MEANING

What does an institution give its members in return? Does it yield order and meaning? This is our suggestion for many of its members, but that suggestion is, of course, to be made plausible by empirical research.

Principles of Analysis

Order is for some sociologists the constituting concept for their science. Morel defines social order as the sum of norms at play in a social entity leading to characteristic resemblance in the behavior of the members in relationships within the institution and in relationships crossing the boundaries of the institution (Morel 1986:21, 52). Thus a democratic order means that, regarding political power in a society, one will find that the members perceive a number of rules of the game valid to secure the specific type of democracy valued by that society (for example majority rule and minority protection). Regarding democracy, a number of behavioral patterns, rights and duties then rule the action scope, and the dominant form of thinking is related to this form of democracy; alternatives (for example, totalitarian or anarchic ways of thinking) are rejected.

By establishing an order we ease the process of integrating social entities. At the macro level, political institutions have a special responsibility in that respect. Concern for integrative institutions deals with questions of how different institutions tend to develop different citizens and different societies. Important "concepts" are good sense, justice and appropriateness. For instance, rights are key aspects of the structure of social belief. The institution is an embodiment and instrument of the community or of the democratic order as a constitutional system, captured by common cultures, collective identities, belonging, bonds, mutual affection, shared visions, mutual trust and solidarity. One can, however, pose a question of "integrity" to investigate whether the political process ensures that participants act in a way dedicated to the common good?

Such questions are ambitious, and they go a little too far for this project. At the micro level, Elster (1989) likewise points to political institutions as being responsible for social order understood as predictability of behavior and as an inclination to cooperate among the members of the society. He points to four mechanisms contributing to that effect: altruism, envy, social norms and self-interest which in complex, interacting processes form the "cement of society". In contrast to March and Olsen, Elster recognizes the importance of personal drives for individual gain.

Meaning implies that the members of the institution see it as something giving them a payoff or fulfilling a need. We are talking about a function that may be cognitive, but it is probably often expressive. Hence, meaning can be utilitarian, giving material return, but it can also be symbolic where the outcome is not tangible goods but meets some important values. In addition, the institution by means of its rules makes it easier for the actors to behave correctly, that is, in the accepted way, whenever an unexpected situation comes up. There is, though, the possibility that someone misinterprets the situation and behaves according to the rules of another institution in which case the result might be disastrous for the one making the misinterpretation (cf. Burns and Flam 1987:42-49).

If meaning has developed among the participants, they tend to share interpretations and preferences within their group, but their ideas may not be shared across groups, particularly if there are cleavages among them protected through contact or resource buffers (March/Olsen 1989:3-14). Organizational principles thus become important vehicles in defining interaction patterns and bases for both trust and mistrust among groups; the institutions are important bases for the interpretation of the surrounding world for the participants.

Generally speaking we can say that the institution induces order, making it possible to predict what may happen under specified circumstances. The institution thereby removes an uncertainty that the members typically see as unwarranted. We can talk of a degree of instrumentality in that regard. An institution fulfills some wants which may be defined objectively or subjectively; subjective wants may be desires for participation, ways of expressing oneself, feeling of security and so on; objective wants could be coordination, protection of minorities and such like. This is not to imply that institutions *must* satisfy such wants. There is no functional model behind these points of view.

The concept of meaning gives us an opportunity to stress the symbolic side of political life. Political scientists have tended to join forces with those who opt for rational actions based on material preferences. This is the way most politicians prefer to make their actions legitimate. But why neglect the symbolic side? After all, many political speeches can be shown to have little tangible content, but much significance in addressing the values of the audience. By confirming the values, the speaker assures their sense of order in the audience and justifies their ideals. March and Olsen (1989) use the concept of appropriateness; institutions are instrumental in defining what it is appropriate to do and think.

From an individual perspective, one may speak of costs and benefits by participating in an institution. Costs could be the use of time, lost alternatives, sub-optimal income and so on. Benefits could be predictability, warranty against great losses and such like. These costs and benefits, then, must be considered by actors before they decide whether or not to join. By saying that, I do not want to imply that actors *must* perform such considerations in order to participate. There is no claim for methodological individualism behind this approach.

Last, not least, one must consider what new knowledge and/or comprehension is achieved. From the perspective of the individual, a number of solutions will often be too unattractive to be pursued. A typical example is the tragedy of the commons (Hardin 1968) where the individual user overuses a natural resource, and consequently the collectivity suffers by losing that resource - examples are grazing, fisheries and pollution of lakes and even oceans. Here a collective solution can bring about an understanding which would not have come about without the institutional setting putting the interests of the collective above the immediate interests of the participants (Ostrom 1990).

Implementing the Principles

The rationale behind the bottom-up approach is that somewhere in the process of implementing public policies, local values and/or interests intervene in order to adapt the policy principles to local circumstances which were - presumably - not possible for the policy-making center to foresee or to accommodate. What happens is action by local actors to make things otherwise, and we need to dig somewhat into how to understand such intervention.

We saw above that several theorists perceive those involved in an implementation structure as necessarily accountable individuals who may subject themselves to democratic control - whether or not they are part of a public system, one might add. Several conceptualizations address this problematic in general terms.

At a fairly abstract level, the term of *social capital* is useful in defining consequences of collective action in the longer run. Where physical capital is the arrangement of material resources to improve flows of future income, and human capital is the knowledge and skills that humans bring to solve any problem, social capital is the arrangement of human resources to improve flows of future income (Ostrom 1995:132). It is created by individuals working with other individuals to make it possible to achieve goals they would probably not otherwise have reached. We may interpret "income" rather broadly as, for example, "benefits", and if we do so, we can say that people creating social capital are crafting some sort of institution which can help solve problems in the future without everyone having to start again from scratch. Robert Putnam and his colleagues (Putnam, Leonardi and Nanetti 1993) go so far as to say that over centuries, certain areas of Italy have built up capacities for collective action, and other areas have failed to do so. Whether or not they are right in those assertions is not important here; the rationale for building institutions is, however.

Social capital creates order in the interactions of people over time, and it also signifies a particular meaning to such actions within an institutional framework. It is important to realize that many such institutions have not been constructed consciously for the benefit of future generations; the long-term spin-off comes whether or not it was intended to be so. When we discuss collective public action bottom-up, we do, however, speak of intentions to do better, wishes to improve a policy problem, and actions that are designed to make a difference. Hence, institution-building bottom-up as we want to analyse it is hardly just an accidental spin-off from daily chores. What may they have in common at the analytic level?

Some analyse meaning as a historical phenomenon:

we ... share the ambition ... to uncover a deeper meaning in social movement. That deeper meaning is what we mean by cognitive praxis. (Eyerman and Jamison 1991:63)

Eyerman and Jamison understand the cognitive praxis as a kind of glue binding the members of a social movement together, and as something to be empirically reconstructed by the observer. They do this, however, by reading their history, thus reconstructing the cognitive praxis from other sources. Our ambition is more to understand contemporary praxis, therefore we must use other methodological tools.

Paul Sabatier uses the concept of *core beliefs* (Sabatier 1986, Sabatier and Pelkey 1987) to select an advocacy coalition which in effect shares these core values regarding desirable policy goals and instruments. This approach will ensure that the group selected is manageable in number and fairly stable over time. This of course makes sense if one wants to find a group that is in agreement, but it is not enough if one wants to identify all the participants that perceive themselves as having a share in the policy problem - they may differ in values and hence compete for influence on the solutions for the policy problem. Sabatier knows this, of course, and uses the concept of policy brokers as intermediaries working to reconcile the differences between advocacy coalitions. This looks a little like a fairly standard interest organization approach, but it is not, given the alternative Sabatier is up against in the case he pursues: the agency perspective within regulatory policymaking.

Core beliefs may be used for identifying a group with a common interest. If we want to understand the intensity of the involvement of the group members, the role of *commitment* as discussed by Robertson and Tang (1995) may become important. In the organizational literature, commitment is a psychological mechanism making the individual feel an attachment to the organization, visible as an identification with the goal of the organization, involvement in actions, and loyalty to the organization. For more than a decade, this perspective has been developed especially under the heading of organizational culture. In rational choice literature, commitment is a conceptual solution to the theoretical puzzle of why people cooperate when there is no direct personal incentive to do so; commitment then is an actor's resolve to carry out a promise to perform in a specified fashion. But increasingly, norms have become part of the analysis as mutually reinforcing expectations among participants in collective action, forcing them from a short-term to a more long-term perspective. Both theoretical perspectives, then, use the term, but based on somewhat different assumptions, particularly regarding the incentives of the individual for being committed:

individual inherent willingness to cooperate in the organizational literature, individual self-interested reasons in the public choice literature.

There is no reason why commitment should be reserved for the organizational sphere; the mechanisms that are discussed can also develop in implementation structures, although formal leadership by its very nature will probably play a minor role - bottom-uppers are nearly by definition in opposition to a formal manager who has to answer for the formal requirements of the activities. Likewise, position holders in the implementation structure may have conflicting commitments; for example, some to their formal mother organization, some to the implementation structure and its cross-organizational colleagues.

Core values and commitment, then, may be important facets of the forces creating meaning and order for the participants in an implementation structure or other institutional arrangements. They are fairly intangible aspects of collective public action, and we should not exclude the more material side of institutional arrangements completely. The rational choice concept of *payoff* is quite useful, since the gain of any individual is easy to understand for any observer as a factor creating meaning for that actor. There is no reason to think that people engage in collective public action for purely altruistic purposes, though it should not be ruled out, depending on the circumstances we want to explore. In the original setting of public choice, payoff is the relation between benefits and costs linked to particular (sets of) action. In a world of economic action, this presents the observer with no problems; everything can be measured in money terms. In the world of collective public action, such unambiguous instruments of measurement are not available; they may apply to some policy problem like, for example, local economic development, but within problems of social services the measurement rod is much more complex, unless one wants to subscribe to a Becker's world of economics, applicable to any side of human interaction[11] (Becker 1986). Payoff, therefore, within our sphere of interest, is the relation between costs and benefits in a broader sense.

INSTITUTIONAL ARRANGEMENTS BOTTOM-UP

We have discussed a number of elements of such an institutional network analysis, forming the conceptual basis for processes of structuration among actors involved in collective public action, that is, collective action linked to uses or possible uses of the public power.

11. "Indeed, I have come to the position that the economic approach is a comprehensive one that is applicable to all human behavior ..." (Becker 1986:112)

The elements in overview are

Policy problem
  - externalities
  - policy sector
  - energy field
Norms and rules
  - community of understanding
  - substance standards
  - procedures
Positions and networks
  - body subjects
  - structural pose
  - implementation network
Order and meaning
  - social capital
  - core beliefs

One may conceptualize the *policy problems* by using variations of the externality understanding of human behavior, thus summarizing a complex interaction of various forces into a generalized pattern. One may also approach the policy problem more along the lines that actors tend to define their activities, namely the policy sector or, as a pattern of communication, the energy field.

Norms and rules are complex elements of the analysis. Norms are attributes of the community of understanding, some might use the term culture, but it may confuse the reader into thinking that culture is the overarching concept, which it is not. Rules are primarily of two kinds: standards of substance putting demands on the quality of the policy, and/or rules of procedure directing processes of interaction towards discourse, possibly authentic discourse.

Positions and networks are in one sense based on roles, but the starting point for the analysis should be based on body-subjects, since those are the ones who communicate. There is no interest in analysing puppets maximizing particular aspects of an understanding of an analytical construct. On the other hand, one might use structural pose to understand how individuals may cope with sometimes conflicting demands of their various activities in different settings. The networks may be understood in similar ways as the implementation structure of implementation researchers.

Order and meaning will to some degree be created by institutional arrangements, but this is not to be understood as a functional consequence or a requirement. It may depend on the availability of social capital which forms the basis for responsive interaction among participants; these must share a number of core beliefs if such interplay is to yield a common meaning.

6. Constructing Research Bottom-up

This chapter deals with the problems of "how-to" do research bottom-up. This means that some meta-theoretical sides of this type of research are to be discussed. First, we locate the development in the social sciences towards postmodernism. Historically, there are no links between the first bottom-up research and postmodernism since most bottom-up projects have been quite modernistic in their research techniques, but over time some convergence has appeared which is worth discussing. Social constructivism seems to be important, particularly in the forms that are applied in evaluation research. Second, we discuss a range of bottom-up studies that have been made; they differ widely, from post-positivistic analysis over critical theory to social constructivist projects. The studies come from a broad range of countries, the USA, Germany, Sweden and Denmark. They give us different lessons, but the lessons are not tied to the nationality of the study, rather to non-national institutional differences. Third, a case of local disagreement over the cut-back of a public service will be discussed both as a top-down and a bottom-up analysis, the latter to illustrate how an institutional analysis may be carried out bottom-up.

TRENDS TOWARDS SOCIAL CONSTRUCTIVISM

In Chapter 2, we have discussed the trends towards postmodern conditions in society. The claim is that there is no such thing as a full-fledged postmodern society, only partial tendencies that differ radically from modernity, which is dominant in many spheres of our lives. Consequently, there are conflicts between the modern society and the postmodern conditions, creating certain dynamics towards change, but also creating some confusion among social actors who lack their acknowledged points of reference. A comparable predicament is now found within the social sciences because of conflicting trends in the paradigms for research; there has always been disagreement among researchers regarding the proper way to pursue research goals, but the differences may be becoming larger.

Paradigms and Postmodernism

In science, research and scholarship, paradigms are used to indicate schools of thought. This is the subject of many book-length treatments in the philosophy of science, so clearly we run the risk of oversimplification in this brief discussion; for a more concise characterization, see Guba and Lincoln (1994). We shall briefly touch upon three paradigms below, the post-positivistic paradigm which is linked to control of modernity, the critical theory and hermeneutic paradigms where many analyse the dark sides of the modern society in order to enhance liberation, and the postmodern trends which, as we shall see, are difficult to characterize. Since postmodernism is at the center of our interest, we will use most of the space for that characterization.

Modernity may be conceptualized as the basis for the *positivistic* research paradigm, the one whose constitution process Weber and Durkheim discussed one hundred years ago, although they disagreed on its desirability. That paradigm has dominated research within the social sciences since then. As we saw in Chapter 2, rationalization is the hallmark of modernity, and it has become the model for analysis within the natural sciences and derivative disciplines like engineering and medicine. The rational model and the understandings of a mechanistic cause-effect process, a "Newtonian" positivistic model, have formed the basis for most scientific activities and structure many models used for educational purposes. Of course, it has not gone unnoticed that Heisenberg and other scientists have found chaos and initiated quantum theory in physics, but still the vast bulk of natural sciences is performed as the traditional Newtonian paradigm prescribes.

In the social sciences, then, organizational endeavors in much of the 20th century have been focused on setting up a comparable paradigm and making "science" the hallmark of social research. Thus, at the universities, many a Department of Government changed its name to the Department of Political Science. And if it didn't, political science was the term its faculty were thinking of. If we go to public administration, Gulick and associates in 1937 published their papers on the *science* of administration (Gulick and Urwick 1937), calling for rational analysis of public administration. Likewise, Laswell and associates in 1951 (Laswell and Lerner 1951) called for a development of policy *sciences* to serve the needs of society for enhancement. These theorists called for the application of rational models or technical rationality, the uses of instruments to resolve social problems in order to solve them as the engineer helps solve the lack of infrastructure by building bridges and tunnels; as the medical doctor applies advanced techniques to cure diseases; and as the agricultural scientist applies techniques to enhance the production potential of farming lands. Typical social science instruments have been statistical techniques (Adams 1994:33) to manipulate large quantities of data in order to categorize phenomena, establish links between them in a cause-effect model, and set up generalizations about the behavioral patterns thus observed.

It is probably not difficult to have social scientists agree on the main trajectory in the development of the social sciences, namely towards a modern science, understood in the terms described above; see, for instance, White and Adams (1994), Hollinger (1994), and Rosenau (1992). They all agree that a change came about with the Enlightenment, and that the scientific community and the modern society materialized hand in hand. Modernity thus has played a very strong role in innovating the social sciences, and *vice versa*. But relatively strong differences come up among observers when one asks for an evaluation of the consequences.

The natural sciences, most agree, have been successful in helping to control nature at some vital points, although there are limits to the power of scientific knowledge when it comes to phenomena like environmental protection and river dam control. But the development and role of the social sciences does not receive any unanimous evaluation.

Most social scientists seem relatively content with the development of the modernistic and positivistic paradigm; they realize that there are limits to how far the scientific community has succeeded in constructing the desired theories, but they faithfully continue to expand partial theories based on statistical evidence, admittedly with limited validity, especially over time. One may label this group *post-positivists*; they do not subscribe to the extremely rigorous demands of positivism, but they carry on the principal ideas and adapt them to circumstances, striving for probabilities rather than strict generalizing laws. Prominent examples would be Simon (1960) and Lakatos (1974). They find social science useful for specific purposes, given that one knows the limitations to that knowledge, and some of them add a possibility of some uses of qualitative research techniques to the methodological repertoire, at least for use in pilot projects. They see the postmodern critiques as exaggerations and tend to ignore them.

The second overarching group of social scientists consists of various sub-groups. One, labeled *critical theorists*, gained special momentum in the 1960s and includes theorists like Habermas (Habermas 1972) and Claus Offe (1986). They are unified by critical attitudes to several facets of Western society. They criticize positivism as a type of science because it does not reflect critically on the interests it serves by its non-reflective reporting on trends in the economy, political systems and social affairs. The objective theories are so only by name, they serve to cover unjust sides of human life;

thus by its very categorization of variables the positivistic science will, for instance, gloss over racial discrimination, suppression of minorities and hide gender differential treatment. Many of the critical theorists have Marxian origins, but their criticisms are in the 1990s not particularly linked to Marxian theory. They share, however, the Marxian interest in putting the object of research into a historical perspective rather than generalizing across time as the post-positivists. The second sub-group may be labeled *hermeneutics*. They are unified by their anti-positivism in terms of rejecting statistical evidence as the primary scientific method, and instead advocate interpretation of historical evidence and of texts. The preferred methods are qualitative; quantitative evidence may be used extensively, but then as evidence towards categorical generalizations or generalizations that explicitly take time into consideration. Prominent examples are Weber and Gadamer. In terms of methodology, the hermeneutic scientists overlap with some critical scientists. The former, however, tend to strive for the very value neutrality the critical theorists have abandoned, but they share the recognition that analysis tends to involve the subject (the researcher) where the positivists set up procedures to objectify the role of the researcher.

There is probably very little we could label highly elaborated *postmodern* research, that is, there is no well established postmodern research paradigm. There is a gradual slide from critical theory and hermeneutics to postmodernism. Most postmodernists defy any categorization themselves, but we may follow Rosenau (1992) and distinguish between *skeptical* postmodernists, who to some degree come out of the critical theorist camp, and *affirmative* postmodernists, who are closer to the hermeneutics. The skeptics are theorists like Derrida and Rorty who see the whole modern project as a sort of misunderstanding, and hence doomed to failure regarding any role of the social sciences in forming society. The whole idea of objectivity is to them an impossibility because knowledge cannot be separated from the way human beings interact. Therefore scientific facts are not just there, but are dependent on the way humans express them, and consequently no scientist has any special legitimacy to present other people with "facts" and analyses, and then go on from there advising how to manage the future. So our understanding of science is turned upside down by those postmodernists.

The affirmative postmodernists as a group share a common ground with hermeneutics. They share a rather strong dissatisfaction with the development of the social sciences and, first of all, they attack the "Big-T" Truth claim, the quest for large-scale generalizations which has been the aim of most participants in the "behavioral revolution" of the social sciences after World War II. They do not, however, see or wish any doom to failure for social scientists and instead search for "small t" truths; social science results that are explicitly restricted to a number of situational variables, and hence are very contingent in time and space terms. Beyond this "antifoundationalist" stance they differ in so many ways that one cannot speak of a school. Some are deconstructivists, some are discourse analysts. Most of them are also united by some sort of social constructivism in their research - the details, again, differ. Most use some kind of qualitative analysis, for example participation, interviews and textual analysis. Most, consequently, do not use statistics in the usual way, that is, for generalizing purposes; they do, however, use statistics for various illustrative purposes and as part of a general qualitative analysis.

In 1992, Pauline Rosenau wrote in her assessment of postmodern trends in the social sciences, explicitly based on her positive stance to modern science:

> The application of post-modernism to the humanities, literature and the arts may be without undue consequences, but its appropriateness for the social sciences is a question of another order. In the humanities, subjectivity and speculation may be playful and interesting, but the social sciences need to be more rigorous and analytical, grounding conclusions on reason and evidence of some sort or another. (Rosenau 1992:168)

She concludes that there are stronger demands on the "truth conditions" of the social sciences than in the humanities. In that assessment lies a demand for social scientists to take responsibility for the uses of their research results in the development of society - while the humanists and artists can play in the corner, it is of no serious significance.

To this author, it seems a little too much to demand that the social sciences must be of such usefulness. The social sciences have always also had the role of forming a basis for critical assessments without necessarily having to prescribe a cure. Furthermore, if one goes through the literature on postmodernism since 1992, Rosenau's assessment seems somewhat premature in its understanding that postmodern science cannot be anything but the outsider's critique, playful and irresponsible. Rosenau's distinction between skeptical and affirmative postmodernists here becomes relevant, and her verdict especially hits the former group, which still refuses to be part of any "responsible" pattern in social science. The latter group, however, seems to have developed towards a more "responsible" status. It now also permeates - without conquering, though - fields like organization theory, policy analysis and evaluation, fields that traditionally have close contacts with practice and therefore have a particular sensitivity to delivering research that is of relevance to practitioners.

In *organization theory*, Gephart *et al.* (1996) sum up that postmodernism has serious consequences for organizational analysis. It deviates from the quest for universal truths or organizational principles and rather seeks local knowledge and insights from which one can develop the capacity for reflection and reflexivity in managers and citizens (Gephart, Thatchenkery, and Boje 1996:359). There certainly is no negativism in such a statement, there is a call for the development of perspectives within the organization, based on own initiatives rather than the great visions from outside theorists. Some of the techniques to achieve this vary from those a modernist scholar would propose, but not dramatically so. First of all, the recommendations require the users to consider reflexively their own position and the relativity of research methods - a demand to put any analysis into a context before conclusions are drawn. The factors analysts discuss, like structure and technology, do not exist independently of how they are observed for use in the analysis. A computer may be sitting on a desk, but the uses of that computer may vary enormously, depending on the skills of the user, and depending on what other members of the organization have put into the files. By reflexive analysis, the gap between analysis and action is reduced. In order to understand one's own organization, one must deconstruct it, but this is in order to initiate, when necessary, a reconstruction of that very organization, based on local logics. Thus, rationality is decentered, not abandoned (Gephart, Thatchenkery, and Boje 1996:363-364).

In *policy analysis*, Fischer and Forrester (1993) have made the case for postmodern analysis of policy and planning, indeed activities that were until then reserved for modern analysis. In their introduction (Fischer and Forrester 1993), the editors anchor their subject in the language in which policy analysts, planners and politicians alike have to situate their topic, and hence they construct it rather than present us with something existing objectively, irrespective of the media of communication. The job for the researcher is

> to attend closely to the day-to-day work analysts do as they construct working accounts of problems and possibilities. Recognizing these accounts as politically constrained, organizational accomplishments in the face of little time and poor data, we can evaluate the analysts' arguments not only for their truth or falsity, but also for their partiality, their selective framing of the issues at hand, their elegance or crudeness of presentation, their political timeliness, their symbolic significance, and more. (Fischer and Forrester 1993:2)

Such an approach, then, has no particular truth claim, nor does it vindicate any completeness of the analysis. It is partial, but important. Hidden in the lines is a critique of the objective understanding of policy analysis. The essays in the Fischer/Forrester volume address broad issues within political and administrative processes, like the contents of policy documents; the solutions they come to; how agendas for action are set; the bargaining processes relating to action, and shifts in political powers; and thus broadly, the role of those processes in a democratic society.

Both organizational and policy analysts have taken up narrative analyses as important methods within their fields. Emery Roe (1994) sets up a procedure for policy analysis based on literary theory, and Barbara Czarniawska (1997) links literary theory to theories of institutions to better understand how the life of organizations develops.

To some this development may seem strange. Why involve methods from disciplines that are remote from the social sciences? One answer is that literary theory, narrative analysis, discourse theory and the like are not far from the techniques that anthropologists and those performing case-studies have used all the time; however, they have not used them from a theoretical stance, but applied interpretive methods all the time without discussing their possible theoretical links. What happens now is that methods from other disciplines are getting integrated in the social sciences in ways that make possible discussions of their theoretical status instead of just having an interpretation which the reader cannot really understand in any depth, since the techniques used by the researcher were not explained.

A third social science field with close connections to practice, namely evaluation, has also voiced criticisms of the modernist paradigm and taken up some postmodern stances. Among the theorists of that field, Guba and Lincoln (1989) probably stand out as some of the most prominent. We turn to the development of evaluation in the following section on social constructivism.

Social Constructivism

The core message of constructivism concerns relativism. There is, however, nothing particularly new in the claims of the relativism of research results. Kuhn (1962) told us that only within a paradigm of research, also in the natural sciences, is there a common understanding of what is right and wrong, and the consensus of the followers of the paradigm establishes its legitimacy. And in the social sciences hermeneutic theorists like Hans Georg Gadamer have told us that research results are dependent on the researcher. That said, it is noteworthy that those claims did not have much effect on the practice of most social scientists for a long time. But in the 1990s, the critical reflections of those and other theorists have become centerpieces of reference. That certainly is the case within social constructivism.

In Chapter 4 on institutional analysis, we touched upon the significance of Berger and Luckmann's (1966) book on the *Social Construction of Reality*. It took 25 to 30 years before that book really became acknowledged in the practices of social science. The short message is that our data and knowledge are constructed in a social process which creates the meaning this knowledge can give us. The data may exist without anyone watching or using them, but as soon as they are used, social processes will come into play, creating a platform for interpreting those data. The claim of social constructivism is that the data have no value for us as human beings until that social process of interpretation has taken place.

A corollary is that all knowledge is relative to the knower and those that participate in social interaction on the knowledge, a process that in itself dissolves the role of being somebody who knows; knowledge becomes part of a relationship between individuals who in the processes may continuously change the contents of that knowledge; it is discursively created. Some claim that knowledge therefore is local, but they then presume that interaction takes place physically between people who are present, but interaction may just as well take place on the Internet. "Local" therefore does not necessarily have any geographical connotations, it may simply indicate restrictions; not everyone can participate and in that sense the processes of social construction of reality are local.

The constructivist understanding has changed scientific activities like evaluation profoundly, from a perspective from the outside, based on objective measurements of performance, to a perspective from stakeholders, that is, those who have an interest in the evaluation - as *agents* who are directly involved in the activities of the organization that is evaluated; the *beneficiaries* like those who directly or indirectly profit from the activities of the organization; and the *victims* like those who are systematically excluded from being beneficiaries (by not being eligible) or who have opportunity costs resulting from the existence of that organization (Guba and Lincoln 1989:40-41). In such a fourth generation evaluation, the stakeholders are used actively to create the necessary data and perspectives for the evaluation. In so far as it is possible, evidence is constructed in a process where goals for the evaluation are reconstructed in a common process; knowledge about the past is reconstructed by consensus, and the criteria for the status and quality of the evaluation are based on credibility and pertinence as they evolve during the evaluation process.

Stakeholder analysis is a good example of the constructivist analysis where concepts, models, and theories are viable only in so far as they demonstrate adequacy in the contexts in which they were created. If the evaluator brings in a report with which the participants cannot identify, the evaluation is a failure. It is also an example of a process that is based on belief in the possibility of creating competence among ordinary members of any organization to perform quite sophisticated processes - and this is where the external evaluator sees the primary challenge: to help stakeholders formulate the necessary components for a successful evaluation.

From stakeholder analysis we can make a connection back to the characterizations of the social sciences above (based on Guba and Lincoln 1994). For our purposes we can exclude the original positivistic paradigm which under present circumstances is more of historical interest. And the hermeneutics are difficult to place in any indisputable way side by side with the critical theorists.

Regarding the *aim* of the inquiry, the post-positivists strive for prediction and control, hermeneutics and critical theorists both seek understanding and critique, the latter group, however, aiming at transformation to promote restitution and emancipation. Constructivists basically desire understanding in order to be able to participate in reconstruction. There is a clear development from classical modernist control, over (sometimes vigorous) critical activities in order to liberate minorities (women, ethnic groups and so on), to the moderate and consensual working methods of constructivists. Critical theorists aim at confrontation, constructivists at compromise, which will then make collaboration possible in order to enhance settings that are seen as dysfunctional to the organization. Thus, post-positivists and constructivists share an interest in enhancing future action for a better society, but their involvements differ, as we shall see below.

The *nature of knowledge* and its quality differs: post-positivists stick to the principles of non-falsifiable hypotheses and they wish to obtain the status of covering laws, but compromise by probabilities in statistical analysis; they apply classical criteria of validity and reliability to their variables and data. The hermeneutic and the critical theorists strive for historical and/or structural insights where understanding of the operation of various forms of social systems is important; they work with many forms of data in a qualitative process and apply criteria of quality according to gains in insight and the degree to which they can establish their results in a historical relationship. Constructivists aim at getting individuals to reconstruct their surroundings in a process of compromise between opposing stories; hence the quality of the project depends on trustworthiness and authenticity. This squares well with their ultimate aims for the research.

There are strong differences in the attitudes regarding *involvement of the scientist*. Post-positivists and most hermeneutics stick to being disinterested observers and informers of holders of power - and anyone else - and thus produce advice for others to implement; they do not get close to the action. Critical theorists may work as advocates and even activists in the well-known role of a transformative intellectual; but first of all, they want to uncover unfortunate sides of modernity; if it comes to a choice between analysis and action, action is for others to care about. The constructivists are participants in processes where they serve as facilitators of many voices in the organizations so that those who may be weaker under normal circumstances gain influence in so far as they are being heard. They will stay on, if possible, and integrate analysis in action-to-come by raising issues that will force local actors to take positions as to changing local circumstances.

Many a post-positivist and hermeneutic researcher would probably some years ago have called the development towards constructivism a normative development, particularly when research turns into stakeholder analysis. On the other hand, it was considered "good practice" to make clear in a research report what the normative stance of the researcher was, in order to acknowledge that influence from norms could not be ruled out completely. Therefore better inform the reader. Constructivism may be understood as a process of strengthening that kind of information, indeed, to make it a core element. Instead of making it clear that norms may play a role, everyone is supposed to have norms and is expected to have those norms play out in the research process. So constructivists take those norms explicitly into account and ask what their significance may then be. Norms are changed from being somewhat suspicious because they are probably being hidden, to something respectable because they are brought to the table and therefore can be dealt with.

PARADIGMS FOR RESEARCH

Bottom-up research may be carried out in a variety of ways; it is not tied particularly to any school of science. It gained momentum in the 1970s, in a period where the social sciences were torn between Marxists and positivists; one might say that some of the ideas in bottom-up projects were ways to enter a middle road between very modernistic understandings of policy analysis, and more radical claims of "power to the people", that is, bottom-uppers accommodated the claims of relevance for actors other than the power-holders at the top of the organization. Still, there was no sign of any particular critical stance to capitalism, to particular types of party politics, or to other actors in the society.

Below we shall take examples from research projects using the bottom-up methodology or perspective in a variety of ways. If we follow the grouping of research above, three stand out as relevant today: post-positivists; hermeneutics and critical theorists; and social constructivists.

Post-positivists

The post-positivists start out with the scientific construction of the policy problem that is to be investigated. This is the responsibility of the researcher, not anyone else. The most general studies deal with the rationale for organizing local governance, based on the policy characteristics of different local government functions, but challenging the view of the desirability of consolidated local government. We have some examples from US metropolitan areas and various analyses of policy fields as a multi-layered system of decision-making; most of them stem from an implementation of the concept of a service industry (Ostrom and Ostrom 1977).

The analysis of public economies
Local government reform has been analysed from many angles. Most, however, are based on ideas of economy of scale that lead to consolidation of districts into larger entities and from one-function to multi-function jurisdictions. The public economy approach differs.

The basic idea is that one must start out with the policy problem - or rather functions of local government - and divide the understanding of the processes of delivering the service into two discrete types of decision: providing the service and producing the service (Ostrom, Bish and Ostrom 1988:85-111). Service *provision* means a process of collective choice where it is decided what to provide, how to finance the service, and the quality and quantity standards that may apply to the service. Service *production* means to actually produce the service within the parameters determined by the service provider. Within local government, this understanding means that the body responsible - the municipality, the county and so on - for the service must make the decisions as to provision, but it does not necessarily have to produce the service. Any organization able to fulfill the demands by the provider can take care of the service production.

This does not mean, as some seem to think, that the service production must be provided by private organizations. Research shows that there is no guarantee that private producers are always cheaper; the real issue is what type of contractual relationship there is between provider and producer (Ostrom, Bish and Ostrom 1988:138-187). The production can be in-house, by private contract, by inter-governmental agreement. It can be arranged by franchise, by voucher, by voluntary organizations, by joint production between organizations. There is no *a priori* determination of what works best; it is up to the producers to prove which economy of scale is right for the particular service. Service production is a question of price and trust - a demand that the service (as specified by the provider) be produced at the lowest costs, but also that the service will actually be produced, once the contract is won.

The production of service, then, may be organized in many ways. Consequently, many different spatial arrangements may be made for service production, depending on the properties of that production that are emphasized. The provision side, then, may be organized so that it best reflects the democratic side of local government; this is a different issue from production and therefore may require other spatial configurations. A crucial feature is how to organize for maximizing the responsiveness to the ideas and problems of any locality.

This way of thinking, then, is bottom-up in both determining service production arrangements and service provision. It is the local problems of production and provision that come to dominate the processes of research, not the views of the organizational leadership. Two large studies have been carried out by the Advisory Commission on Intergovernmental Affairs (ACIR) to substantiate pros and cons of a fragmented metropolitan area: one of St. Louis (ACIR 1988), and one of Pittsburgh (ACIR 1992). They were based on an initial theoretical study, a rather surprising venture by a public commission (ACIR 1987).

The research techniques used to assess the organizational patterns are not bottom-up in the sense of the other studies reported on below - but the general methodology certainly is. By and large, the techniques are to set up statistical measures of efficiency (internally in departments and so on) producing the right service for the citizens of the jurisdictions, and in equity in the distribution of taxes. In addition, the organizational patterns of cooperation between the providers, between the producers and between providers and producers, were mapped out.

We shall quote some conclusions from the Pittsburgh study (ACIR 1992:81-88). First of all, the study rejects the popular belief that fragmented governmental arrangements cannot be coordinated. Coordination is ensured by, first, the overarching county council providing a number of countywide services and services that require a large population base but that are separate from other services that are normally grouped together (for example, certain police services). Furthermore, there is widespread cooperation between government entities to enhance information dissemination between local governments and to help organize common projects. There is relatively little contracting out and instead cooperative measures between localities, helped by a strong public entrepreneurship. The main problem of the area is fiscal equality; this, however, is not so much due to the fragmentation of local government as to a reluctance at higher levels of government to equalize incomes of lower levels.

These studies, then, are helpful in illustrating the bottom-up claim that forms of organization should be adapted to situational and policy circumstances. One general organizational form applied across all problem areas is not an appropriate solution. The result is that specific problems are then to be solved by the managerial top, a very difficult managerial challenge. These analyses stress the role of active citizens in making the decisions (principles) of provision, and then look for organizational solutions to their policy specifications.

The principles of public economy in metropolitan areas were also applied in a discussion of how to organize for education (Davis and Ostrom 1991). Behind the analysis was a public American debate about public or private education as two alternatives - hierarchy or market? Davis and Ostrom show that analysing in terms of two such alternatives is neither fruitful nor sensible, and it does not square with the reality in school systems. They identify four existing types of educational systems: a large-scale public district system regulated by the state; a purely private system; a small-scale system of school districts, and a multi-tiered public economy system. They add a voucher system and conclude about all the educational systems that none is perfect, all have flaws in some direction. There is no such thing as a perfect institutional arrangement. Of these, however, a multi-layered system has the best prospects because it best reflects the behavioral diversities in the production and particularly in the provision side of education. That is, as soon as we are speaking of needs that go beyond the running of any particular school, we should go beyond the localized system in order to create enough room for diversity and thereby equality for local minorities.

Specific policies

In the presentations below, we have focused on the policy problems and the implementation structures. Once the policy problem has been conceptualized, the rest of the analysis more or less follows, and many research methods can be applied. But conceptualizing the policy problem becomes the nuts and bolts of the analysis.

In terms of specific policy fields, there are two main types that have attracted bottom-uppers: industrial and manpower policies, and the practices of field workers within various public health areas. These policies were among the initial testing grounds for bottom-up research, done by the research team in Wissenschaftszentrum Berlin. They have the same characteristics: they deal with some central elements of the welfare state and the mixed economy, and they have distinct inter-organizational qualities in their formal design. Therefore, they attracted researchers that differed from the received view of implementation.

The first European study (Hjern and Hull 1987, summarized in Hjern 1987) has more or less become the classic reference of all bottom-uppers searching for an implementation structure - the equivalent of analysing a service industry, as in education above. Using the ideas of network analysis and extending them to larger areas, the authors mapped out the élite structure linked to the policy problem of making small firms grow. Many programs have more or less such an aim, and therefore one had to analyse across programs if one were to grasp what actually happened in four West European countries included in the study.

In analytical terms, the core of the analysis was the creation of a number of implementation functions: relating to how to understand the policy problem, how to prioritize alternative ways to go, how to create resources for the strategy and how to evaluate the results. The actors of firms were asked to identify their contacts related to the first three of those functions, which of course had to be specified in the language of the firm rather than at the above general conceptual level. Individuals so identified were asked about their role and further contacts, and thus step by step this "snowballing" method uncovered the individuals involved in making small firms grow - the "assistance structure" during the last three years.

One main result of the project was the realization that firms use programs because of their availability and not because they fit the local problems particularly well. The role of the firms, their brokers and the implementation officers of public programs then became one of adapting particular programs to local problems, almost no matter what the formal goals of the programs were.

An interesting result is that in West Germany, only one area out of four actually had an implementation structure related to making small firms grow. Many programs addressed the problems, but only had effect *vis-à-vis* the growth of small firms in one site, the city of Borken. The authors conclude that if a top-down approach had been used, it would have had to conclude that in Borken there was poor execution of the goals of the specific programs under scrutiny since they did not operate the way the program initiators had planned them to do. Bottom-uppers, of course, see the results as a success story.

Carlsson (1993) has analysed three types of Swedish policies for revitalizing small Swedish towns and villages in the Northern, rural areas - one of making local development productions commercially viable; one of reversing trends of population decline; and one of promoting town development "from below". At least two cases are selected from each policy. Like Hjern and Hull, he identifies implementation structures which vary from case to case; some are totally dominated by public agencies, some are strongly influenced by local actors; still they all somehow relate to the formal public policy. The actual local policy is the result of a process of common creation by different actors relating to several, often formally unrelated programs. The policy creation processes vary from case to case. Even if separate cases have the same policy problem or make identical political decisions, a "policy gap" identifying differences in collective action patterns can be identified; none of the institutional patterns are similar. New patterns of institutional arrangements are created side by side with the formal political-administrative ones (Carlsson 1993:209-210).

Carlsson determined the policy problem by letting the actions of local actors be definitive, marking the policy problem as seen by the implementor. Whatever the intentions of the formal policy makers have been, it is the intentions of local actors that are decisive, and consequently it is the local processes of organizing that are important to understand and hence to investigate (Carlsson 1993:178). This kind of approach, then, is a first step away from having the researcher decide how to conceptualize the policy problem.

Hanberger (1992) has analysed some Swedish attempts to make local business more international in its outlook and production strategies, the analysis including interventions from public agencies. The research strategy followed that of Hjern and Hull (1987) by systematically choosing actors in 100 business firms and 5 local governments and then - by the "snowballing method" - taking departure from the contact network of the responsible actors of those organizations in regard to the policy problem as those individuals perceived it. By this inductive process, Hanberger mapped the network related to the task of creating a relationship with the environment in order to enhance the trade of the firm - this he labeled "local business environment"; he was particularly concerned with the international trade pattern. Contrary to the received view that local business environment is, by and large, linked to the area of a (Swedish) municipality, he shows that the administrative divisions do not make sense for many business firms; their contact network goes beyond and sometimes does not even include the business strategy office of the town hall, especially not if the firm is not located in the administrative center town of the municipality.

Many Swedish municipalities seem to have followed a course of developing an international strategy. They involve themselves in analysing their own resources and linking the international environments of local businesses. Hanberger's thesis is that such a strategy is insufficient. Business firms do not restrict their contact network to the municipality, but use any other actor that seems relevant for their strategies, irrespective of physical location. But the firms value a good local business network environment

(Hanberger 1992:33) whereas there is less indication that they value the international strategy of their municipality very highly. Local governments therefore should do more to develop a local networking policy.

The methodological starting point is important for the results. In terms of a confrontation with a top-down analysis, Hanberger (1992:86-87) has shown that the statistics of the Swedish Government would have misled the analyst if he started out with such an official source for selecting cases. Fifteen per cent of the firms he analysed did not show in the files of business firms of the Statistical Bureau, and of those that were included some indicated that they did export, but this information was not conveyed by the Statistical Bureau.

Bostedt (1991) carried out an analysis of the implementation of occupational health organization in three Swedish municipalities. When interviewed about the role of the formal organization, employees expressed the view that it was not well suited for solving complex problems like fresh air, serious physical harm and psychological problems. Bostedt then defined an implementation structure based on four functions - definition of needs and demands for action, priority-setting between demands, mobilization of resources, and evaluation of the interventions. Less critical tasks like noise from machinery were solved by the formal rules, but the employees did not take a strong interest in those.

The actual implementation structures, then, were three, not four. A number of shop floor employees took care of small-scale plant problems. More complex tooling problems and psycho-social problems were moved higher up the hierarchy, large-scale problems were pushed to the top of the organization, and external agencies became involved. These three implementation structures used part(s) of the formal occupational health organization, but the formal structures were not decisive for the outcome of the processes. Bostedt does not attempt to check whether these implementation structures do the job better than plants where the formal organization works as scheduled. He does, however, indicate that the degree of success for the implementation structure in the organization depends on ability to adapt, flexibility in solutions, and some ability to act autonomously *vis-à-vis* the formal organization. In addition, the complexity of the problems in hand play a role.

Kettunen (1994) analysed the implementation of environmental health in three Finnish municipalities, starting with the perceptions of the health inspectors and going on to the actors they mentioned as participants within four problem fields - zoning as a means for a clean environment within the municipal area, clean water, control of food production and sale, and protection against environmental accidents (for example, from transport of hazardous waste). Only those identified in the first round were interviewed in order to keep the number at a manageable level; that is, no extensive snowballing method was used.

The author reflects on the special advantages of the bottom-up methodology versus the top-down approach:

> ... the case might not be quite the same. ... There are reasons to presume that a top-down oriented description would be narrower, limiting itself to the legally structured formulation of goals and measures. The starting point would lead to the conclusion that implementation of environmental health care works badly because the legal sanctions are rarely used. (Kettunen 1994:182-183)

Since the conclusion of the bottom-up cases is that the objective is reached by local negotiation, first with shop-owners regarding individual cases, and then with other health inspectors in the region to set "reasonable" standards (Kettunen 1994:124-125), the method for analysis certainly did matter.

Kettunen proceeded by identifying three steps in the local policy process related to environmental health, and hence risk for individuals in the locality: identifying a policy problem, assessing possible consequences of the problem, and solving the adverse consequences thus identified, if any (Kettunen 1994:67-68). In most cases, the problem identification took place as a mix of using nationally set standards for environmental hazards and a local procedure for applying those standards to, for example, water quality or food processing. Also to some degree, the assessment was a question of using generally recognized laboratory methods and standards, but precisely when and how to pick samples is decided locally, according to factors like special local features of risk; thus surface water must be assessed more often than well water for drinking purposes. Finally the solution of minimizing risks is very much up to local initiatives; typically, as indicated above, problems were negotiated rather than dealt with by disciplinary action.

What can we learn from those studies? They are examples of the policy problem being analysed in somewhat different ways[12]. The starting point from the bottom-up redefines the whole area of research: what are the needs of the businesses wanting development in general or even international development of their market? Certainly one can expect some differences from formal public program goals. The value of some of these studies for bottom-up research lies in their application of the policy problem within formal organizations. The limitations of those studies lie in the fact that the

---

12. Both Carlsson and Hanberger have been part of the research environment linked to Benny Hjern's professorship instituted by the Swedish Research Council of the Humanities and Social Sciences.

starting point is with the formal actors; the researchers have tried to overcome the difficulties by redefining the policy processes taking place in relation to specific problems that arise in the daily procedures. The studies then
show that there is quite some variation in the actor network developing
within some problem fields, whereas in others it is by and large the same. In
Kettunen's case, variance indicates that local implementors follow specific
strategies to cope with issues, not that they deviate from an implementation
accountability (Kettunen 1994:180).

Hermeneutics and Critical Theorists

There are some differences between the researchers quoted in this section,
primarily because of their opposite stances to the involvement of the researcher. Below we touch upon the role of the active citizens and public
administrators - as types of local political entrepreneurs. Analysis of field
workers or "street-level bureaucracy" is no new research interest (Lipsky
1980). But research into the practices of field workers and their interaction
with "clients" is still a fairly limited area of research, or perhaps it is not
reported on much in the international literature. Maybe no wonder, since the
theme is highly sensitive within organizations, and often research reports on
the topic are kept within the boundaries of the organization, strictly for purposes of management and staff.

In some discussions of bottom-up research two alternative perspectives
are considered important. The first one holds that bottom-up is a research
perspective which lets the research start at the bottom - with policy
problems, with the street-level bureaucrats and with the clients of the services, but beyond that there is no commitment to any specific values on the
part of the researchers. The second perspective holds that there is an intrinsic
value linked to the starting point being bottom-up; the researchers have special commitment to attempt to solve the problems as they emerge from that
perspective.

We discussed this in Chapter 5 under the concept of *empirical constitutionalism* (Hjern and Hull 1982). If we take a look at trends in public
policy, the changes towards more experimental modes in the public sector
may support that stance. Experimentation means more uncertainty regarding
the specificity of goals, and more open attitudes as to which course a policy
may take. Experimentation takes place in settings of considerable uncertainty
regarding a means-ends type of policy; this means that policy-makers know
that there is a need for action, but precisely with what aims is a matter of dispute or rather uncertainty except for the very broad idea of making things

better. Consequently, there is probably even greater uncertainty regarding choices of instruments except for a general feeling that a number of actors at the street-level bureaucracy level may have ideas that should be tried out. Significant changes have taken place in local government in the Nordic countries based on such experimentation in the second half of the 1980s and the first years of the 1990s (Baldersheim and Ståhlberg 1994). Basically, the model all countries followed was that local governments were invited by the central government to apply for specific exemptions from parliamentary law; in many cases, permission was granted, and the local government could then pursue, for instance, new ways of economic development, or new principles for governance of local schools.

Gradually, then, a mood of experimentation has developed among politicians and officers. At the town halls, the change has been felt as a certain animosity towards traditional efficiency goals, stated in quantitative terms, and instead a general comprehension of a necessity for more "soft goals", stated in more ambiguous terms. Lars Hulgård quotes some examples from a survey among local government officers:

> Quantitative goals cannot stand alone. We are a service organization - expectations and experiencing play large roles.

> Straight measurement of outcome is no longer applicable since the target group of unemployed people functions so badly that a substantial effect in employment cannot be measured. Hence development at a personal level is necessary - and the measurement of such a kind of work desirable (Hulgård 1998, 67, PB translation).

In the first case, the officer states that a service-producing organization does more than just deliver a specific service; the way it is done has great significance. In the second case, the officer expresses a certain despair that the clients of his agency are so hard hit by unemployment that they cannot return directly to the labor market; they need counseling and other channels for personal development before they can even speak to a recruitment officer. So one can conclude that quantitative measures do not suffice, and there is a great need for the development of new ways to evaluate soft goals and processes that involve the development of such goals. The latter perspective may be particularly interesting in experimental programs since those responsible for them may be dependent on those who are willing to become partners in actually shaping the program by supplying ideas that become the implementation of that program as they evolve (Hulgård 1998:74). Responsibility then is to be understood as being able to select other people to fulfill roles that are created as the contents of the program are created.

The role of the traditional - post-positivistic - evaluators, then, is challenged, too. Cases in point are some programs for evaluating community
care for the mentally ill; the Danish Ministry of Social Affairs explicitly
wanted evaluations to be made from the angles of the users, and the
evaluators were to become actors in a development of a social policy so that
the results of the evaluations by their very participation were fed into the
processes of setting priorities for the mentally ill in the future. A special task
for the evaluators, therefore, was to be able to handle situations of conflict
that might arise when some other participants in the programs might disagree
with their dual roles (Hulgård 1998:82).

What to do, then, as an evaluator, when goals are unclear or *de facto*
ignored? An example from the evaluation of a neighborhood council may
illustrate such a process (Engberg 1998, Hulgård 1998); in this case, the
researchers did not intend to (and did not later) intervene in the processes
after the evaluation report was turned in. In order to put the case of the
neighborhood into a perspective from the start of the evaluation, the researchers set up four criteria for evaluating the activities - based on the
Scandinavian literature on decentralization and democratic experiments:
legitimacy (acceptance by the population), influence (on concrete policies),
participation (local identity and recruitment to office), and efficiency (using
resources in a more coherent fashion) (Engberg 1998:105). Although these
criteria were to some degree useful, other dimensions entered the analysis as
it unfolded.

The council had a formal goal, formulated by the municipality council
which had set up the statutes for the neighborhood council, but since it was
so general in its formulations, and since it was obvious from the start of the
evaluation that not much had been done to actively fulfill the general
declarations, the evaluation team asked two questions to members of the
council: What did you do? How did you make a difference in the neighborhood? A number of major cases, as seen by actors in the council, were thus
identified. The files were analysed and, based on that information, a number
of actors were identified and interviewed. They were asked about whom they
had interacted with, and by this snowballing technique the actual
implementation structure was identified by unwrapping the network of
people involved.

In this way the cases which the neighborhood council initiated could be
used towards a performance evaluation; that evaluation, then, could be confronted with the formal goals for the evaluation - or any other goals, for that
matter, such as the ones taken from the research on Scandinavian democracy
mentioned above. The purpose of the evaluation, then, became to describe

actions and put them into perspective by the opinions of actors within and outside the council; in the neighborhood and at the town hall. Those who were interviewed found that there were two basic themes for the actions of the council: a social project aiming at social integration of the neighborhood, and a democratic project aiming at more participation in the processes of the neighborhood (Hulgård 1998:87). Of those, the social integration activities were the most successful, but democratic participation was also enhanced. In total, the council had improved integration of the area by supporting the creation of activity networks.

A success story? One may interpret the results in several ways. Story "A": On many counts positive results regarding integration, but not as seen by all participants; in particular, the office holders of another council of the area, the tenants' organization, were criticizing the council for initiating activities which they thought belonged to the turf of the tenants' organization. Story "B": Using the criteria from democratic theory, the success was, first of all, linked to legitimacy at the élite level (ordinary tenants did not know much about the council) and participation, again among those who were interested in local affairs, But as the evaluation evolved, it became clear that successes were more linked to the social dimensions mentioned above. In other words, the evaluation process created by itself new understandings (Engberg 1998:115-116), which the evaluation team did not have the time to pursue within the formal time limits of the evaluation, as had been agreed upon with the formal initiator of the evaluation, the municipality council.

It seems, then, that within a policy developmental or experimental sphere, the use of empirical constitutionalism can aid processes of searching for better policies. However, it requires to some degree consensus during the research process: those involved must be in agreement with the researcher regarding research findings; not in every detail, but in the overall picture. If there are great differences, the reporting back and ensuing discussions of the research get more or less blocked. The policy frame must be about the same (Schön and Rein 1994).

An illustrative case follows. In a policy document to the Nordic Committee of Civil Servants for Regional Development (NÄRP) Benny Hjern argued that if one wanted to develop the border regions of the Nordic countries, typically spanning two countries, one must start out with a localized understanding of a strategy for particular projects. Formal national entities, however, confound rather than help such a strategy:

> The discussion in this report on activity across national borders shows that altogether, it can be understood as a veritable laboratory for those who want to

learn about the borders of the Nordic states as obstacles for local interaction within various fields of regional development (Hjern 1990:9, PB translation)

They are not geared for project management, and certainly not across formal boundaries, hence a strong campaign for "learning to deregulate" was recommended (ibid). The task was to tear down the - invisible, but effective - walls between the implementation networks of national agencies and depend on local action by local project organizations which, staffed by full-time personnel, would organize activities across such boundaries. They would then construct the empirical constitutional basis for action across state borders, which state agencies by their very working procedures prevent. By such a step, Hjern recommends the formalization and intensification of what is already going on, namely activities across normal organizational and state boundaries, and thereby letting the empirical constitutionalism become real constitution.

Social Constructivism

The variance among projects in this section is very high. Below we shall present the reader with three examples of research that have been identified as constructivist, and which apply a bottom-up perspective. Two of them are Danish, one Dutch, but, as we shall see, the nationality is less important than an understanding of the institutional context or rather the interpretation of that context by the actors and the social construction of room for action. So basically, these processes could have been played out anywhere - some details would differ, but the message to be understood concerns precisely such variance extending beyond national structural contexts.

The first example concerns the construction of perceptions of democracy. Jensen (1998a) started out a project on democracy in tenants' associations in low-income housing areas by asking how democracy is defined, intending to examine how the tenants actually participated in the democratic processes. In order to better understand the formal rules which were available to anyone interested in participation from pamphlets and so on, she interviewed a number of people supposedly intimate with the system: researchers, officers in the Ministry of Housing, tenants, elected representatives of tenants, janitors and administrators. She also participated in a course on democracy, observed an administrative office in a low-income area for one week, observed tenants' meetings and so on. This was a striking experience in that there were great differences among these people as to what tenants' democracy was about. Three versions were discernible among tenants: one group saw democracy as an offer to realize yourself: those who wanted to do things had ample opportunity to arrange events. Another group saw democracy as part of the administrative system and did not distinguish between employees and elected representatives, so they took their dissatisfactions with decisions made by the political board, that is the leadership, to the employees at the administrative office, and wanted to file a formal complaint at that office about its political bosses. A third group saw democracy as a lifestyle, a symbol signalling collective responsibility in the area. Each model of democracy had its roles which the actors reflexively constructed in their daily praxis (Jensen 1998b).

In addition, the original perception of tenants' democracy underestimated the role of the administration as an active co-producer of the ideas of what democracy is and ought to be; its role in the daily praxis of democracy. The administration performs activities like information dissemination, education and development, and it is important in daily praxis, in the interplay between tenants, representatives and employees. This the more so because the administration over a decade or so has become professionalized - from a group of janitors to a segment of visionary project consultants and administrators with a strong nose for tenants' politics.

Thus, the researcher experienced a move from working with predefined categories on democracy to working with a number of actors actively constructing and reconstructing a democratic system which was anchored in a formal system of rules, but its practice was not identical with that system. So the research question was changed from "How does democracy function?" to "How are the conceptions of actors regarding democracy being produced?" (Jensen 1998a:174). The identification of the three basic understandings and the realization of the possible roles of the administration meant that a snowballing technique, constructed for action patterns relating to policies, would not make sense. Instead, sites were selected based on various structural characteristics of the administrative organizations and the degree of political decentralization. Within the sites selected, individuals were taken out for semi-structured interviewing based partly on randomization of tenants and selection of active individuals.

Since the subject became human conceptions of democracy, there were no Big-T Truths (discussed above) to search for, and the truths that came out were constructed in a complex process between interviewees and researcher. They were then judged on the basis of their *empirical resonance* - were the understandings the researcher wrote out on the basis of the interviews recognizable by other people? - and their power in terms of *interpretive transfer* - that is, communicability to the Academy and particularly its usefulness if transferred to another research object (Jensen 1998a:182-185). There is, then, no idea of grand generalizations, but a demand for recognition, and maybe additional uses by lay men and/or researchers.

The second example is based on the snowballing methodology and concerns health care for the elderly (Pedersen 1998). In the area of research, roles in health care for the elderly are divided between several public and semi-public organizations. The municipalities run home care for those elderly people who are still in their homes but having difficulties in managing certain facets of their daily needs; these services affect the largest number of people. Homes for the elderly are also run by municipalities or by non-profit organizations on contracts with the municipalities. Hospitals are public, run by the county councils; some of them have geriatric departments. GPs and medical specialists are formally private, but practically all their services are paid for by the national health system, administered by the municipalities and counties.

Some of the hospitals have geriatric departments taking care of those elderly who are hospitalized for causes that are not clearly to be treated by other departments (like surgery). Furthermore, a number of elderly people are temporarily in such departments because there is no adequate care available in their home municipality. Typically there is no immediate vacancy in a home for the elderly. No research has previously been done in how this "system" actually works as an implementation network.

A bottom-up strategy aimed at analysing the ways priorities are set for the elderly regarding care started from the policy problem as seen by the elderly. The research team of three involved in the project - a Research Nurse, an MD PhD-student and an Administrative Science PhD-student - developed a methodology to avoid a purely arbitrary process of selection (Kjerholt, Himmelstrup and Pedersen 1995). Using a county hospital as their starting point, they chose three municipalities of that area with different organizational structures for home help and identified 24 elderly (more then 75 years old) individuals living in those municipalities each falling into one of three categories: some who had been hospitalized, some who had had a falling accident in the home, and some who had just qualified for admission to a home for the elderly. At the initial encounter, the elderly had a physical examination, and those individuals who had been involved in the treatment were interviewed. Participatory observation took place when applicable. Further contacts were made after one month and again after a further two months, and everybody who had been involved directly and at upper or other levels of management was interviewed.

Thus 24 implementation structures were mapped out to make the basis for a comparative analysis of how priorities are constructed by the practices of all those involved in the processes, on the basis of medically comparable events[13]. The social construct of the network becomes clear from the case of "Carlo" who had pains in his stomach one night. The visiting night MD in the area asked for admittance to the hospital on the grounds of suspicion of a malign disease, and at the hospital he was treated for an ulcer. Carlo's own opinion was that he had lost weight for quite some years and therefore could no longer eat hot food. Carlo's family doctor and the home care people thought that his greatest problem was worry about his wife who suffered from dementia. So which is right? Malign disease, ulcer, psychological problems or weight loss? The answer depends on the perspective chosen - is it a physical problem, a psychological problem, or a social problem? The patient himself wanted to be able to eat (Pedersen 1998:227-228), and the story shows how everyone wants to help, but constructs different understandings of the situation. Ultimately, then, the outcome of the process depends on who participates in the encounters, and how they resolve their differences.

The theoretical expectations were that in spite of the medically similar problems, the actual implementation structure would vary due to institutional factors: who gets involved, what norms are applied, how does a network evolve, and how does a sense of meaning develop from the processes of interaction. Furthermore, there is a need to set the "coping strategies" of street-level bureaucrats into a larger perspective. An institutional analysis is well suited for such a purpose. Many institutional forces may come into play; doctors, nurses, home helps and patients are differently situated within complex patterns of the health organization, and the cases show how there is no single way to understand channels of influence; they vary with the situations and the capacity of actors to bring in strategic resources in the process.

The third example concerns the implementation of a policy of social renewal (Kensen 1998) where the Dutch national government asked localities to come up with ideas for new ways of carrying out such policies - in a spirit of experimentation very similar to that of the Nordic countries, as we saw above. Since the national government did not want to limit the action scope in the localities, the understanding of social renewal had to become a local matter, and therefore it was an obvious object for research from the bottom-up. Not everyone thought so, though. Kensen criticizes another research group in that field for starting with a fixed and general definition of social renewal in order to have a standard for evaluating success or failure in the local policies for social action. By such a starting point, they begged the

13. Individuals with aphasia, very poor hearing abilities and severe dementia were excluded since they do not satisfy the research demand of interviewing individuals capable of strategic behavior.

question and neglected the request from the national government for diversity in the localities (Kensen 1998:203).

Kensen has several examples of such diversity. In the first municipality, a social worker thought that social renewal was to be understood as (limited) self-governance for the citizens, and as citizen participation in policy development and implementation. Her colleagues, however, were not in full agreement. In another municipality, a social worker thought that social renewal was the same as a previous policy for distressed areas - because the new policy was referred to the department that used to deal with that policy. Thus social renewal became old wine in new bottles, and this triggered a heated debate among politicians and local government officers who disagreed about this interpretation. And so on. Kensen found differences *among* municipalities, and different opinions *within* municipalities - variations like a) a new way for the municipality and its officers to address a policy; b) recreating respect for the work of social workers; c) (limited) self-governance for citizens and citizen participation; d) nothing new (*sic*); e) citizens can take care of themselves; f) authorities must serve people; g) the pool of jobs; h) new version of policy for distressed areas (Kensen 1998:206).

How were these differences found? The basic elements of the research were streams of communication aimed at creating understanding of the social renewal; the concept got its meaning by rewriting, defining and articulating, and since words are part of a social community, this process of working with meanings can be seen as a process of negotiating, rejecting, adapting and exchanging; in short, processes of human reaction. The process of selecting people interacting in this way comes close to that of snowballing, but the research interest is linked to the creation of meanings, not to particular solutions to policy problems. The researcher, then, searched for differences as much as for similarities, an important distinction from other projects on social renewal which wanted to put the policies into a uniform definition. By looking for differences it became clear what social renewal could not be (Kensen 1998:216-18); it was not what the local social welfare organizations could offer; it was not something where results could be mandated beforehand; it was not something reserved for public authorities; it was not something that necessarily required more means or more capacity. It was something that by the very process had become anchored in the personalities that participated, based on their experiences and their language. It was found, not by official definitions, nor by the sole use of official policy documents, nor by concrete evaluation of the consequences of local policies. It was found by the researcher participating in dialogues with interviewees and actively constructing an understanding of differences, and then translating them into the scientific discourse.

We have, then, above seen three different ways of social constructivism in research. They have in common that differences, rather than similarities, are sought for. Being close to everyday life, they have some rather banal results, as one might expect from any kind of research, and some rather striking results, depending on the expectations of the reader. The research is comprehensive, and reports are long because the contents do not invite for (statistical) generalizations. The research techniques are based on dialogue where the researcher seeks to obtain common understanding; an understanding which is then often tried out in communication with other people knowledgeable about the topic. Thus the research results are constructed using various forms of social interaction which include rather than exclude the researcher.

PUTTING THE PIECES TOGETHER

Until now, this chapter has illustrated some of the variety within the social sciences regarding uses of bottom-up research. Bottom-up is not something that any school of metascience can claim as its own. The perspective has been used to some degree by all camps. This section will draw upon the institutional approach that came out of the previous chapters and illustrate them with a case of disagreement concerning a local public service (Johannessen, *et al.* 1996).

The Case Top-down: From Library to Depot

Let us first look at the case as it is reflected by formal minutes, papers in archives, newspaper stories and some interviews (Johannessen, *et al.* 1996:48-52). We take the top-down perspective of the main organization, the municipality.

The case concerned a cut-back process in a municipality of 7000 inhabitants where most people lived in the center town, but there were some living in four small villages of 200 to 300 people, and one larger of 700. The process started in 1994 when the municipality council decided that for the next four-year budgetary cycle, cut-backs on running costs would be necessary. In September, the staff was asked to prepare suggestions for cut-backs, and we shall follow the events within the library field. In this municipality, as in most organizations, cut-back processes tend to be segmented; changes are made by departments and budgetary subdivisions in an incremental (or, in this case, decremental) way rather than through an overall analysis of what the basic priorities of the agency as a total entity are, and what they should be if changes in the overall resources become necessary. So, the largest determinator of this year's budget is the budget of last year (Wildawsky and Caiden 1997:45), both in overall size and distribution between sub-divisions. The head librarian was asked to cut back by 100,000 Dkr, with the provision that the book account was not to be cut. He returned with a proposal that the main library cut back its opening hours by three hours a week, and that the branch library in the village of Baarse - the village with 700 inhabitants - was to be closed down from January 1, 1995. Total cut-backs were 15 hours a week for an (acting) librarian, and 6 hours for an assistant reshelving returned books. These 23 hours, however, did not only refer to the branch library.

On the political side, there was a municipality council with four five-member standing committees of politicians, all members of the municipality council. The committees made most of the decisions, some of them subject to final approval by the council (or its executive committee). The committee on schools and cultural affairs handled libraries. The mayor (member of the council and elected to function for the whole four-year term of the council) functions as both political and administrative leader and thus has a very strong position, and particularly so in this case since his party had the majority of seats in the council. The mayor had a meeting with his party colleagues at the committee and advised them not to close the branch library. Two weeks later the head librarian had an alternative ready: decimating the book account and firing one book reshelver, plus some additional minor library changes, and stopping the local children's theater. The committee did not favor that alternative.

Before the committee had decided what to do, the municipality council finalized the framework budget, detailing a cut of 100,000 Dkr, with the proviso not to cut the book account. The council had not been informed about the probable outcome of such a decision, namely the closing of the Baarse branch library. Two weeks later the committee chose the original proposal to close the branch library from January 1995, but since the acting branch librarian's contract ran out by the end of November, it was decided to close the branch then.

The local newspaper routinely gets all agendas for meetings at the town hall, but since the idea of closing the branch library had figured under the nondescript heading of "Budget 95", the journalists had not realized what was at stake. A decision to reduce personnel, however, must be approved by the executive committee of the council, so when the agenda for its meeting (8 November) came out at the start of November, the journalists realized what was under way. A front page story on 5 November (three weeks before closure was scheduled) ran: "Branch library in danger of getting closed". People in Baarse immediately rallied to protest; the chairmen of the local associations gathered with the district member of the municipality council and wrote a letter of protest to the executive committee. They added some figures showing that costs per book lent were half of those of the main library, and pointed to the fact that the municipality plan stated that the branch library was to be upheld for the whole time-horizon of the plan.

The executive committee sent back the decision to the cultural committee, partly because there was a breach of formal procedures (the municipality plan), partly because the minority (among those the district member from Baarse) was vigorously against. The committee then had a meeting with the representatives of the village; during that meeting the local representatives gained the impression that the decision might be revoked, and it was agreed to have a hearing in the village two weeks later.

At the hearing with about 70 participants (there were about 250 households in Baarse), the chairman of the committee initially made it clear that the decision could not be revoked, but the committee would be prepared to discuss a solution involving a branch library run by voluntary efforts from the community. This initial speech created a confrontational mood. The villagers vowed that they would fight the closing; they proclaimed a no-confidence stance to the municipality council and foresaw that the next step would be closing the school, and that this was a first step towards the death of the village community. From the town hall contingent, the town manager reproached the village for not understanding the municipality as a whole, and a member of the cultural committee called the villagers a "hen house", much to the consternation of the villagers. At the closing of the meeting, some villagers declared a willingness to consider voluntarism.

The final decision was then made by the cultural committee: an extension of the branch library until February 1995, and a possibility for continuation by voluntary members of the village; there would, however, be no subsidies to running costs from the municipality. The decision was approved by the executive committee and later the council, but the opposition voted nay. At working meetings comprising the cultural committee, the head librarian and a group from the village, an accord was worked out that the room of the branch library would remain available at the local school, books would be there from the main library, the municipality would pay for utilities, cleaning and insurance, and the villagers would provide voluntary staff to run the branch which was downgraded to a "depot".

Seen from the top-down perspective, then, the case concerned how to keep the best library services if one had to cut back. The municipality was willing to sacrifice easy access, favoring a high standard in the main library. As a spin-off of a difficult process, the municipality maintained access in the village at next to no cost in terms of money, but without professional expertise to help in more complex matters than getting a book from the shelves. So the municipality nearly got what it wanted; there were warning signs, though, that the villagers might cause trouble, and one had to involve them better in future decisions. The municipality normally had very few party political cleavages, but in this case, it became unavoidable. It was, however, notable that the opposition member of the cultural committee stuck to the committee decision and did not vote with his party.

The Case Bottom-up: Maintaining the Community

We now turn to a discussion of the case of the book depot from a bottom-up perspective. The source is the report of Johannessen, *et al.* (1996:47-67), but the data are organized somewhat differently in the interpretation made below, and my interpretation of implementation structure deviates from that of the report; this, however, is mainly a difference regarding the structure of the analysis, not regarding the substantive conclusions. If we were to do a full story, the information above should be repeated in the new contexts, but for reasons of space we assume that the reader is familiar with the information from the story top-down. The information below mainly came out of interviews with 23 individuals where the interviewing rationale was to inter-actively construct the understandings of those individuals of what had taken place, and how the interviewees saw their roles and possibilities (Johannessen, *et al.* 1996:30). The individuals were selected on the basis of a reading of papers and newspapers, plus additional information from those interviewed. The snowballing method was seen as superfluous in this case.

As one might expect, the case is extremely complicated if one wants to follow all the arguments made in the process. For instance, there were many policy discussions linked to the technicalities of staff allocation between the main library and the branch, since all staff members were employed at the main library. The total of 23 hours cut-back did not concern the branch alone. Furthermore, there were disagreements as to how many books were actually lent to the village, and how many were lent to the school children at the school that housed the branch. Finally, there were a number of interests linked to alternative uses of the room for the branch, for instance, the school had interests in taking over the room. We shall not go further into those matters.

If we take the perspective of an institutional analysis of collective action, the point of departure is the *policy problem*. At the town hall, there were several actors involved; the head librarian, the cultural committee, the mayor, and other local government officers. The question one may pose is what a library branch means to different actors in the process.

A main actor among the town hall officers was the head librarian who drafted the alternatives for decision by the committee. As a professional, his perspective was to preserve the level of service in the municipality as a whole, and if that was not possible, to protect the high-quality main library.

The perspective of the politicians of the committee was different. They had a broad range of activities to oversee, and the library branch was only one small cog in the wheel. They did not see the closing of the branch as that great a problem. It was not far to the main town, most went there at least once a week, and for those without a car there was one bus every hour. Furthermore, the elderly and the handicapped had special services by having books brought to them. Finally, they thought that the level of service was low in the branch anyway, so the loss was tolerable.

Other leading officers held a perspective of the municipality as a whole. They saw general policy problems of parochialism, where people would demand the same service as those living in the center, without paying the other costs of living there. In that sense, they did not take a stance regarding the branch *per se*, they had a more general organizational perspective.

The mayor also had a general organizational policy problem perspective. His principles as both administrative and political head of the municipality were that it was important to reach consensus. If a committee agreed, he would not interfere. If they disagreed, he would recommend that any decision be referred back to them until they reached a consensus. The problem with the library branch, then, was one of breaking the consensus and, in addition, to having a part of the municipality become rebellious, creating fertile soil for those who would cash in politically on such a matter. He saw the active villagers as chauvinists creating such undesirable conflict.

If we turn to the village, there were many activists there, but whereas the town hall saw them as one united front against the town hall, the villagers themselves saw at least two distinct groups which in this case chose to cooperate, but which in other matters might not quite agree and probably would take different political courses of action.

The first group liked to live in a village and saw village life as the best of all, thriving in social networks and associational life. They were quite suspicious of outsiders and saw the town hall as something close to the root of all evil. They were morally upset and indignant over the way the town hall communicated the intent to close the branch and saw the event as yet another chance to fight the municipality. Their animosity was possibly anchored in the past when Baarse was an autonomous parish commune (parish communes were merged in 1970 into larger entities, municipalities, in the whole country, and as a result about four fifths of them disappeared).

The second group had a policy conception for the village; the village needed a number of public services on site such as a school, the child care center and the library, and in addition a general store, a bank and various types of industry - plus associations to organize activities. These people, then, saw the closing of the branch as a first step in a strategy to strip the village of public services, and if that happened, other services would flee, too, and the village would be deprived of its economic basis in a vicious circle of decline. The village would die. Therefore, the second group was always ready to fight. The outcome of the process became very favorable for the village, no matter what stance; the depot is now run by three volunteers, and many people stop by daily to get a cup of coffee and talk - when a librarian ran the place, that was not even conceived as an option. So by now, the depot has become a village coffee shop!

Based on the different perspectives on the policy problem one can see why the conflict was played out, and what the rationales were for the actors. At the town hall, only the head librarian had any interest in the library as such. The members of the cultural committee were concerned with their budgetary turf and wanted to see it damaged as little as possible, and here the branch was only a minor brick. The other actors had an organizational perspective of the municipality as a whole in budgetary terms, and the protest from the villagers did not come as a surprise, especially not to the mayor, but they were determined not to accept the protests. They saw the villagers as mavericks *en bloc* and did not at all perceive the quite different rationales behind the actions of the two groups. The two groups acted in unison in this case, but only because it fitted into the agenda for possible action of both parties.

In the discussion above, we have touched on the second element of institutional analysis that seems quite important to sort out in this case, namely what creates *order and meaning* for the actors.

The head librarian had a professional perspective. His job is to get the best possible library, and most professional librarians would agree that this means the highest level of service in terms of a broad range of books. This, in turn, requires centralization of services in order to create economy of scale. If everything is spread thinly in small villages, there is no way of offering a large range of services to them, at least not with the technology that was available in 1994. For the head librarian, then, it made no sense to cut back on the main library. As far as he was concerned, one could do without the services in the village as long as the main library was accessible.

One could suppose that his committee of politicians had mixed motives of politics and administration. But there was no party politics in the committee visible until very late in the process. It did make sense to them, first of all, to create consent as far as possible, and to maintain their autonomy as a committee. Their rationale was to maximize services they were asked to administer, and in that perspective a library branch was a minor event. Likewise, the rationale for the mayor was to keep the basic agreement that was in the municipality council; political fights were very rare, and he intended to keep it that way. That said, when the case became politicized he knew that he still had a comfortable majority so that he could press through decisions even then. But since from the very beginning he advised his party colleagues in the committee to avoid a confrontation with the village people, it is quite clear that consent in the organization was his first priority and his platform as a political and administrative chief. His chief officers followed the same rationale; as "budgetary animals" their main concern was to create a budget that followed the desires of the municipality council, and in this case it also got primacy *vis-à-vis* some village radicals.

Those village radicals, then, were not quite so radical. They were trying to protect what they saw as their interests (none of the eight leading figures used the branch very much), but with somewhat different rationales. One group did this for the particular cause, a goal-oriented action in order to preserve the library; they knew how to link this to formal elements - the municipality plan which, they thought, was a guarantee for them. It turned out not to be, but it secured a hearing process which the town hall would rather had not taken place. The other group participated, not so goal oriented, but as parochials who would not miss a chance to express their anxiety and outrage to the town hall people.

Moving on to the third element of the institutional analysis, *positions and network*, one can say that a number of networks became intertwined in this case. One cannot speak in general of one policy network since the basic rationales did not coincide, but for this purpose, forces were joined.

In the village, there was a number of associations which immediately took action when the case became known on 5 November. Leading members of eight associations met with the district councilman and formed a coalition to formulate a letter of protest. As the process evolved, one of them became the leading spokesman and negotiator, and he tacitly obtained delegated authority on behalf of the community. He belonged to the more conflict-oriented group in the neighborhood but, when he became spokesman, he worked out a compromise and had no difficulty in this *ad hoc* change in pose. An organizational outcome of the case has been that the chairmen of the associations now meet on a regular basis in order to coordinate their activities in the locality, and their attitudes to initiatives from the town hall. Thus the issue of a policy for the village has become formalized in a practical manner with the district politician and the leaders of a bank, an industrial enterprise and a public organization forming the leadership. A number of loose local networks have become focused and joined into a policy-oriented core network.

At the town hall, the formal organization played an important role in the second half of the process, that is, after the issue became politicized, but until then the informal network of politicians working in agreement was dominant. The committee of schools and cultural affairs was the dominant group together with the head librarian. The latter became a sort of scapegoat since he was unable to bring up an alternative that did not create a consensus, but he became important in the final phase when the details of the compromise with volunteers had to be worked out. The council member from Baarse was in one sense linking the town hall to the local network, but since he belonged to the opposition and was part of the move to politicize the case, he never came to function as an active member towards a solution; he did, however, provide the villagers with important information. In the final phase, a formal network was created, its members being the head librarian, the school principal of the Baarse branch school and one of the Baarse association members; these people worked out the compromise.

The last element of the institutional analysis consists of *norms and rules*. The formal rules of a municipality had some importance; budgetary procedures prescribe a deadline for the municipality budget which may not be exceeded, therefore the proposed cut-back became mandatory before the committee had found a way to implement it, and it could not circumvent it because there were strings attached to the general frame - books were not to be touched. The formal rules also outplayed the committee as the executive committee would not approve its decision, and then other rules prevented the planned closure by 30 November. The village had no formal rules for collective action, but informal rules were pluralistic; if someone took an initiative on behalf of the community, others would yield support, if asked to do so.

Regarding norms, the basic norm of not deciding for citizens without informing them, was broken by the town hall, strengthening the villagers' distrust. Furthermore, one can say that two systems of norms - those of the village as an entity and those of seeing the municipality as a whole - clashed and resulted in a formal victory for the municipality-as-a-whole view, but at the same time, the potential for the village has been strengthened by the formation of the village policy network in Baarse. If the norms of consent at the town hall are to be pursued, one will probably in the future see more negotiations between the village and the town hall before proposals are put forward. Indeed, the mayor has plans that all villages (five in all) might do better by forming a neighborhood council to look after the interests of the area. If he succeeds, he will have prevented a future confrontation between one village and the town hall, and in its place he will have created a general forum for village points of view.

Top-down versus Bottom-up

What did we learn from the two ways of treating the case? Some differences have come out, based on the two perspectives.

The top-down case told about a cut-back problem linked to a minor budgetary adjustment with the committee of schools and cultural affairs, where some protesters in the village fulfilled the expectations of the top leadership and rallied in an unholy alliance with the one council member from the village. The council member was a leading member of the opposition and thereby saw a chance to shake the political foundation of the mayor who had worked intensely to create a municipality of consent rather than political conflict.

The bottom-up case showed a more complex picture, and it tells a different story. To the villagers, the case was not really about the library branch, but about the future of village life. There were two groups, not one, that joined forces to ensure that, from one perspective, their community would have a future with the necessary services, and from the other perspective, that the town hall was taught a lesson not to fool with the villages.

The town hall never saw, or at least did not recognize, the potential of the village perspective until the report from Roskilde University was written and presented to a group of local government officers. To quote the town manager: "I can comprehend the state of affairs, but I cannot approve of it" (Johannessen, *et al.* 1996:65). That statement is an example of social constructedness *par exellence* - the town manager sees and listens, but refuses to include the observations in his practice. The report may have been useful in letting the town hall better understand the diversity of village demands, rather than just seeing them as angry mavericks. If they work on the matter, they may reach some level of mutual approval. It does, however, require the will to do so among the actors.

7. Conclusion

Under postmodern conditions the traditional methods of policy analysis, emphasizing the role of formal organizations in developing and implementing public policies, have severe shortcomings. At the local level, in particular, organizational forms vary to such extents that organiz*ing* rather than organiz*ation*, that is, a process perspective rather than a structural perspective, becomes important to understand as the driving rationale behind the actors. From a formal perspective, there is a bewildering mix of public and private action taking place. In order to avoid such perplexity, we have used the phrase "collective public action" as a conceptual vehicle to approach what is going on when people use public means to pursue their own course of action, whether within or outside the original scope set up by the organization administering those means.

We have discussed various aspects of institutional analysis as methodologies for analysing collective public action. In this last chapter, we sum up the arguments and point to further steps towards the analysis of collective public action in the locality.

ANOTHER STATE

If anything, state theory is linked to the modern society. The modern state has been understood as a powerful agent, increasingly based on a democratic conception which has gradually included more and more of the adult population. It has a strong bureaucratic apparatus which mirrors the rationalization of society. The bureaucratic staff is increasingly educated at the institutions of higher learning which have severed their previous ties to religion and thus are able to teach on the basis of scientific knowledge.

Under postmodern conditions, part of the state still remains modern, but other parts change into something more fragmented, less unified, with its autonomy under serious attack; in short a Swiss cheese rather than an elephant. But note that it is the form of the state that is changing. The core, *the public power*, has not changed much, if at all. The public power distinguishes the state from all other phenomena in the society by offering and sustaining the legitimate right to regulate all relationships between citizens, to extract resources and redistribute them among interests and to back up any intervention by use of force. This right has not changed. Changes relate to the *locus* or rather *loci* of this power - the public power now relates to many organizational forms. Organizationally, the fragmentation has taken place, from a hierarchy of powers to many networks, nationally and internationally, with the number of actors changing over time as situations and problem fields change.

Nationally, decentralization to localities has taken place, empowering groups of citizens in ways they have never seen before in relation to their status as users of public services. Internationally, new regimes of regulation come about as (Western) states give up their sovereignty in favor of supranational norms for behavior. This in turn empowers citizens even more; a good example is ethnic minorities who get recognition and possibilities to resort to bodies of appeal which formerly did not exist.

These new institutional arrangements, based on public powers, are at the center of the concern of this book, the discussion has mainly involved the local versions of the fragmentation. The public power is squarely rooted in some constitution, but the number of constitutions has increased. The roots of the public power are legal constructs, but the way daily practices implementing the public power organize for action goes beyond the normal conceptualizations of lawyers. The realization of the public power is done by fragmented institutional arrangements whose configurations may change over time, and the precise forms of implementation are currently negotiated in order to make adaptation to new situations possible. There is a continuing struggle among interests in the society to become a part of the public power, to get legitimation and material resources.

This, of course, is a challenge for existing public organizations which face increasingly differentiated demands from citizens, new forms of interaction as much out of the organization as within, and challenges to management which increasingly finds that authority is something which is negotiable and may even be reversed by use of external links.

Some may say that some of the examples of research in Chapter 6 are more modern than postmodern. That is a matter of degree, as stressed several times in this book. Social constructivist research qualifies for being considered as different from the traditional - read modern - types of research that are found elsewhere. Social constructivists witness the problems of modern organizational theory to grasp what is going on; they stress the need to approach the research in new ways, alien to the categories found in most textbooks on research methodology. So they qualify as important actors in the processes of taking steps towards new ways of analysing behavior linked to public policy.

THE NEED FOR COLLECTIVE PUBLIC ACTION

Collective action is understood as an activity involving more than one individual to achieve a common goal, without those involved competing or dominating one another. The more fragmented the world becomes, the more there may be a need for many people to act collectively for mutual benefit. Such collective action is a sign of new ways of coordinating activities and pooling resources in an individualized environment. The new social movements have by some theorists been understood as *the* indication of a postmodern society. More forms should be recognized as postmodern. One might take the development of implementation theory, evaluation analysis and organizational theory as signposts. Increasingly, research has shown that the modern organization does not work as prescribed, and that people cooperate in other ways in order to solve the problems of firms and individuals out there. This should be recognized as special forms of collective action - within new implementation structures, if you will; hence the concept of *collective public action* where collective action is linked to the public power as discussed above.

Some theories have had and still have problems with conceptualizing such behavior. Most theories based on methodological individualism have as a starting point the axiom that individuals pursue individual goals only, and hence collective action remains a puzzle. But some researchers, active in constructing theories of institutional development, have formulated models that make such behavior feasible due to particular institutional arrangements. Still, motivations are somewhat blurred since preferences remain exogenous to the model. Methodological collectivists, on the other hand, make so many factors endogenous that it is difficult to grasp how changes come about; actors tend to disappear in broad understandings of processes of mediation. I suggest an approach somewhere in between those two extremes, namely the *strategic actor using institutional arrangements as both constraints and assets for future action*, working actively to change guards into servants. At the same time, however, they *act by constantly reformulating their strategies and hence preferences* into what is feasible rather than keeping an unreachable goal. This is what *actor-cum-institution* is about.

It is true that new technologies make distance a troubled concept. Information - or rather data - is available regardless of location through the Internet and satellite communication by TV. But regarding collective action, this only changes the level of informed action. Only very special forms of collective action can be made by electronic means, among which vociferous protest via e-mail is one. But active communication requires moderators, as soon as we get beyond very few individuals interacting, and hence some sort of organization is required. And there are several steps from communicating about collective problems to staging collective action. The latter mostly requires some degree of personal presence - or, in a virtual organization, the moderators working to coordinate. Even on the Internet the moderator is felt to be an individual by the participants, even though there is no physical contact. Therefore, the body-subject still is of great importance both in a narrow and a broad sense.

INSTITUTIONAL ARRANGEMENTS BOTTOM-UP

In research, institutional analysis suffers from the division between methodological individualists and collectivists in the sense that their rigid conceptions tend to dig trenches instead of building bridges. But there are some bridge contractors.

The gist of the argument is the need to understand the dynamics of institutions as both resources and constraints instead of only analysing institutional rules constraining actors or institutional cultures condoning specific traits of action. A focus on dynamics cannot leave out the particular actors instigating and mediating changes in behavior, triggering reactions from other actors and thus participating in new modes of handling situations calling for action.

Analysing such processes is demanding, and there is no fool-proof research design, nor is there one overshadowing all other approaches. It is clear, however, that many of the methodologies linked to the concepts of the modern society will not suffice. The modern categories of class, gender, age, and occupation may not be obsolete, but since they yield generalized knowledge they convey less meaning under postmodern conditions where organizational forms are changing all the time and therefore cannot be treated as invariant and independent variables. The analysis must grasp differences according to various policy problems, and various behavioral norms and institutional rules implemented by varying numbers of actors in different roles and interrelations. Precisely being part of such a development is a driving force for participants in that their understanding of their own and other actors' situation depends on the institutional processes. Meaning is created through participation, it is not something being handed down by a superior authority or induced by peer pressure.

Activity patterns, conceptualized as communication between body-subjects, are what the researcher must strive to lay bare as processes of institutional action. But in order to understand the creation of meaning, such analysis must be carried out in some accommodation of the bottom-up approach. First, the perspective from the top often does not cover the understanding among field workers and users of services. Second, the view from the top may be seriously flawed because the actual institutional processes are not visible and hence are not understood from that angle. Third, and consequently, actual institutional processes in the field may change so much and so rapidly that a top-down perspective is out of date.

This calls for a bottom-up analysis, where departure is taken from the experiences in the field. This will capture most of the problems mentioned above. And if those problems are not there, no harm is done, because in that case the top-down perspective will anyway be fulfilled, since there is no discrepancy. Therefore, a bottom-up analysis is safe to catch what is going on - which may be according to the rules from the top - while a top-down analysis runs the risk of only finding the tip of the iceberg. The change towards postmodern analysis has opened new possibilities for the researcher to analyse public action on the basis of social constructivism. This puts new emphasis on intersubjectivity - for the research objects to recognize and appreciate what the researcher communicates about the matter, and for the scientific community to understand the case on conceptual grounds, to enhance future theoretical understandings.

The chapters have shown a variety of ways to do bottom-up analysis. Departure is taken from the individuals involved in the policy problem. The absolutely most critical issue, then, is how the researcher approaches the policy problem - this is where the scope of the whole analysis is determined. Some do it by digging into the "technologies" of the policy problem, and then go on to analyse how various actors create the actual policy by more or less coordinated action. Others prefer to analyse the processes (of the organization) as some of the main actors see them and then discriminate between them to find the most crucial cases for a bottom-up analysis. The networking method shows how interaction patterns are set up, and the task of the researcher then is to be a participant in constructing an understanding of the meaning participants ascribe to being an active part of problem solving. This is where social constructivism has become important, and the researcher gives up the stance of standing outside the processes that are researched.

In most cases, such bottom-up analysis changes the perspective of the analysis away from the specific program objectives of formal public programs. This does not mean that such objectives must be disregarded, but it is important to realize how actors in the locality define their problems and then use any means for solving them. This may be in perfect harmony with the official program objectives, but often it is only so to some degree. In such cases a task for the research may be to tease out the differences and help form an analytic basis for discussing whether public programs should be changed or whether local action should be acknowledged in other ways; or whether some action should be taken to prevent such local action in the future.

This raises the question of normative issues.

NORMATIVE ISSUES

A bottom-up analysis as used in this book is a methodological invention. It does not prescribe a particular stance on the part of the researcher, but it does require a certain ability to extract and comprehend ways of thinking that may be quite remote from the values of the investigator.

The research advocated here is not meant to have any particular degree of big-T Truth to it. It is meant to reflect, as faithfully as possible, the understandings of actors regarding their conditions within the network that is under scrutiny. Other actors may have other perceptions, and the task is, in the first instance, to make them clear to the observer, realizing that observing is not a neutral activity. Consequently, the small-t truth is constructed in an interaction process between several people; it happens in a process towards creating meaning for those involved.

Implementation researchers are likely to face many activities that do not correspond to the received view of how things ought to take place. This calls for caution and a need to respect the right of people to be and do otherwise. But there must be limits to what the observer should accept. If one analyses a remote and small community, chances are high that the values of the majority there do not correspond with those of the observer, who, being employed by a university or research institution, is likely to come from a city environment. The researcher then must learn to report on activities and to understand what is being done despite having different values and ideas of the state of the world.

This means that to some degree, one must apply the principle of empirical constitutionalism (Hjern and Hull 1982). But norms are what they are - we cannot escape them. Therefore, the researcher must beforehand make up his mind what will be acceptable to the eye and soul when empirical research is being carried out. If those individual norms are being overstepped out there, one must refrain from further analysis and reconsider the choice of bottom-up analysis as a methodological tool. Or reconsider the wish to do research at all.

Another aspect should be made clear. Bottom-up analysis as advocated here is a methodological tool and is an interesting research perspective. But it does not mean that everything in the world should be understood bottom-up. Nor does it mean that, for example, policy advice should necessarily have that perspective. It is one perspective among many. It makes sense as a methodological choice, at described above, but it does not always make sense as a policy prescription. For instance, a number of problems which require swift reaction cannot be dealt with from the bottom, unless adequate time is available, which it is not when the demand is "swift". Nor can the location of a major infrastructure like a bridge or the location of a polluting industry be dealt with from the bottom; it is safe to predict that any locals will advocate possible locations for that structure - but elsewhere. NIMBY (Not In My Back Yard, a well-known stance from locals attending town meetings on the location of roads, institutions for the insane, refugee centers and so on) is a well-known defense mechanism. It may be legitimate to have it from an individual perspective, but it may also be legitimate for a majority to overrule that principle if there is a considerable gain for the general public, as long as appropriate procedures are followed.

Likewise, there are differences in perspectives among staff and managers, and those differences of course color the outlook and the thinking about solutions to problems that arise. Making the analysis bottom-up does not mean that one must support any and all ideas from the staff regarding the management of that organization. Chances are high that the bottom-up researcher will have a very good understanding of both staff and management, but in so far as policy advice may be a zero-sum game, he or she must be free to choose between sides, all aspects taken into consideration.

References

ACIR (1987), *The Organization of Local Public Economies*, Commission Report A-109. Washington, DC: Advisory Commission on Intergovernmental Relations.

ACIR (1988), *Metropolitan Organization: The St. Louis Case*, Commission Report M-158. Washington, DC: Advisory Commission on Intergovernmental Relations.

ACIR (1992), *Metropolitan Organization: The Allegheny County Case*. Washington, DC: Advisory Commission on Intergovernmental Relations.

Adams, G. A. (1994), "Enthralled with modernity: The historical context of knowledge and theory development in public administration", in *Research in Public Administration. Reflections on Theory and Practice*, ed. J. D. White and G. A. Adams, pp. 24-41. London: Sage Publications.

Almond, G. A. (1988), "Return to the state", *American Political Science Review*, **82**(3), 853-75.

Andersen, N. Å. (1995), *Selvskabt forvaltning*. København: Nyt fra Samfundsvidenskaberne.

Arvidsson, H., Berntson, L. and Dencik, L. (1994), *Modernisering och välfärd - om stat, individ och civilt samhälle i Sverige*. Stockholm: City University Press.

Ashford, D. A. (1986), *The Emergence of the Welfare States*. Oxford: Blackwell.

Atkinson, M. M. and Coleman, W. D. (1989), "Strong states and weak states: sectoral policy networks in advanced capitalist economies", *British Journal of Political Science*, **1**, 47-67.

Axelrod, R. (1984), *The Evolution of Cooperation*. New York: Basic Books.

Baldersheim, H. and Ståhlberg, K. (1994), *Towards the Self-Regulating Municipality*. Dartmouth: Aldershot.

Barrett, S. and Fudge, C. (1981), "Examining the policy-action relationship", in *Policy and Action. Essays on the Implementation of Public Policy*, S. Barrett and C. Fudge, pp. 3-32. London: Methuen.

Barry, B. and Hardin, R., eds. (1982), *Rational Man and Irrational Society? An Introduction and Sourcebook*. London: Sage Publications.

Barzelay, M. (1992), *Breaking Through Bureaucracy. A New Vision for Managing in Government*, in collaboration with B. J. Armajani. Berkeley:

University of California Press.

Bauman, Z. (1992), *Intimations of Postmodernity*. London: Routledge.

Becker, G. (1986), "The economic approach to human behavior", in *Rational Choice*, ed. J. Elster, pp. 108-22. Cambridge: Basil Blackwell.

Berger, P. and Luckmann, T. (1966), *The Social Construction of Reality. A Treatise in the Sociology of Knowledge*. New York: Doubleday Anchor.

Berrefjord, O., Nielsen, K. and Pedersen, O. K. (1989), "Forhandlingsøkonomi i Norden - en indledning", in *Forhandlingsøkonomi i Norden*, ed. K. Nielsen and O. K. Pedersen, pp. 9-39. København: Jurist- og Økonomforbundets Forlag.

Beyme, K. v. (1987), "Institutionstheorie in der neueren Politikwissenschaft", in *Grundfragen der Theorie politischer Institutionen*, ed. G. Göhler, pp. 48-60. Opladen: Westdeutscher Verlag.

Birnbaum, P. (1988), *States and Collective Action: The European Experience*. Cambridge University Press.

Blackler, F. (1992), "Formative contexts and activity systems: Postmodern approaches to the management of change", in *Rethinking Organization. New Directions in Organization Theory and Analysis*, ed. M. Reed and M. Hughes, pp. 273-94. London: Sage Publications.

Bogason, P. (1986), "Cross-national problems in multi-level spatial planning: Theory and practice", *Scandinavian Housing and Planning Research*, 3(1), 13-24.

Bogason, P. (1992), "Strong or weak state? The case of Danish agricultural export policy 1849-1906", *Comparative Politics*, **24**, 219-27.

Bogason, P., ed. (1996), *New Modes of Local Political Organizing: Local Government Fragmentation in Scandinavia*. New York: Nova Science Publishers.

Bogason, P. and Toonen, T. A. J., eds. (1998), *Comparing Networks*, vol. 76 no 2, Special Issue of *Public Administration*.

Bogason, P. and Toonen, T. A. J. (1998), "Introduction: Networks in public administration", *Public Administration*, **76**(2), Summer, 205-29.

Bostedt, G. (1991), *Politisk institutionalisering. Organisering av lokalt arbetsmiljö*, Ph. D. Diss., Forskningsrapport 1991:4. Umeå: Statsvetenskapliga Institutionen, Umeå Universitet.

Buchanan, J. M. and Tullock, G. (1962), *The Calculus of Consent*. Ann Arbor: University of Michigan Press.

Burns, T. and Flam, H. (1987), *The Shaping of Social Organization. Social Rule System Theory with Applications*. London: Sage Publications.

Campbell, J. L., Hollingsworth, J. R. and Lindberg, L., eds. (1991), *Governance of the American Economy*. Cambridge: Cambridge University Press.

Carlsson, L. (1993), *Samhällets oregerlighet. Organisering och policyproduktion i näringspolitiken.* Stockholm: Symposion Graduale.

Christensen, J. G. (1988), "Withdrawal of government: a critical survey of an administrative problem in its political context", *International Review of Administrative Science*, **54**(1).

Clegg, S. (1990), *Modern Organizations. Organization Studies in the Postmodern World.* London: Sage Publications.

Coleman, J. S. (1987), "Norms as social capital", in *Economic Imperialism*, eds. G. Radnitzky and P. Bernholz, pp. 133-55. New York: Paragon.

Coleman, J. S. and Fararo, T. J. (1992), *Rational Choice Theory. Advocacy and Critique.* London: Sage Publications.

Crawford, S. and Ostrom, E. (1995), "A grammar of institutions", *American Political Science Review*, **89**(3), 582-600.

Crook, S., Pakulski, J. and Waters, M. (1992), *Postmodernization. Change in Advanced Society.* London: Sage Publications.

Czarniawska, B. (1997), *Narrating the Organization. Dramas of Institutional Identity.* Chicago: The University of Chicago Press.

Damgaard, E. (1986), "Causes, forms and consequences of sectoral policymaking: some Danish evidence", *European Journal of Political Research*, **14**, 273-87.

Damgaard, E. and Eliassen, K. A. (1978), "Corporate pluralism in Danish law-making", *Scandinavian Political Studies*, **1**(4), 285-313.

Davis, G. and Ostrom, E. (1991), "A public economy approach to education: choice and co-production", *International Political Science Review*, **12**(4), 313-35.

DiMaggio, P. J. and Powell, W. W. (1983), "The iron cage revisited: Institutional isomorphism and collective rationality in organizational fields", *American Sociological Review*, **48**, 147-60.

Dunleavy, P. (1991), *Democracy, Bureaucracy and Public Choice.* New York: Prentice Hall.

Durkheim, E. (1965), *The Division of Labor in Society.* New York: Free Press.

Dye, T. R. (1992), *Understanding Public Policy.* Englewood Cliffs, NJ: Prentice Hall.

Elmore, R. E. (1979), "Backward mapping: Implementation research and policy decisions", *Political Science Quarterly*, **94**(4), 601-16.

Elster, J. (1989), *The Cement of Society. A Study of Social Order.* Cambridge: Cambridge University Press.

Elster, J. and Slagstad, R., eds. (1988), *Constitutionalism and Democracy.* Cambridge: Cambridge University Press.

Engberg, L. A. (1998), "Induktion og deduktion i bottom-up debatten.

Metodeovervejelser i forbindelse med en undersøgelse af Grantoften Bydelsting", in *Samfundsforskning bottom-up. Teori og metode*, ed. P. Bogason and E. Sørensen, pp. 94-118. København: Roskilde Universitetsforlag.

Evans, P., Rueschemeyer, D. and Skocpol, T., eds. (1985), *Bringing the State Back In.* Cambridge: Cambridge University Press.

Eyerman, R. and Jamison, A. (1991), *Social Movements. A Cognitive Approach.* Cambridge: Polity Press.

Fabbrini, S. (1988), "The return to the state: critiques", *American Political Science Review*, **82**(3), 891-99.

Farmer, D. J. (1998), "Public administration discourse as play with a purpose", in *Papers on the Art of Anti-Administration*, ed. D. J. Farmer, pp. 37-56. Burke, VA: Chatelaine Press.

Fielding, N., ed. (1988), *Actions and Structure. Research Methods and Social Theory.* London: Sage Publications.

Fischer, F. (1995), *Evaluating Public Policy.* Chicago: Nelson-Hall Publishers.

Fischer, F. and Forrester, J. (1993), "Editors' introduction", in *The Argumentative Turn in Policy Analysis and Planning*, ed. F. Fischer and J. Forrester, pp. 1-17. London: UCL Press.

Fischer, F. and Forrester, J., eds. (1993), *The Argumentative Turn in Policy Analysis and Planning.* London: UCL Press.

Fox, C. J. and Miller, H. T. (1995), *Postmodern Public Administration. Towards Discourse.* London: Sage Publications.

Franz, H.-J. (1986), "Interorganizational arrangements and coordination at the policy level", in *Guidance, Control and Evaluation in the Public Sector*, F. X. Kaufmann, G. Majone and V. Ostrom, pp. 479-96. Berlin: De Gruyter.

Friedmann, J. (1967), "A conceptual model for the analysis of planning behavior", *Administrative Science Quarterly*, **3**, 225-52.

Fukuyama, F. (1992), *The End of History and the Last Man.* New York: Free Press.

Gardner, R., Ostrom, E. and Walker, J. (1990), "The nature of common-pool resource problems", *Rationality and Society*, **2**, 335-58.

Gephart, R. P., Thatchenkery, T. J. and Boje, D. (1996), "Conclusion. Reconstructing organizations for future survival", in *Postmodern Management and Organization Theory*, ed. D. Boje, R. P. Gephart and T. J. Thatchenkery, pp. 358-64. London: Sage Publications.

Gibbins, J. R. (1989), "Contemporary political culture: an introduction", in *Contemporary Political Culture. Politics in a Postmodern Age*, ed. J. R. Gibbins, pp. 1-30. London: Sage Publications.

Giddens, A. (1984), *The Constitution of Society. Outline of the Theory of Structuration.* Cambridge: Polity Press.

Giddens, A. (1990), *The Consequences of Modernity.* Cambridge: Polity Press.

Glaser, B. and Strauss, A. (1967), *The Discovery of Grounded Theory.* Chicago: Aldine.

Göhler, G. (1987), "Institutionslehre in der deutschen Politikwissenschaft nach 1945", in *Grundfragen der Theorie politischer Institutionen*, ed. G. Göhler, pp. 14-47. Opladen: Westdeutscher Verlag.

Göhler, G. and Schmalz-Bruns, R. (1988), "Perspektiven der Theorie politischer Institutionen", *Politische Vierteljahresschrift*, **29**, 309-44.

Granovetter, M. (1992), [1985] "Economic action and social structure: The problem of embeddedness", in *The Sociology of Economic Life*, ed. M. Granovetter and R. Swedberg, pp. 53-81. Boulder, CO: Westview Press (Original work published in 1985).

Graymer, L. and Thompson, F. (1982), *Reforming Social Regulation.* Beverly Hills: Sage Publications.

Guba, E. G. and Lincoln, Y. S. (1994), "Competing paradigms in qualitative research", in *Handbook of Qualitative Research*, ed. E. G. Guba and Y. S. Lincoln, pp. 105-17. London: Sage Publications.

Guba, E. G. and Lincoln, Y. S. (1989), *Fourth Generation Evaluation.* London: Sage Publications.

Gulick, L. and Urwick, L., eds. (1937), *Papers on the Science of Administration.* New York: Institute of Public Administration.

Habermas, J. (1972), *Knowledge and Human Interest.* Boston: Beacon Press.

Hanberger, A. (1992), *Lokalt samarbete och global integration*, Forsknings-rapport. Umeå: Statsvetenskapliga Institutionen.

Hanf, K. and Toonen, T. A. J., eds. (1985), *Policy Implementation in Federal and Unitary Systems.* Dordrecht: Martinus Nijhoff.

Hardin, G. (1968), "The tragedy of the commons", *Science*, **162**, 1243-48.

Hardin, R. (1982), *Collective Action.* John Hopkins University Press: USA.

Hardin, R. (1995), *One for All: The Logic of Group Conflict.* Princeton, NJ: Princeton University Press.

Harsanyi, J. C. (1986), "Advances in understanding rational behavior", in *Rational Choice*, ed. J. Elster, pp. 84-107. Oxford: Basil Blackwell.

Hegner, F. (1986), "Solidarity and hierarchy: Institutional arrangements for the coordination of actions", in *Control, Guidance and Evaluation in the Public Sector*, ed. F. X. Kaufmann, G. Majone and V. Ostrom, pp. 407-29. Berlin: De Gruyter.

Heidenheimer, A., Heclo, H. and Adams, C. T. (1989), *Comparative Public Policy. The Politics of Social Choice in Europe and America.* New York:

St Martin's Press.

Hernes, G., ed. (1978), *Forhandlingsøkonomi og blandingsadministration*. Oslo: Universitetsforlaget.

Hernes, G., ed. (1983), *Økonomisk organisering*. Oslo: Universitetsforlaget.

Hirschman, A. O. (1970), *Exit, Voice and Loyalty*. Cambridge, MA: Harvard University Press.

Hirschman, A. O. (1982), "Rival interpretations of market society: Civilizing, destructive, or feeble?", *Journal of Economic Literature*, **20** (December), 1463-84.

Hjern, B. (1987), *Policy Analysis: An Implementation Approach*. Paper presented at APSA 1987 meeting, Umeå University, 3-6 September (Mimeo).

Hjern, B. (1990), *1992 och Nordens regionalpolitiska gränsregioner. Utvärdering för Nordisk Ministerråd*, CERUM Working Paper 1990:2. Umeå: CERUM (Mimeo).

Hjern, B. (1992), "Illegitimate democracy: A case for multiorganizational policy analysis", *Policy Currents*, **2**(1), February, 1-5.

Hjern, B. and Hull, C. (1982), "Implementation research as empirical constitutionalism", *European Journal of Political Research*, **10**(2), 105-17.

Hjern, B. and Hull, C. (1984), "Going interorganisational: Weber meets Durkheim", *Scandinavian Political Studies*, **7**(3), 197-212.

Hjern, B. and Hull, C. (1987), *Helping Small Firms Grow: An Implementation Approach*. Beckenham, Kent: Croom Helm.

Hjern, B. and Lundmark, K. (1979), "Blandekonomi och post-weberiansk förvaltningsteori: Administrativa lärdomar av svensk regionalpolitisk forskning", *Statsvetenskapligt Tidskrift*, **4**, 257-66.

Hjern, B. and Porter, D. O. (1983), "Implementation structures: A new unit of administrative analysis", in *Realizing Social Science Knowledge*, ed. B. Holzner, K. D. Knorr and H. Strasser, pp. 265-77. Wien-Würzberg: Physica-Verlag.

Hoffman, J. (1995), *Beyond the State. An Introductory Critique*. Cambridge: Polity Press.

Hollinger, R. (1994), *Postmodernism and the Social Sciences. A Thematic Approach*. London: Sage Publications.

Hood, C. and Schuppert, G. F., eds. (1987), *Delivering Public Services in Western Europe: Sharing Western European Experience of para-Government Organization*. London: Sage Publications.

Hulgård, L. (1998), "Bløde mål og evaluering bottom-up", in *Samfundsforskning bottom-up. Teori og metode*, ed. P. Bogason and E. Sørensen, pp. 66-93. København: Roskilde Universitetsforlag.

Hummel, R. P. (1990), "Circle managers and pyramidal managers: icons for the post-modern public administrator", in *Images and Identities in Public Administration*, ed. H. D. Kass and B. L. Catron, pp. 202-18. London: Sage Publications.

Inglehart, R. (1997), *Modernization and Postmoderization. Cultural, Economic and Political Change in 43 Societies*. Princeton, NJ: Princeton University Press.

Jensen, L. (1998a), "Bottom-up. Forskning med hovedet under armen?", in *Samfundsforskning bottom-up. Teori og metode*, ed. P. Bogason and E. Sørensen, pp. 169-98. København: Roskilde Universitetsforlag.

Jensen, L. (1998b), "Cultural theory and democratization of functional domains", *Public Administration*, **76**.

Jessop, B. (1989), "Putting states in their place: State systems and state theory", in *Recent Advances in Political Science*, A. Leftwich. London: Croom Helm.

Jessop, B. (1990), *State Theory. Putting Capitalist States in Their Place*. Cambridge: Polity Press.

Johannessen, S., Larsen, D., Neufeld, J. J. and Stockholm, K. (1996), *Politik i det lokale. Beretningen om Bårse Bogdepot*. Roskilde: Institut for Erhvervsøkonomi og Samfundsvidenskab.

Jørgensen, T. B. (1977), *Samspil og konflikt mellem organisationer*. København: Nyt fra Samfundsvidenskaberne.

Kenis, P. and Schneider, V. (1991), "Policy networks and policy analysis: scrutinizing a new analytical toolbox", in *Policy Networks. Empirical Evidence and Theoretical Considerations*, ed. B. Marin and R. Mayntz, pp. 26-59.

Kensen, S. (1998), "Undersøgelse af de lokale tolkninger af et policy-begreb", in *Samfundsforskning bottom-up. Teori og metode*, ed. P. Bogason and E. Sørensen, pp. 199-221. København: Roskilde Universitetsforlag.

Kettunen, P. (1994), *Implementation in a Multi-Organizational Setting. Local Networks in Environmental Health Policy*, Annales Universitatis Turkuensis Ser. B, Tom 207. Turku: Turun Yliopisto.

Kickert, W. J. M., Klijn, E.-H. and Koppenjan, J. F. M., eds. (1997), *Managing Complex Networks. Strategies for the Public Sector*. London: Sage Publications.

Kiser, L. L. and Ostrom, E. (1982), "The three worlds of action. A metatheoretical syntesis of institutional approaches", in *Strategies of Political Inquiry*, ed. E. Ostrom, pp. 179-222. London: Sage Publications.

Kjerholt, M., Himmelstrup, B. and Pedersen, A. R. (1995), *Design for Projektet: Ældresektorens Udvikling, Sundhedsprioritering Set Bottom-Up*. Roskilde: Institut for Samfundsvidenskab og Erhvervsøkonomi (Mimeo).

Klandermans, B. (1991), "New social movements and resource mobilization:

The European and the American approach revisited", in *Research on Social Movements. The State of the Art in Western Europe and the USA*, ed. D. Rucht, pp. 17-44. Frankfurt am Main: Campus Verlag.

Klijn, E.-H. (1997), "Policy networks: An overview", in *Managing Complex Networks. Strategies for the Public Sector*, eds. J. M. Kickert, E.-H. Klijn and J. F. M. Koppenjahn, pp. 14-34. London: Sage Publications.

Kuhn, T. S. (1962), *The Structure of Scientific Revolutions*. Chicago: Chicago University Press.

Lakatos, I. (1974), "Falsification and the methodology of scientific research programmes", in *Criticism and the Growth of Knowledge*, ed. I. Latakos and A. Musgrave, pp. 91-196. Cambridge: Cambridge University Press.

Laswell, H. D. and Lerner, D., eds. (1951), *The Policy Sciences: Recent Developments in Scope and Method*. Stanford: Stanford University Press.

Laver, M. (1981), *The Politics of Private Desires*. Harmondsworth: Penguin.

Lehmann, E. W. (1969), "Toward a macrosociology of power", *American Sociological Review*, **34**(4), 453-65.

Lindblom, C. E. (1965), *The Intelligence of Democracy. Decision Making Through Mutual Adjustment*. New York: The Free Press.

Lindblom, C. E. and Cohen, D. K. (1979), *Usable Knowledge. Social Science and Social Problem Solving*. New Haven: Yale University Press.

Linder, S. H. and Peters, B. G. (1987), "A design perspective on policy implementation: The fallacies of misplaced prescription", *Policy Studies Review*, **6**(3), 459-75.

Lipsky, M. (1980), *Street-Level Bureaucracy: Dilemmas of the Individual in Public Services*. New York: Russell Sage.

Lukes, S. (1973), "Methodological individualism reconsidered", in *The Philosophy of Social Explanation*, ed. A. Ryan, pp. 119-29. Oxford: Oxford University Press.

Lundquist, L. (1987), *Implementation Steering. An Actor-Structure Approach*. Lund: Studentlittratur.

March, J. G. and Olsen, J. P. (1983), "Organizing political life: What administrative reorganization tells us about government", *American Political Science Review*, **77**(2), 281-96.

March, J. G. and Olsen, J. P. (1989), *Rediscovering Institutions. The Organizational Basis of Politics*. New York: Free Press.

March, J. G. and Olsen, J. P. (1994), "Institutional perspectives on political institutions", paper presented at IPSA Conference, Berlin (Mimeo).

March, J. G. and Olsen, J. P. (1995), *Democratic Governance*. New York: The Free Press.

Marin, B. and Mayntz, R., eds. (1991), *Policy Networks. Empirical Evidence and Theoretical Considerations*. Campus: Frankfurt am Main.

188   *Public Policy and Local Governance*

McCarthy, J. D. and Zald, M. N. (1987), "Resource mobilization and social movements: A partial theory", in *Social Movements in an Organizational Society. Collected Essays*, ed. M. N. Zald and J. D. McCarthy, pp. 15-42. New Brunswick: Transaction Books.

McSwite, O. C. (1998), "The new normativism and the discourse movement: A mediation", *Administrative Theory and Praxis*, **20**(3), 377-81.

Mintzberg, H. (1981), "Organization design: Fashion or fit?", *Harvard Business Review*, January/February, 103-16.

Mitchell, W. C. (1988), "Virginia, Rochester and Bloomington", *Public Choice*, **56**, 101-20.

Moe, T. M. (1984), "New Economics of Organization", *American Journal of Political Science* 28:4:739-777.

Morel, J. (1986), *Ordnung und Freiheit*. Innsbruck: Tyrolia Verlag.

Nielsen, K. and Pedersen, O. K., eds. (1989), *Forhandlingsøkonomi i Norden*. København: Jurist- og Økonomforbundets Forlag.

Niskanen, W. A. (1971), *Bureaucracy and Representative Democracy*. Hawthorne: Aldine-Atherton.

Nordlinger, E. A. (1988), "The return to the state: Critiques", *American Political Science Review*, **82**(3), 875-85.

O'Neill, J. (1973), "Scientism, historicism and the problem of rationality", in *Modes of Individualism and Collectivism*, ed. J. O'Neill, pp. 3-26. London: Heinemann.

Offe, C. (1986), *Disorganized Capitalism*. Cambridge: Polity.

Olsen, J. P., ed. (1978), *Politisk organisering*. Oslo: Universitetsforlaget.

Olsen, J. P. (1991), "Political science and organization theory. Parallel agendas but mutual disregard", in *Political Choice. Institutions, Rules and the Limits of Rationality*, ed. R. Czada and A. Windhoff-Héritier, pp. 87-119. Frankfurt am Main: Campus.

Olsen, J. P. (1992), *Analyzing Institutional Dynamics*, LOS-Senter Notat. Bergen: LOS-center.

Olson, M. (1965), *The Logic of Collective Action*. Cambridge, MA: Harvard University Press.

Osborne, D. and Gaebler, T. (1993), *Reinventing Government. How the Entrepreneurial Spirit is Transforming the Public Sector*. New York: Plume.

Ostrom, E. (1986), "A method of instititutional analysis", in *Control, Guidance and Evaluation in the Public Sector*, ed. F. Kaufmann, G. Majone and V. Ostrom, pp. 459-75.

Ostrom, E. (1990), *Governing the Commons: The Evolution of Institutions for Collective Action*. Cambridge: Cambridge University Press.

Ostrom, E. (1995), "Self-organization and social capital", *Industrial and*

Corporate Change, **4**(1), 131-59.

Ostrom, E., Gardner, R. and Walker, J. (1994), *Rules, Games and Common-Pool Resources*. Ann Arbor: University of Michigan Press.

Ostrom, E., Parks, R. and Whitaker, G. (1978), *Patterns of Metropolitan Policing*. Cambridge, MA: Ballinger Publishing Company.

Ostrom, V. (1974) [1973], *The Intellectual Crisis in American Public Administration*. Alabama: University of Alabama Press (Original work published in 1973).

Ostrom, V. (1986), "Methodological individualism and multiorganizational analysis", unpublished paper, Bloomington, Indiana: Workshop in Political Theory and Policy Analysis (Mimeo).

Ostrom, V. (1991), *The Meaning of American Federalism*. San Francisco, CA: Institute for Contemporary Studies Press.

Ostrom, V., Bish, R. and Ostrom, E. (1988), *Local Government in the United States*. San Francisco, CA: CGS Press.

Ostrom, V. and Ostrom, E. (1977), "Public goods and public choices", in *Alternatives for Delivering Public Services*, ed. E. S. Savas. Boulder, CO: Westview.

Page, E. C. and Goldsmith, M., eds. (1987), *Central and Local Government Relations. A Comparative Analysis of West European Unitary States*. London: Sage Publications.

Parsons, T., Bales, R. and Shils, E. (1953), *Working Papers in the Theory of Action*. New York: Free Press.

Pedersen, A. R. (1998), "En præsentation af sneboldsmetoden", in *Samfundsforskning bottom-up. Teori og metode*, ed. P. Bogason and E. Sørensen, pp. 222-37. København: Roskilde Universitetsforlag.

Pedersen, O. K., Andersen, N. Å., Kjær, P. and Elberg, J. (1992), *Privat Politik. Projekt Forhandlingsøkonomi*. København: Samfundslitteratur.

Pedersen, O. K. and Nielsen, K. (1988), "The Negotiated Economy: Ideal and History", *Scandinavian Political Studies*, 11:2.

Piore, M. and Sabel, C. (1984), *The Second Industrial Divide*. New York: Basic Books.

Porter, D. O. (1990), "Structural pose as an approach for implementing complex programs", in *Strategies for Managing Intergovernmental Policies and Networks*, eds. R. W. Gage and M. P. Mandell, pp. 3-28. New York: Praeger.

Pressman, J. L. and Wildawsky, A. B. (1973), *Implementation*. Berkeley, CA: University of California Press.

Putnam, R., Leonardi, R. and Nanetti, R. Y. (1993), *Making Democracy Work: Civic Traditions in Modern Italy*. Princeton, NJ: Princeton University Press.

Radnitzky, G. and Bernholz, P. eds. (1987), *Economic Imperialism. The Economic Approach Applied Outside the Field of Economics.* Paragon House Publishers: New York.

Rasmusen, E. (1994), *Games and Information. An Introduction to Game Theory*, 2d ed. Oxford: Blackwell.

Rhodes, R. A. W. (1997), *Understanding Governance. Policy Networks, Governance, Reflexivity and Accountability.* Buckingham: Open University Press.

Rittberger, V., ed. (1993), *Regime Theory and International Relations.* Oxford: Clarendon.

Robertson, P. J. and Tang, S.-Y. (1995), "The role of commitment in collective action: Comparing the organizational behavior and rational choice perspectives", *Public Administration Review*, **55**(1), January/February, 67-80.

Roe, E. (1994), *Narrative Policy Analysis. Theory and Practice.* Durham, NC: Duke University Press.

Rohr, J. A. (1986), *To Run a Constitution. The Legitimacy of the Administrative State.* Lawrence: University Press of Kansas.

Rose, R. (1979), "Ungovernability: Is there fire behind the smoke?", *Political Studies*, **27**(3), 351-70.

Rosenau, P. M. (1992), *Post-Modernism and the Social Sciences. Insights, Inroads and Intrusions.* Princeton, NJ: Princeton University Press.

Rucht, D., ed. (1991), *Research on Social Movements: The State of the Art in Western Europe and the USA.* Frankfurt-am-Main: Campus.

Sabatier, P. A. (1986), "Top-Down and Bottom-Up approaches to implementation research: a critical analysis and suggested synthesis", *Journal of Public Policy*, **6**(1), 21-48.

Sabatier, P. A. and Pelkey, N. (1987), "Incorporating multiple actors and guidance instruments into models of regulatory policymaking", *Administration and Society*, **19**(2), 236-63.

Salamon, L. (1981), "Rethinking public management: third party government and the changing forms of government action", *Public Policy*, Summer, 1-16.

Savas, E. S., ed. (1977), *Alternatives for Delivering Public Services: Towards Improved Performance.* Boulder, CO: Westview.

Scharpf, F. W. (1988), *Decision Rules, Decision Styles and Policy Choices.* Köln: Max-Planck Institut für Gesellschaftsforschung. Discussion Paper 88/3.

Schön, D. A. and Rein, M. (1994), *Frame Reflection. Toward the Resolution of Intractable Policy Controversies.* New York: Basic Books.

Schotter, A. (1981), *The Economic Theory of Social Institutions.* Cambridge: Cambridge University Press.

Scott, K. J. (1973), "Methodological and epistemological individualism", in *Modes of Individualism and Collectivism*, ed. J. O'Neill, pp. 215-20. London: Heinemann.

Scott, R. W. (1995), *Institutions and Organizations*. London: Sage Publications.

Selznick, P. (1957), *Leadership in Administration*. New York: Harper and Row.

Selznick, P. (1996), "Institutionalism old and new", *Administrative Science Quarterly*, **41**, 270-77.

Sharpe, L. J., ed. (1993), *The Rise of Meso Government in Europe*. London: Sage Publications.

Simon, H. A. (1960), *The New Science of Management Decision*. Englewood Cliffs, NJ: Prentice-Hall.

Simon, H. A. (1987), [1986] Rationality in psychology and economics", in *Rational Choice. The Contrast Between Economics and Psychology*, ed. R. M. Hogarth and M. W. Reder, pp. 25-40. Chicago: University of Chicago Press (Original work published in 1986).

Streeck, W. and Schmitter, P. C., eds. (1985), *Private Interest Government. Beyond Market and State*. London: Sage Publications.

Tarrow, S. (1994), *Power in Movement. Social Movement, Collective Action and Politics*. Cambridge: Cambridge University Press.

Taylor, M. (1982), *Community, Anarchy and Liberty*. Cambridge University Press: Cambridge.

Taylor, M. (1987), *The Possibility of Cooperation*. Cambridge University Press: Cambridge.

Thelen, K. and Steinmo, S. (1992), "Historical institutionalism in comparative politics", in *Structuring Politics. Historical Institutionalism in Comparative Analysis*, ed. S. Steinmo, K. Thelen and F. Longstreth, pp. 1-32. Cambridge, MA: Cambridge University Press.

Therborn, G. (1995), *European Modernity and Beyond. The Trajectory of European Societies 1945-2000*. London: Sage Publications.

Titmuss, R. M. (1970), *The Gift Relationship: From Human Blood to Social Policy*. London: Allen and Unwin.

Wamsley, G. L., Bacher, R. N., Goodsell, C. T., Kronenberg, P. S., Rohr, J. A., Stivers, C. M., White, O. F. and Wolf, J. F. (1990), *Refounding Public Administration*. Newbury Park, CA: Sage Publications.

Weaver, K. R. and Rockman, B. A., eds. (1993), *Do Institutions Matter? Government Capabilities in the United States and Abroad*. Washington, DC: Brookings.

Weber, M. (1978), *Economy and Society. An Outline of Interpretive Sociology*. Berkeley, CA: University of California Press.

White, J. D. and Adams, G. B., eds. (1994), *Research in Public Administration. Reflections on Theory and Practice*. London: Sage Publications.

White, O. F. J. and McSwain, C. J. (1990), "The Phoenix project: raising a new image of public administration of the past", in *Images and Identities in Public Administration*, ed. H. D. Kass and B. L. Catron, pp. 23-59. London: Sage Publications.

Wildawsky, A. and Caiden, N. (1997), *The Politics of the Budgetary Process*, 3d ed. New York: Longman.

Williamson, O. (1975), *Markets and Hierarchies: Analysis and Antitrust Implications*. New York: Free Press.

Willke, H. (1992), *Ironie des Staates. Grundlinien einer Staatstheorie polyzentrischer Gesellschaft*. Frankfurt am Main: Suhrkamp.

Wittrock, B. and Wagner, P (1990), "Social science and state development: The structuration of discourse in the social sciences", in *Social Scientists, Policy and the State*, ed. S. B. and A. Gagnon, pp. 113-37. New York: Praeger.

Index